THE
POWER
OF A
GOOD
FIGHT

THE
POWER
OF A
GOOD
FIGHT

How to Embrace Conflict to Drive Productivity,
Creativity, and Innovation

LYNNE EISAGUIRRE

A Pearson Education Company

For Elizabeth and Nicholas.
May they have only good fights.

International Standard Book Number: 0-02-864269-4
Library of Congress Catalog Card Number: 2002103793

04   03   02   8   7   6   5   4   3   2   1

Interpretation of the printing code: The rightmost number of the first series of numbers is the year of the book's printing; the rightmost number of the second series of numbers is the number of the book's printing. For example, a printing code of 02-1 shows that the first printing occurred in 2002.

Printed in the United States of America

Note: This publication contains the opinions and ideas of its author. It is intended to provide helpful and informative material on the subject matter covered. It is sold with the understanding that the author and publisher are not engaged in rendering professional services in the book. If the reader requires personal assistance or advice, a competent professional should be consulted.

The author and publisher specifically disclaim any responsibility for any liability, loss, or risk, personal or otherwise, which is incurred as a consequence, directly or indirectly, of the use and application of any of the contents of this book.

Author's note: Throughout this book, I have drawn heavily on examples from my clients. However, to protect their privacy and ensure confidentiality, I have changed their names, descriptions, and other identifying characteristics. I am grateful to them for their examples and their trust in me.

For marketing and publicity, please call: 317-581-3722

The publisher offers discounts on this book when ordered in quantity for bulk purchases and special sales.

For sales within the United States, please contact: Corporate and Government Sales, 1-800-382-3419 or corpsales@pearsontechgroup.com

Outside the United States, please contact: International Sales, 317-581-3793 or international@pearsontechgroup.com

CONTENTS

APPENDIXES

INTRODUCTION

I always liked a good fight.

—Franklin D. Roosevelt

Many people, when they hear the title of this book, *The Power of a Good Fight*, say, "What do you mean a *good* fight, Lynne? I've had many fights in my life, but I've never had a *good* fight."

A good fight is one that builds trust, builds relationships, helps us stay on purpose, and positions us for leadership in our organization. A good fight helps us see the value of conflict. A good fight can lead to innovative solutions to issues that we would never have discovered without working our way through the dispute. The question then becomes, *how can we encourage more good fights and fewer bad fights?* This is a question I've researched for many years.

HOW I CAME TO STUDY CONFLICT

Many people in my audiences ask how I came to study conflict. After law school, I practiced litigation with a large Denver law firm. I tried a wide variety of commercial and employment cases. I joke that because I spent 10 years standing in front of federal judges, it's almost impossible to insult me because I've been insulted by professionals. (Not that you're not a professional, but it's probably not your job to insult people.)

Working in the trenches of legal disputes made me realize that litigation was not the best solution to most problems. Even when we won at trial, the process took too long and cost too much. I discovered that even though some people certainly had legitimate claims, they could have been resolved at a much earlier stage if people knew how to harness the creative power of conflict instead of avoiding disputes or creating destructive clashes.

I became interested during the 1980s in the entire field of Alternative Dispute Resolution, including mediation and arbitration. I pursued additional training in mediation and arbitration and integrated these techniques into my regular trial practice. Clients started to hire me as a mediator and I served as an arbitrator for the American Arbitration Association.

After practicing litigation for 10 years, I decided to pursue my interests in writing and teaching on workplace issues. Yet, during the 1990s, workplaces felt more like war zones than work zones to me. I authored a book on sexual harassment, then I started conducting training and consulting on sexual harassment. While working on a book on diversity issues for the same publisher, I started to meet client requests for diversity and EEOC (Equal Employment Opportunity Commission) training. Because of my experience in employment law, my clients asked for my assistance on other employee matters such as preventing conflict and workplace violence. Consulting, training, and cleanup of employee messes seemed to create a never-ending stream of business.

Yes, I disliked the defensive, unproductive, and uncreative conflict approach that I found in most workplaces. How did the workplace get so hostile? How could constant and personal strife possibly contribute to the bottom line? How could destructive disagreements make organizations and employees happier and more productive? The unresolved battling all seemed like a waste of time and energy. My idea of embracing conflict productively was a foreign concept.

Having grown up on a ranch, I'd always worked, helping out with chores and taking care of animals and a large garden, in addition to housework. My first paying job at 16 involved cleaning restrooms, selling snacks, teaching swim lessons, and lifeguarding at a public swimming pool. From there, I progressed to waitressing, dishwashing, dorm counseling, and clerical work as I worked through high school, college, and law school. As an attorney and law clerk, I'd worked in public and private settings, for the U.S. Congress, federal government, as a university professor, and as an associate, contract attorney, and partner in a law firm. Along the way, I'd also founded and managed two of my own businesses, one of which employed dozens of people as well as involved outside stockholders, contract workers, and vendors.

However, *nothing* in my 30 working years prepared me for the world of work I found in the new millennium.

NEEDS FOR THE MILLENNIUM WORKPLACE

Downsized, right-sized, reorganized, and demoralized, most employees seemed to me to be more suspicious than productive, ready to file internal grievances or sue at the least provocation.

And no wonder. Most had been loyal, hard-working, integral parts of an enterprise. They expected some measure of security in exchange for their hard work. In the new workplace, instead, they found they could be terminated on a moment's notice, frequently after being reassured the day before that their jobs were secure.

Mergers and acquisitions created more "Working Wounded,"[1] as author Bob Rosner called them. Even though research revealed that 70 percent of mergers fail—usually because of the failure to address people issues—organizations continued to pursue them.

Those who stayed viewed their bosses with a wary distrust. Organizational mission statements, the latest "program du jour," and *Dilbert*-style consultants were greeted with equal disdain. Dozens of new "trainings"—from sexual harassment to new computer programs— were launched by harried human resource departments who struggled to keep up with the legal realities of the changing workplace climate as well as the continuing demands for new skills.

Employers were beginning to wake up to the coming labor shortage, but spent more time grumbling about the lack of good employees and fading employee loyalty than trying to solve the problem and improve employee retention and morale.

The intensely competitive business environment created even more of a need for innovation, yet many business leaders instead avoided conflict and fostered conformity, as author Gary Hamel argues in *Leading the Revolution*.[2]

I was convinced there had to be a better way and that something much more radical than another new training (and I agree with whomever first said that training is for dogs, not people) was needed. After much research, reading, writing, and hours of interviews with workers and bosses in the trenches, I decided that drafting more policies, more lawsuits, or EEOC regs couldn't possibly help. What was needed was something totally new: a whole new alliance between the parties; a new set of expectations.

Employers also needed to offer a different attitude toward employees—one of partnership and alliance rather than parental arrogance. Employees need to be educated to understand the real-world requirements of the organization. Employees and bosses needed to understand that conflict was a normal part of the workplace.

> What was needed, I determined, was to give co-workers a new set of skills and a new way of thinking about conflict. What was needed was a more creative approach to conflict, one that neither avoided disputes nor fanned the fire of anger in destructive ways. What was needed was the ability to harness the energy of conflict to fuel innovation.

First on the list of skills of any co-worker, manager, or leader in this new world of work is creative conflict management and consensus building skills. This book is a step toward helping you develop those tools. It will work only if you embrace it, use it, and adapt my suggestions as necessary to make them yours. As an employee or leader, this book will help you navigate the new territory. (Remembering, of course, that the map is not the territory.)

Before you begin your journey, I urge you to work on acquiring what the Zen masters call "beginner's mind." What they mean by this is to empty our minds of old ideas so that we are sincerely open to new ones. The following may help illustrate this point. Zen masters tell a story about three bowls.

One bowl is turned upside down so that water simply flows over it; it cannot contain anything. Another is upright, but full of debris—also unable to receive. The third is upright and empty. As you read this book, ask yourself:

> Am I willing to come to this experience with an upright, empty bowl, truly open to embrace and use new ideas about conflict?

> Am I willing to consider that conflict is not a sign of dysfunction, but that it could be a powerful force for success in my organization?

The workplace continues to change at a rapid pace. Diversity, outsourcing, work group teams, and mergers between companies that used to be competitors increase workplace conflict. And yet, most of us lack a creative conflict approach. Most of us are afraid to embrace and harness the powerful force of conflict. We either run from it or create destructive disputes. A recent survey of recruiters and CEOs ranked good "people skills" as the number one attribute they sought in employees. Other research has pointed to "interpersonal conflict" as the reason most people leave jobs. An American Management Association study found that managers spend 25 percent of their time refereeing conflicts. As individuals, we spend 50 percent of our time each day negotiating. And yet, how much of our time do we spend learning how to harness the force of creative contention?

In order to thrive and survive in the fast-paced future of work, we must be able to embrace and use conflict, as well as to develop the ability to build broad support for our work and ideas through the use of strong consensus building skills. Leaders and co-workers must also learn to be *confrontable*, to welcome others' feedback and criticism in order to drive innovation and creativity.

This book takes you step-by-step through the process of acquiring the attitudes, skills, and systems you and your organization will need for the millennium workplace.

HOW TO HAVE A *GOOD* FIGHT

There are three keys we need to remember to have a good fight:

1. Assume leadership
2. Be on purpose
3. Prepare for conflict

This book will delve into all three of these keys, but briefly, the first key, *assume leadership*, means that we need to consider the costs of raising and not raising conflict. We need to understand that while healthy conflict is a normal, natural, and productive part of life, unhealthy and *destructive* conflict is not. We need to constantly ask ourselves, *how important is the conflict?* If we decide the issue is important, we don't assume it's unfair that we have to make the first move, but instead, we need to make sure we are proactive. We also need to take the lead in improving our own conflict approach as well as to urge others in our organization to do the same. We need to learn to embrace conflict as a healthy chance to change what's not working into something more successful.

The second key, *be on purpose*, is the power that drives us through whatever obstacles we need to overcome in order to embrace the conflict. Conflict innovation takes work and skill. The more skill we have, the easier the work will be. If we have a broader purpose in life that is big enough and wide enough to include whatever conflict or negotiation we're currently struggling to embrace, that purpose will help us make the challenging effort to skillfully and elegantly harness the power of contention. That purpose will help us look for the creative edge in conflict.

The third key is *prepare for conflict*. What I mean by this is that we must plan both before conflict happens and when in the midst of a dispute. For this we need to consider which of the *top 10 steps to conflict success* (refer to Chapter 11) we need to follow and perhaps role-play a possible approach.

A PRACTICAL APPROACH

Other helpful books on conflict resolution are available. Many, such as *The Mediation Process* by Christopher Moore,[3] focus on third-party conflict resolution. While this book will briefly touch on that issue, we will primarily focus on *direct conflict resolution*—the situation where you, the reader, are directly involved in the conflict. In addition, many books on conflict tend to be detailed and academic. While excellent, most leaders and other workers do not have the time to study academic texts on conflict.

Other useful books, such as Fisher and Ury's *Getting to Yes,*[4] focus on negotiation and assume that you can walk away if the deal doesn't work. The problem with these approaches is that most people assume that negotiation is something different from the every day conflict processes in which most of us engage. As I like to say, however, *conflict is simply a negotiation that we don't know we're having.* These so-called negotiation skills are of limited use for most people in workplace situations since they assume we can leave the conflict by leaving the job. While technically true, continuing to leave jobs because of destructive conflict skills or because of the fear of confronting conflict, is an expensive option—both in terms of time and money. These books also focus on resolving the conflict rather than using the conflict to drive creativity.

This book will focus instead on: *using conflict as energy to mold problems into innovation solutions*.

It will also offer practical solutions and skills to learn how to value conflict and productively embrace contention. It is meant to be a "user-friendly" overview of the issue with techniques you can begin using today to immediately improve both your attitude about conflict and your own approach.

CONFLICT RESOLUTION OPTIONS

There are many ways to approach conflict. Certainly, one of the most popular options throughout history has been to resort to war or other forms of violence. At the opposite end of the spectrum are those who simply assume we should always give up: surrender our own interests and needs, accommodate, or perhaps spend time together in the hot tub (also known as the California method) and avoid conflict. Appealing to a higher authority—manager, leader, mediator, or judge—is also a popular, although costly, approach.

This book will focus on other options. We will focus on learning to value conflict and create productive disputes. We will explore an *interest-based* conflict approach. This is the concept that a skillful and productive conflict process can actually create new and more innovative solutions that we might not have seen without working our way through the problem. An interest-based conflict approach is different from conflict resolution or negotiation systems that assume one party will necessarily lose and another party will win. Those methods seek to help gain the most advantage and win the most in the situation.

We will also address forms of cooperative decision-making as opposed to *third party assistance* with negotiation that involves help from a therapist, trainer, or mediator. We will avoid *third party decision-making*, which usually involves the use of a judge, arbitrator, leader or other decision-maker with the power to enforce his or her decision.

I will continue to challenge your attitude toward conflict, encouraging you to recognize the creative force you'll gain through skillful conflict management. If you diligently work your way through this book, you'll increase your ability to have many good fights.

HOW THIS BOOK IS ORGANIZED

The Power of a Good Fight is organized into four parts:

Part 1 will help both you and your organization adjust your attitude and approach to conflict, assisting you in welcoming conflict as a precursor to change and creativity.

Part 2 will help you gain flexibility in your own approach to conflict as well as assist you in understanding why others use different styles.

Part 3 will give you a practical and systematic approach to productively use conflict.

Part 4 will help you lead your organization through the changes it will need to make in order to avoid bad fights and encourage good ones.

ACKNOWLEDGMENTS

Books may be written by authors, but actually delivering a copy into a reader's hands takes much more than one person's work. I'm indebted to my agent, Michael Sneal, who saw the potential of this book early on and guided me skillfully through the proposal process. Renee Wilmeth at Alpha Books helped me shape and refocus the book, while remaining cheerful and optimistic—everything a writer wants an editor to be. Nancy Lewis helped further develop and polish the manuscript. Thanks to Christy Wagner for her skillful and speedy management of the process.

On the home front, my hard-working and upbeat assistant, Debra Harris, typed and proofed endless versions of this book without complaint. In addition, Alyssa Graves also provided valuable help with research. O. C. O'Connell offered research and last-minute editorial assistance without complaint. I'm thankful also to my many clients who trusted me with their personal stories.

Long-time friends Peter Clarke, Susan Hazaleus, Cheri Tobin, and Laura Wing helped shore up my attitude. My fellow "villagers," residents of my co-housing community in Golden, Colorado, offered in-the-trenches-training on the realities of dealing with thorny conflicts and the consensus process.

My parents, Joe and Wilma Eisaguirre, and siblings, Kim Jones and Lew Eisaguirre, provided moral support and their usual unflagging belief in my abilities—as well as teaching me much of what I know about good fights!

Thyra Wilson and Allison King cared for my children with devoted attention so that I would have the time and energy to work. John Evans provided moral support as well as extra child care. And of course my kids, Elizabeth and Nicholas, worked cheerfully on their own books so that I would have the time to write mine. I love you more than any of my writer's words can ever express.

CONTACT THE AUTHOR

Lynne Eisaguirre presents speeches, workshops, and consulting services on conflict and negotiation, diversity, team building, leadership, and employee retention. She is known for her lively and interactive approach. If you would like to know more about these or other services please call 303-216-1020 or visit her company's website at www.workplacesthatwork.com.

TRADEMARKS

All terms mentioned in this book that are known to be or are suspected of being trademarks or service marks have been appropriately capitalized. Alpha Books and Pearson Education, Inc., cannot attest to the accuracy of this information. Use of a term in this book should not be regarded as affecting the validity of any trademark or service mark.

PART 1

The Power of Attitudes: How to Embrace Conflict to Drive Productivity, Creativity, and Innovation

CHAPTER 1

LEADING THE WAY: HOW TO LEVERAGE CONFLICT INTO SUCCESS

If two people on the job agree all the time, then one is useless. If they disagree all the time, then both are useless.

—Dale Carnegie

A group of eight gather around the conference table to discuss the merits of several companies that are vying to become the new IT provider for the division. Not 10 minutes into the meeting, things turn ugly. The accounting manager sulks because billing functions aren't even among the top ten system features being evaluated. The IT manager is indignant that the operations people keep interrupting her presentation to explain the kinds of reports they need in order to measure performance against budget. When the IT manager directs the discussion in favor of a particular system, the vice president of operations lashes out that his staff is not getting the chance to participate in the selection process. The CEO detaches himself from the fray. The meeting ends in disarray and open hostility.

And the person who contributes most to the deadlock? The CEO. His style of conflict resolution is to avoid it. He refuses to assume leadership in conflict. As a result, not only do conflicts continue to fester without resolution, but his organization is losing its creative edge and its most innovative employees who resign in disgust at the lack of forward progress on their projects.

Sound familiar? Unfortunately, you're not alone; scenes like these are repeated in the hallways and offices of workplaces everywhere.

According to the American Management Association (AMA), your best people are spending about 25 percent of their time dealing with unproductive conflict in the work place. That's about two hours a day your staff is burning up fussing about disagreements instead of creatively approaching and harnessing conflict to focus on core objectives, sales numbers, production schedules or bonus triggers. Can your organization afford that?

And the more teamwork your organization needs in order to function, the higher the number of potential unproductive conflicts. In the information field, for example, AT&T—with different business units offering part of the whole—has to combine the pieces a customer needs. This requires an incredible amount of teamwork. AT&T estimates that employees spend 80 percent of their time responding to a customer's request for complex systems, fighting, and negotiating among themselves. Workers spend only 20 percent of their time actually devoted to listening to and selling to customers. These ratios are not unusual for many companies.[1]

If you want your organization to thrive, you and your team must learn to expect conflict, confront it, and skillfully harness the power. You must learn how to have *good* fights. Contrary to popular misconception, these are learned skills and attitudes, not personality traits. Adapt the attitude and practice the skills and you can become one of the most respected leaders in your organization. Why? Because innovation and productivity will improve, collaboration will increase, staff members will feel valued, turnover will decline, and you'll beat the budget.

It's that simple. Move toward success by recognizing and understanding the causes of destructive conflicts.

If you're going to be viewed as a *leader* in your organization and survive and thrive at work into the next century, you must develop your own conflict approach *and* develop a reputation for leadership in conflict management and consensus building.

Today, unproductive conflict increasingly disrupts most workplaces, lowering productivity and morale.

What this book asks you to do is to assume *leadership* in conflict resolution. By that I mean I will encourage you to be the person who first steps up to the plate to embrace conflict. In order to do that, you'll need to change your most basic attitudes about the role of conflict in the workplace.

Many professionals tell me that they chose their profession—HR, sales, marketing, or information technology—because they like people *or* because they want to avoid dealing with people.

Either way, they view conflict as the enemy. I constantly hear my clients complain about wanting to move to a job where there is "less conflict" or where "things are less political." My experience is that conflict-free organizations are rare. Even if you do find one, an apparently calm organization may not deliver on the professional's true needs. Conflict—skillfully resolved—tends to develop more creative, innovative, and vibrant organizations.

We need to move toward embracing conflict as a friendly force to be directed and used, not avoided like the enemy. Leadership involves learning to value conflict.

THE VALUE OF CONFLICT

Why should we value conflict? Because research has shown it's necessary in order to drive innovation and creativity. According to author and business expert Gary Hamel in *Leading the Revolution*,[2] this is the number one issue most businesses must face in order to stay competitive today.

Many researchers have found a direct link between the relationship of constructive conflict and innovation. For example, Robert I. Sutton, professor of management science and engineering at Stanford University, author of "Weird Ideas That Work: 11½ Practices for Promoting, Managing and Sustaining Innovation," notes that most experienced executives predict that creativity should flourish in a fun, low-stress workplace where conflict is minimal, managers mind the budget, and people use their time productively. Yet that's not usually the case. After studying creative companies for more than 10 years, Sutton has found them to be "remarkably inefficient and often terribly annoying places to work where 'managing by getting out of the way' is often the best approach."[3]

Sutton finds that managing for creativity means "taking most of what we know about management and standing it on its head …. It means taking perfectly happy people and goading them into fights among themselves."[4]

His research and decades of other research prove that good fights succeed by increasing the range of a company's knowledge, by causing people to see old problems in new ways, and by helping companies break from the past. These conditions produce the rich soil for creative work.

START WITH HIRING

Researcher Sutton, for example, emphasizes that creating constructive conflict needs to start during the hiring process. In fact, he suggests hiring people who make you uncomfortable—even those you don't like—in order to find a few useful misfits who will ignore and reject the organizational model, increasing the variety in what people think, say, and do. This is exactly the opposite of what most people manage, which is to hire people who "fit in" based upon a manager's chemistry with the people.

I remember, for example, the hiring process we used at the large Denver law firm where I was a partner. We received many resumes from young graduates of prestigious, traditional east coast law schools who thought it would be fun to move to Colorado to ski. We doubted, however, that they would fit into our litigation-driven law firm environment, which tended to favor smart aleck, entrepreneurial self-starters. In order to screen out any suspected wimps, we would, after formal interviews of the most promising candidates, take them to dinner at an old Denver restaurant called The Buckhorn Exchange.

This colorful eatery was known for animal heads on the walls—from anteaters to elephants—and an exotic menu ranging from snake to Rocky Mountain Oysters. We would sit in the bar drinking shots of tequila with worms in it and munching peanuts, throwing the shells on the floor. If they survived and even seemed to enjoy this unique environment, we concluded that they might indeed thrive at our firm. If they seemed uncomfortable, we passed them by. This interview-screening tactic resulted in hiring many people like us, but we lacked diversity and ultimately, I believe, limited the creative potential of the firm.

We will return to the idea of diversity and conflict in Part 2.

PROVOKE GOOD FIGHTS

Managing for creative sparks by provoking good fights and avoiding bad ones has produced some of the most famous product innovations of our time. For example, 3M's former CEO William McKnight once ordered a young employee named Richard Drew to abandon a project he was working on. McKnight scoffed at the product Drew was trying to develop, saying it would never work. Luckily for 3M, Drew disregarded the order and went on to invent masking tape and lay the foundation for 3M's defining product, Scotch tape.

Similarly, in his book *The HP Way*, David Packard brags about an employee who defied a direct order from him. "Some years ago," he writes, "at an HP laboratory in Colorado Springs devoted to oscilloscope technology, one of our bright, energetic engineers, Chuck House, was advised to abandon a display monitor he was developing. Instead, he embarked on a vacation to California, stopping along the way to show potential customers a prototype. House was convinced he was onto something so he persisted with the project, even persuading his R&D manager to rush the monitor into production. The resulting $35 million in revenue proved he was right. Packard continues: "Some years later, at a gathering of HP engineers, I presented Chuck with a medal for 'extraordinary contempt and defiance' beyond the normal call of engineering duty."[5]

Such scenarios could never have occurred if Packard and HP hadn't created an environment that welcomed good fights.

One of Professor Sutton's most well-supported ideas for managing creativity is that you should find some *happy* people and then encourage them to fight. He emphasizes that he's not talking about fueling personality conflicts or relationship issues; battles between people who loath one another stifle innovation. *"The fights you need to cause are all about ideas."*[6]

Bob Taylor, a psychologist turned research administrator, encouraged this kind of conflict among the computer scientists from various universities who were responsible for the technologies that made the computer revolution possible, including personal computers, the Internet, and laser printers. When they met at their annual conferences, "I got them to argue with each other," Taylor recalls with unashamed glee. "These were people who cared about their work. If there were technical weak spots, they would almost always surface under these conditions. It was very, very healthy."[7]

All of this healthy conflict, Sutton found, generates a lot of new ideas. Of course, it's hard to generate a few good ideas without also generating a lot of bad ones. Evidence of this phenomena can be found in the voluminous records maintained by an overworked staff at the U.S. Patent and Trademark Office. That office awards a new patent every six minutes, although most of these never see the light of day as a marketable product.

The key to success is to reward idea generation itself, as did former Time Warner chairman Steve Ross. He claimed that people who didn't make enough mistakes should be fired. Few leaders share his philosophy. Most companies neither tolerate nor reward failure.

If organizations could tolerate the tension induced by failure, think of how many more innovations would come to fruition. In 1939 DuPont chemist Roy J. Plunkett was researching refrigerants when he discovered tetrafluoroethylene resin. It took 10 more years of research before that substance became known around the world as Teflon.

GOOD FIGHTS FUEL CREATIVITY AND PRODUCTIVITY

How, you may be wondering, can something that feels so terrible to most people, and makes many so angry, actually be good for the organization? Because when you allow conflict, you encourage employees to be themselves. Employees who feel comfortable bringing all of themselves into the workplace are also more productive and innovative. They feel free to bring up problems, challenge management, and question bad decisions. Conversely, if managers foster conformity and obedience, employees won't flag potential problems or create new ways of doing things.

For example, one of my clients develops, manufactures, and sells complex medical implant devices costing thousands of dollars per item. In order to make any single sale, the clinical team and the sales team must coordinate and execute a delicate dance of cooperation. The clinical experts tend to be cautious "by-the-book" team players. The sales team tends to pay more attention to whether they make their sales numbers on any given month. Working in pairs of one sales person and one clinician to approach hospitals, the inherent tension between their objectives tended to simmer below the surface, lowering productivity, creativity, and enthusiasm.

The sales team would gripe and moan among themselves about the rigidity of the clinicians and how much their attitudes affected sales. The clinicians would whine to their managers about the smallest infraction of the rules by their sales partners. Finally, one sales associate told a new clinician that she was incompetent and would ruin any chance of her own sales success.

The clinician—deeply offended—repeated the slur to her manager, and World War III broke out between the sales team and the clinicians. Yet the open warfare finally brought the long-simmering issues to the table for resolution. I worked to mediate the dispute between the parties. Although they were initially resistant, the two teams were finally able to sit down and talk openly about their differences. This ultimately lead them to collaborate more effectively and discover more creative ways of working together. That pair went on to transcend their original conflict and become the top-selling team in the entire department.

A hundred years ago John Dewey, the great thinker, writer, and the founder of our modern education system, wrote: "Conflict is the gadfly of thought. It stirs us to observation and memory. It instigates to invention. It shocks us out of sheep-like passivity, and sets us at noting and contriving .... Conflict is a *sin qua non* of reflection and ingenuity."

For those of us who are persuaded by academic research, a significant body of studies has shown that conflict among management teams is not only inevitable, but also valuable. For example, Professor Kathleen M. Eisenhardt[8] studied technology companies and garnered some interesting results. When she finished her research, all the participating companies fell into one of three categories. Companies in the first group were those with little conflict. Interestingly, these organizations were less effective and took longer to bring new products to the market. The second group of companies in her study had lots of conflict, but it was often *personal* in nature. These companies were also relatively ineffective because their conversations were divisive and angry. The third contingent was able to minimize interpersonal conflict while effectively managing *substantive* conflict. As a result, those companies emerged as the most productive and innovative.

The Disney organization has an international reputation for creativity and innovation. Michael Eisner, Disney CEO and Chairman, believes that Disney's constant stream of new products is fueled by "creative friction."[9] "Disney," he says, "is a company built on a powerful combination of institutionalized creative friction—an environment that produces a constant stream of ideas—and good, old-fashioned common sense which 'edits' those ideas for broad commercial appeal. No matter what business you're in," Eisner asserts, "creativity 'has a way of cleaning up the balance sheet and making the income statement shine very brightly.'"

Eisner even uses this approach to creative problem-solving when Disney needs to come up with a solution that costs money. As he often quotes Woody Allen: "If show business wasn't a business, it would be called show show." Everything they do must be both creatively and fiscally responsible, whether they're talking about an acquisition, a corporate financing, or a movie scene. The collision between creativity and finances can lead to a lot of fights, yet the underlying Disney culture that fosters hashing out solutions creatively yields results.

As an example, Eisner mentions one of the first movies his team made at Disney. It was called *Outrageous Fortune* and starred Shelley Long. The script called for a scene in an apartment where the main character asks her parents for money to go to ballet school. The entire movie was over budget and the financial people thought the scene should be cut. The writer disagreed and a conflict ensued. The creative friction resulted in an innovative solution: Shelly Long made her request into the intercom in front of her parents' apartment building. No sets. No additional actors. She begs through a phone buzzer in an already-built exterior. When she finishes, a check floats down from the apartment. Eisner estimates the scene cost about $4.82 to make and was:

> ... so much better and so much funnier than what the script originally called for because somebody had a different point of view about how it could be done. There was a nice resolution of conflict that made sense in terms of creativity and cost.[10]

This kind of creative friction helps organizations avoid the dangers of "groupthink," the Orwellian term Irving Janis created.[11] Janis described this phenomena as "a mode of thinking that people engage in when they are deeply involved in a cohesive in-group, when the members' strivings for unanimity override their motivation to realistically appraise alternative courses of action."[12] The Groupthink tendency is really troublesome for creativity. Groups have illusions that everyone else is in agreement, which leads it to self-censor doubts and pressure dissenters. As a result, the group aborts divergent thinking and seizes too quickly upon options. Many of Janis's observations came from examining critical decisions of U.S. foreign policy making where groups critically needed creativity.

The Bay of Pigs disaster was one of his examples. Pulitzer Prize–winning historian Arthur Schlesinger Jr. called the 1961 invasion of Cuba by 1,400 expatriates one of the "worst fiascoes ever perpetrated by a responsible government."[13] Within three days, all of the invaders had been killed or captured. The major assumptions President Kennedy and his National Security Council held were entirely misguided. They believed that the Cuban population would spontaneously raise up to support the brigade of invading expatriates. They underestimated the ability of Castro's large, well-trained army and airfare to respond. And—to add insult to injury—the invaders landed in a big swamp.

How could a group of such smart people make such a dumb decision? At least part of the answer lies in the *groupthink*. Schlesinger, a member of Kennedy's group, later berated himself for his silence during the meetings:

> Though my feelings of guilt were tempered by the knowledge that a course of objection would have accomplished little save to gain me a name as a nuisance. I can only explain my failure to do more than raise a few timid questions by reporting that one's impulse to blow the whistle on this nonsense was simply undone by the circumstances of the discussion.[14]

Interestingly, Kennedy himself later analyzed the fiasco and appointed his brother and attorney general Bobby Kennedy to be a special "devil's advocate" during all such future discussions. Historians credit his recognition of the problem with his success in handling the Cuban missile crises.

Richard Tanner Pascale's study of innovative companies found that they embraced paradox and tension. He points to Honda as an illustration of a company with "a contention-management system that facilitates, rather than suppresses, conflict."[15] Because Honda is decentralized, it has conflict between its separate companies and departments. It decided to manage this contention in a productive way.

One of many approaches Honda used is called *waigaya*, which means "noise" in Japanese. During these regular meetings, subordinates are encouraged to openly, though politely, challenge their bosses. Takeo Fujisawa, Honda's co-founder, explains that fostering such open debate is like conducting an orchestra:

> As president, you must orchestrate the discordant sounds into a kind of harmony. But you never want too much harmony. One must cultivate a taste for finding harmony within discord, or you will drift away from the forces that keep a company alive.[16]

With waigaya, Honda has cultivated communication skills of the participants and the facilitator to keep the meetings productive.

Honda also intentionally creates cross-functional teams composed of young and new employees who have the right blend of personality and knowledge and are likely to see the problem in new and creative ways.

As these examples of successful conflict illustrate, if you want to change the way you are perceived in your organization, you need to plan for conflict, improve your own skills, and assume leadership in modeling conflict management and consensus building skills.

CHAPTER 2

THE LEADER AS DETECTIVE: HOW TO UNCOVER THE CAUSES OF GOOD AND BAD FIGHTS

Too often we enjoy the comfort of opinion without the discomfort of thought.

—John F. Kennedy

Mark Jacobs stared out of his office window into the darkening light. It was after six o'clock, but he hadn't moved since he returned from the staff meeting at five. All his team members did nothing today but squabble over things that seemed insignificant: when they would have the next meeting, why some reports went before others, who would get to choose the new software providers. He couldn't get them to focus on the real issue: they were behind on their production schedule, and what were they going to do about it? Why couldn't they work together to solve the problem? Why did every little dispute ignite a new round of warfare? What was all this conflict about, really? Why did every discussion degenerate into person sniping?

Mark's musings and confusion over causes are not unusual. In order to harness the power of attitudes about conflict, we need to discover the causes in our organization. If we don't, it's much more difficult to value conflict. Instead, we will continue to think that life is unfair or that people are just too difficult. We especially need to uncover masked conflict.

What kind of conflict causes *good* fights instead of *bad* ones?

Productive conflicts concern ideas, not personalities. Productive conflict is open instead of hidden. Why do we have so many bad fights today? Let's consider the contributing factors.

THE CAUSES OF CONFLICT

Certainly media violence, including movies and the Internet, is one cause of more conflict. We're seeing a whole generation of workers moving into the workplace who have been raised on violent images as a model for managing conflict.

Change in the workplace is another reason. We're working in a time where mergers, acquisitions, sales, and the creation of entire new enterprises all occur at lightning speed. All this change and the resulting conflict is not necessarily a bad thing. In fact, as psychologist Harville Hendrix has written, "Conflict is an indicator of growth trying to happen." Yet when we resist the change, we fail to embrace the conflict and we become mired in it. Many people fear change, and fear spawns more conflict.

The increasing diversity in most workplaces also creates conflict because we have not effectively trained most workers to work with people who are different than they are. As we will discover in Part 2, we can learn to use differences to generate creative sparks.

In addition, the use of e-mail and other technology also causes conflict. I don't know why this is, but people will say things in e-mail that they would never say in person.

When we fail to talk face-to-face, we miss subtle nuances of emotions and expressions that help us understand what the person talking really means. Abrupt statements by e-mail or fax can create more unproductive conflict.

In addition, as psychiatrist Edward Hallowell has postulated in his book, *Connect*,[1] many knowledge workers spend their day staring at computer screens rather than having human contact. His research shows that this is actually causing chemical changes in our brains, leading to depression and mood swings. People in this state frequently have more unproductive conflicts.

Many workplaces are moving toward a less hierarchical structure and toward a more team-oriented environment. This can be a good thing and yet it requires a more sophisticated set of skills, especially conflict management and consensus-building skills. Finally, most of us are too busy; productive conflict takes time.

All these reasons point to more conflict in the workplace and yet, after the participants in my workshops have listed all of these reasons, I frequently list one overwhelming cause: life.

Life causes conflict, especially because life isn't fair and we all have to deal with change and loss. When we're not conscious about our own grieving process, we may project our feelings onto others in the workplace and cause unproductive conflict. We all have different needs and interests than those with whom we live and work. Most of us have been raised and educated with the idea that we cannot embrace conflict, work through it, and have all of our different needs and interests met at the same time. Sometimes this is true.

Yet more often, if we're willing to be honest about our needs and creatively explore ways of meeting everyone's needs, we can satisfy many of our interests much of the time. We can actually develop a more creative idea than what we planned before working through the dispute.

We have to presume that it's up to us to assume leadership in conflict. We have to assume it's up to us to serve as models of skillful and creative conflict management.

The bottom line: We can't wait until we move to an organization without conflict, until the difficult people leave, or until the current emergency is over to improve our own approach to conflict. We have to start *now*.

ASSUME LEADERSHIP IN CONFLICT

In order to succeed, you must first examine your own view on conflict. Do you avoid conflict and, therefore, allow disagreements to fester?

Be careful if this is your personal conflict resolution style. Conflicts can devolve into a *negative spiral of conflict*. When we reach the bottom of the spiral, some important psychological changes occur:

- We're unable to see the opposing party or parties clearly.
- Our perceptions of others will be clouded.
- We'll suspect every action, no matter how innocent.

Psychologists call this *selective perception*. If, for example, I'm having a conflict with Jane and I walk down the hall and see Jane talking to Jim, whom do you think I will assume they're talking about? Me, of course!

What's significant about this change to selective perception is that we don't even realize this is happening. We'll continue to insist that we see the situation accurately. At that point, conflict is difficult to manage creatively and frequently results in personality clashes, litigation, or escalates into violence—tragic, unnecessary and expensive outcomes. Therefore, the key is to assume leadership and be the first to try to embrace the issue.

There are other conflict resolution styles, including an aggressive, competitive—what I call *pit bull*—style. This style may result in temporary victories, but damages the relationship and the organization over time, because a person who uses this style does not seek to meet the *needs* and *interests* of the parties involved. A person using this style doesn't really value conflict, they're just steamrolling over the opposition. Even if people submit to the will of the pit bull, there may be foot-dragging, time-wasting, and perhaps even sabotage down the road. More on conflict resolution styles in Chapter 4.

If you triangulate conflict, you may need to learn to talk directly to the person with whom you have the problem, rather than to others. Complaining to third parties about the conflict results in what I call *triangulation strangulation:* The conflict process is *strangled* rather than resolved. If you need to ventilate, choose a trusted advisor—coach, counselor, or priest—outside the organization. This style is another way of avoiding—rather than valuing—conflict. We will return to a more extensive discussion of style in Part 2.

Consider the possibility of welcoming conflict and developing the balanced approach outlined in this book. Try to discover the *needs* and *interests* of all parties involved and invent creative solutions that address those needs rather than becoming polarized on *positions*.

Learning to work skillfully with conflict and to add consensus-building skills in your organization will help move you into leadership as a strategic business partner and leader in your organization. One of the first jobs you need to assume is to uncover what causes good and bad fights.

THE MASK OF CONFLICT: IDENTIFYING CONFLICT IN ORGANIZATIONS

One of the first steps in assuming leadership in conflict is to learn to identify issues before they escalate out of control because other issues often mask conflict. If conflict is masked, we're not really seeing the value of conflict.

For example, can you identify the hidden expressions of conflict in the following statements:

Why can't they do their jobs?

Why do we always have to clean up their messes?

That's not *my* job!

Because we're all dependent upon each other in the workplace, and each worker's efforts impact the success of another, unresolved conflict creates a climate of blaming, whining, and griping.

Our department always gets the shaft. We have to get our share!

No one appreciates our effort.

The sales guys get whatever they ask for!

All organizations have limited money and resources. If leaders fail to address and skillfully embrace these issues, turf battles and perceptions of unfairness and favoritism emerge. Every department will feel that it needs more than it's getting.

Don't bother to complain. No one listens.

You know what happened to the last person who spoke up!

Just stay away from him and you'll do fine.

Expressions of apathy and cynicism infect organizations where it is normal to have conflicts around limited promotional opportunities, small pay raises, or ineffectual leaders. When individuals aren't rewarded for creative conflict management and collaboration, they'll spew forth negativity.

If they weren't so difficult (or stubborn or gossipy), we'd have a better place to work.

Negative judgments about co-workers or managers are expressions of unproductive conflicts. If people don't respect each other, they'll blame and complain. These kinds of attitudes are long running spirals of conflict.

All organizations must struggle to resolve issues of limited resources, time, abilities, and personnel, yet the conflict-skilled organization with strong models of collaboration and creativity can find direct ways to master these challenges. Leadership involves recognizing conflict and embracing it even when it's masked. Masked conflicts create simmering and ultimately bad fights.

IS IT A GOOD FIGHT OR A BAD FIGHT?

When you're in the trenches during a conflict, how do you know if it's a good fight or a bad fight? Good fights share several overarching characteristics: they honor the value of conflict; they are open, not masked; they concern ideas, not personalities; and they involve the skillful expression and management of emotion.

Generating good fights starts with attitudes that value conflict. Professor Linda L. Putnam summarizes her research on conflict and that of others, stating that within organizations, a good fight "balances power relationships, promotes flexibility and adaptiveness, and prevents stagnation of work units."[2] Good fights then, are fought by people who realize the power and value of controversy.

For instance, one of my clients is an enormously successful financial services company that specializes in throwing life preservers to companies that are sinking. They look at creative ways to restructure the foundering company's debt, consolidate operations, and plug leaking cash flow holes. Early on, the two founders realized that in order to succeed in their risky market, they would have to meticulously examine every potential deal for hidden flaws. They recognized that eagerness to close deals could cause them to make borderline, if not outright unsound, decisions. If that happened, they would sink right along with their clients. They needed to develop a process that would ensure that they used sound business practices so they harnessed the creative ideas of every person on staff. Every complex deal was subjected to a brutal cross-examination. The originating deal-maker would explain the proposed transaction to the assembled group, and everyone else would be invited to hash, critique, and otherwise challenge the speaker's ideas. It was the equivalent of throwing a piece of luggage into the gorilla's cage to see if it survived. Newcomers to the process quaked and worried, labeling the apparent chaos as "running the gauntlet."

Yet once a new employee sat through several such sessions, they became passionate converts. They realized that if a proposal survived the ordeal, the deal would almost certainly be a success because all possible calamities had already been anticipated. They learned to value the painful, yet creative brainstorming sessions.

When groups are in conflict, the good fights focus on the value of the process, realizing that through the dispute they can enhance their understanding of complex problems, learn to broaden their perspectives on organizational life, and experience success in managing differences.

Of course, these benefits can only occur if the fight is open, not masked. The second characteristic of a constructive conflict is that it brings the issue out into the light. Destructive conflicts lurk in the shadows or act as an undercurrent, working against the success of the organization. As psychologist and researcher Robert Baron has theorized, "conflict often serves to bring problems that have previously been ignored or neglected out into the open."[3] If workers understand the value of conflict, they will be much more likely to discuss issues openly and raise concerns to management.

The third broad characteristic of good fights relates to the content of the conflicts. According to conflict theorists, good fights are called cognitive conflict—the clash between opposing points of view or perspectives, instead of personalities or personal slights. Cognitive conflict enhances the quality of decisions because it forces a more thorough evaluation of the issues and increases the decision-maker's desire to understand others' ideas. Open discussion of conflicting points of view characterizes more successful organizations and leads to a stronger commitment to the group.[4]

Therefore, one way to determine if you're in a good fight is to ask if it's about ideas, points of view, and perspectives—not people or personality conflicts.

The fourth broad characteristic of good fights is the combatants skillfully manage the expression of emotion. While—as we will discuss more extensively in later chapters of this book—emotions must be honored and appropriately expressed—the unartful explosion of emotion during conflict creates bad fights. Why is this so? As Professor of Psychology Baron observes, "Conflict situations frequently require the careful, systematic processing of complex information."[5]

When we're out of control emotionally, however, we can't manage effectively "cognitive tasks during conflicts." As Baron emphasizes, "[G]rowing empirical evidence suggests that the following adage contains a considerable grain of truth: 'When emotions run high, reason flies out the window.'"[6]

Simply put, when we're upset during conflict, we can't think clearly and the likelihood of a bad fight increases. While we will grapple with skillful emotional expression during conflict in other sections of this book, Baron suggests several techniques for forestalling strong negative emotions.

Positive framing—encouraging the participants to focus on the potential gain of managing the conflict—is one way emotions are calmed. Another, he suggests, is by giving participants the information about the rational basis for their opponents' position. In other words: Information is power. When combatants understand why an opponent has adopted a particular stance, their reactions are less emotional and more favorable. Baron also suggests coaching participants to manage their own anger or frustration by inducing positive emotional states that are incompatible with the negative emotion through the use of visualization and imagery. Finally, he mentions that several recent studies suggest that exposing persons in conflict to treatments such as "mild flattery, a small gift, or humorous comments from an opponent," help reduce negative emotions and promote good fights.

In other words, your mother was right! You do "catch more flies with honey than with vinegar" and "a spoonful of sugar helps the medicine go down."

As we go through this book, we will continue to explore how you can detect good vs. bad fights. But keep in mind the four broad characteristics: recognizing the value of conflict; open, not masked; ideas, not personalities; and skillful emotional expression, not damaging emotional explosions.

WHY FAIRNESS IS NOT THE ISSUE

When I suggest to people that they need to welcome conflict and embrace its creative potential, I frequently hear a chorus of "it's not fair." People believe, "I'm not really the problem, it's *those* difficult people over there."

What I've noticed is that we assume that the difficult people are those who seem to have a different conflict management style than we do. If we're aggressive about confronting people, for example, we tend to point to those who avoid conflict as the problem. If we're loyal and accommodating, we see people who are always raising issues as the "difficult people."

Mostly, we all seem to think that it's simply *not fair* that we should be the one to have to assume leadership and develop the skills to lean into conflict. We believe that it's not fair that we work with people who cause conflicts or who avoid conflicts. We haven't really accepted the reality that *life causes conflicts*. Believing that life *should* be fair is, in my experience, the number one reason that people avoid creatively valuing and managing conflict.

For example, I was coaching a woman I'll call Esmerelda who started a job at a new law firm and immediately began criticizing everyone. I suspect that she was one of those people who sat in the first row in fourth grade, constantly yelling: "Call on me, call on me, call on me!" She was a tiny woman with a tall personality.

It's good to give people feedback and offer suggestions, but in most organizations, it's better to wait a while when we're new. Esmerelda was the kind of person who would not only advise you on how to write your brief, but would also tell you how to wash out your coffee cup and, when you were in the bathroom trying to have a little peace and quiet while you combed your hair, she would be telling you how to fluff it.

The firm's managing partner asked me to coach Esmerelda. The firm wanted to try to work things out because Esmerelda was brilliant and she billed tons of hours.

After a few sessions with Esmerelda, I was ready to give up. "It's not fair!" Esmerelda would wail. "I'm not the problem! I work harder than anyone else and I'm brighter than anyone else. I shouldn't be the one who has to change."

Everything I suggested was met with the stubborn response that others, not she, were the problem.

She finally got to me. I lost patience and said something that wasn't very diplomatic: "Esmerelda, most of us learn at about age four that life is not fair. What happened to you?"

This was not a nice thing to say, but it got her attention.

After that, I started thinking, was that true? Did I really learn at age four that life isn't fair? I decided that my own epiphany came at age 11 when I had one of those life-changing experiences.

I attended the kind of small rural school where if you weren't at the Friday night game there was nothing else to do. Not exactly the end of the world, but you could see it from there.

I had a lot of energy as a child, and I didn't think it would be fun to sit in the stands on Friday night. This was before girls' athletics, so being on the field was not an option. From the time I was in kindergarten, I decided that I would become a cheerleader. My friends and I practiced all through grade school.

Finally, we reached junior high and could actually try out for cheerleading. We were so excited. We practiced even harder. The big day arrived. The gym at school was full of kids, teachers, and the principal. The kids yelled, jumped, and screamed as only junior high kids can do.

I did my cheer in front of the judges and I was great. Perhaps not as great as Esmerelda, but I was great. The next day the list was posted. For some reason, at this school, the teachers selected the cheerleaders. I'm not sure why, perhaps they believed it made the event less of a popularity contest.

My friends were there with me as I stood in the school hall running down the list of names. My name was not there. I was devastated. Even worse, the girl who had been selected was Tilly Titlebaum. She was nice, but she was not as good a cheerleader as me.

I went home sick. My mother put me in a hot bath to calm me down. I cried for three days.

When I finally stopped crying, I realized that I still did not want to sit in the stands every Friday night. So I looked at my options and decided to become a baton twirler. The only problem was, I didn't know how to twirl a baton. But I spent the summer practicing and in the fall was selected to be a majorette. I pranced out in front of the stands at least some of the time.

Life isn't fair. People in authority make bad decisions—such as the teachers in this case. How often has someone in authority made a bad decision about *you*? I'll never know why they did, but I think that event was the start of a certain cynicism that perhaps led me to wanting to become an attorney. (Attorneys are professional cynics.) I've often joked that I became an attorney so that I could sue Tilly Titlebaum for impersonating a cheerleader.

Seriously, even though life isn't fair, we still need to take responsibility for assuming leadership in our life and in conflict. Believing that "it's not fair" is one of the primary hurdles to using the energy of creative contention. As one of my former law partners put it to his clients who expressed their disappointment in the outcome of a trial: "You may find perfect justice in the next world, but not in this one."

We need to realize that both others and ourselves in our organization are constantly battling these feelings of unfairness and loss, and that these unrecognized and unaddressed feelings can frequently lead to unproductive and uncreative conflicts. We need to provide leadership so that our organizations can address these issues directly and skillfully.

We need to stop avoiding conflict and welcome the creative potential in dealing skillfully with thorny issues. We need to change our thinking and attitudes about conflict and assume leadership. If we do, we will build trust, relationships, and creativity in our organizations. This is especially true if we stay on purpose during conflict, the subject of our next chapter.

CHAPTER 3

THE POWER OF PURPOSE: HOW TO USE YOUR MISSION AND VALUES TO EMBRACE CONFLICT

I have fought a good fight, I have finished my cause, I have kept the faith.

—2 Timothy 4:7

In 1945, a young inventor looked around the ruins of his homeland. He took $1,600 in savings, hired seven employees, and rented a room in a bombed-out Tokyo department store. They spent weeks sitting in the rubble trying to figure out what kind of business the new company should pursue. They brainstormed, fought, and sat until they agreed upon a path. With that, Masura Ibuka founded Sony Corporation.

Today, that global entity reveals the power of purpose.

A clearly articulated mission paves the road to organizational success as surely as the yellow brick road illuminated the way back home for Dorothy and the gang. It's easy for you or your organization to become hopelessly lost in destructive conflict without a landmark to guide it back to its focus. A defining focus serves as an organization's global positioning compass and gives it the drive to do the hard work of moving from conflict to connection, and then from connection to creativity.

Creating a strong network of connection is a safety net that allows people to take risks, embrace conflict and challenges, and raise the performance bar.

That's why the first key to valuing conflict is perhaps the most important—being clear about your goals. It's difficult to change your attitude and embrace conflict without a clear sense of values and purpose. You may be thinking: *This is a lot of work, Lynne. All this conflict management stuff. I don't have time for this! I've got 99 voicemails to return. I've got 110 e-mails to return. I don't have time.*

I find that the only way to stay clear during conflict is to have a deep understanding of what I'm about, both in my work life and my personal life. Similarly, we need to make sure our organizations are clear about their purpose and goals. If our organizations are clear about how conflict relates to their mission, we will be able to harness the value of conflict.

ORGANIZATIONAL GOALS AND CONFLICT

Conflict and creativity researchers agree that common goals, missions, objectives, and values are necessary to use conflict to fuel innovation and productivity. Researcher Eisenhardt, for example, in studying companies that managed conflict well, found that these teams minimized destructive conflict by framing strategic choices as collaborative, rather than competitive. "They did so by creating a common goal around which the team could rally. Such goals do not imply homogeneous thinking, but they do require everyone to share a vision."[1]

Eisenhardt found that teams "hobbled" by conflict were those that lacked common goals. Similarly, creativity researcher Dorothy Leonard[2] found that a "thoughtful, common mission statement does serve to unite people" during the conflict process. She warns, however, against the kind of generic mission statement—"to be a world class company"—for example, that many organizations create, but that has no real meaning for people.

Leonard found that the kinds of mission and purpose statements that help make conflicts constructive are those that are specific and distinctive. Those that, for example, unite the group against a common enemy such as earth-moving equipment giant Komatsu's slogan, which was "Beat Caterpillar." Similarly, during World War II, the British produced radar, faster airplanes, and computers in an unprecedented collaboration born of the common mission to defeat Hitler. She notes, however, that once the war was won, British science, government, and labor returned to internal squabbling and both innovation and the economy sagged.[3]

Common enemies can be other forces, Leonard stresses. At Northwestern Medical Hospital outside Chicago, for example, patients were dying of a hospital-borne infection. A task force was formed with infectious disease specialists, a pharmacist, computer technicians, admissions personnel, and even maintenance personnel—departments who normally battled each other over money and other resources. Faced with a common enemy, the group worked through conflict to develop creative solutions.[4]

Some groups find fighting *for* an objective to be more inspiring than fighting *against*, Leonard notes.[5] Office supply giant Staples, Inc., states its mission as "Slashing the costs and hassle of running your office!" and every employee receives a wallet-size card with that mission inscribed on it. The informal mission of Intuit is equally simple: "to make customers feel so good about the product they'll go and tell five friends to buy it." Apple started out with the goal of putting a computer on every desk.

My own client, Sun Microsystems, has an informal mission: "to kick butt and have fun." All of these missions keep these organizations on purpose during the inevitable conflicts.

If you're going to encourage the sparks of creative abrasion, your organization must be clear about its values and purpose in order to build a creative synthesis.

USING CONFLICT TO FUEL A TURN-AROUND

In fact, one of the best ways to turn an organization around is to both embrace conflict and to be clear about your values, mission, and purpose while doing so. That clarity and healthy conflict frequently fuels major changes and results in tremendous success. In tandem, they give an organization the power to jettison its unhealthy baggage and achieve unexpected positive outcomes. Such was the case with the Mercy Atlantic Healthcare System.

Mercy is a large regional network made up of seven hospitals and a full spectrum of outpatient services, including home care, home infusion, durable medical equipment, and hospice. For Mercy, the twin drives of welcoming conflict while staying true to their purpose and values created success. Mercy's experience can serve as a useful template in valuing conflict.

The system was floundering financially. An expensive merger with a smaller system had left them low on cash and long on cultural conflicts, while mistrust ran rampant throughout the organization. A new CEO named Tom Hoffman was hired from out of state. He brought with him his longtime friend, colleague, and confidant Bob Randolph to be the chief financial officer. Just days before Hoffman's arrival, a patient died unexpectedly at one of the organization's hospitals. It was the third surprising death in the last two years.

The morale of employees was at an all-time low as they faced an uncertain future and criticism by the local press. Clearly, the company needed an infusion of creativity and innovation to manage its problems. The new CEO came in committed to redevelop and change the culture; he was specifically committed to breaking down organizational walls between work units as well as opening up decision processes to encourage participation from everyone.

Hoffman's predecessor had enforced an intense command-and-control culture that encouraged bad fights over protecting turf. There was enormous financial pressure on the organization due to falling Medicare reimbursement, cut-rate managed care contracts, and a poorly planned joint venture with a brand-new urgent care center that was empty. Power was used to advance the self-interests of the previous CEO and some managers who followed his lead.

One of the senior vice presidents, for example, was a particularly untrustworthy and sneaky executive, utilizing a deadly "cobra" style (see Chapter 4). The executive frequently encouraged his senior manager to go to the CEO and denigrate her performance, plans, and practices. Once the manager became aware of the situation, she tried to go around the executive, but she was repeatedly blocked. Her team became so discouraged and frustrated that all their creativity and problem-solving skills ebbed out of them, and their division's performance went from barely making their budget to a disastrous free-fall slide. They were so demoralized and tired of being falsely criticized that they lost the energy to implement solutions and take the reasonable risks necessary for them to succeed. Their work performance was dismal, and their creativity was nonexistent.

When Hoffman learned of the situation, he canned the executive and made it clear to all employees that he counted on them to use their judgment, including taking thoughtful risks. As the group came to believe that it really was a part of their "job description" to risk reasonable mistakes, their performance improved dramatically. These improvements led to significant financial gains.

Dismissing the deadly senior vice president and setting a different tone sent a message about the company's values and mission and set the stage for building a better work climate. The managers of that particular division became so energized that within 18 months they became the superstar performers of the entire company.

Hoffman soon discovered, however, that Mercy's entire executive management was also seriously at odds, as was evident by unproductive conflicts over decisions, recurring turf issues, and the withholding of information by managers.

Hoffman assumed that his management difficulties were "people problems" that would disappear if executives could just be given the right psychological advice to help them fix their personal character defects. Yet outside consultants convinced him that changing the organization wasn't just a matter of fixing individuals; it had to involve assessing the entire cultural context to grasp how effectively it functioned in decision-making, cooperation, and human resource utilization. To attack the most irritating symptoms, such as the bad behavior or misalignments without understanding what triggered, them would make the problems worse instead of better.

What Mercy's surveys and focus groups revealed was that while Hoffman had jettisoned the practices of the old regime, people didn't know what to do now. The work environment didn't include any new coherent mission, cultural values, or standards of expected behavior.

Based on the service they provided, Hoffman sought to bring the mission of service back to the core of Mercy's operations. He wanted all decisions to reflect that purpose. He began by personally embracing a goal of servant leadership, holding himself and all the other executives accountable as stewards for the much larger community. He and his executive team began to think of themselves in service roles, responsible for managing the assets of their share holders and helping employees do their jobs. Hoffman insisted that from now on everyone at Mercy was to hold him accountable for acting consistently with his values and purpose. Anyone who disagreed should confront him directly. He invited constructive conflict.

Consistent with their purpose, the executive team decided on a set of core values for conducting their business that emphasized integrity. Because there had been so much mistrust, sabotage, and indirect communication, they emphasized rebuilding employees respect. Hoffman wanted to create an organization where people at all ranks took initiatives to solve problems creatively without fear of reprisal. He encouraged good fights.

Conflict resolution training was delivered to all the managers, but even that wasn't enough. He soon realized that the executive team was still mired in interpersonal conflicts. These bad fights were not being addressed openly, much less managed.

To his surprise, Hoffman learned that his own style created problems. Even though he gave lip service to the idea of a more open, participatory work climate, he intimidated his fellow executives, and they felt afraid to confront him when they had a difference of opinion.

Hoffman was so committed to the vision and what it would take to get there that he moved ahead at a pace that was too fast for some members of his team. For other members, Hoffman's own commitment to integrity and his management style triggered significant personal conflict. The more open process required them to assume leadership in conflict. They balked mightily. Some teams didn't want to be held accountable for their own performance, so they found fault with their peers and made excuses.

Personal style difference compounded the problem, leading to communication conflict and suspicions of others' motives. Hoffman now had to build a greater degree of trust among his executives and managers. He started by openly addressing their styles and differences, an important tactic we will address in Part 2.

Although addressing the interpersonal issues among the executive team was sometimes uncomfortable, the open discussions—while staying true to their values and purpose—allowed Mercy to create the kind of team they wanted. Decision-making became more efficient; executives were quicker to voice concerns or differences of opinion. They also spent more time asking about each other's ideas and began to appreciate the value their individual differences brought to the team, which resulted in more productive conflicts. The executive time now shared a strong vision and created more good fights and fewer bad ones.

This shared vision and new culture created better decision-making where the free flow of ideas was expressed and valued. The creative collaboration and conflict management produced rich rewards. The organization reached the elite level for health-care systems. It was awarded the highest commendation from the Joint Commission on Accreditation of Healthcare Organizations. It achieved budget numbers. Every member of Mercy, from janitors to CEOs, earned bonuses. None of this could have been accomplished without the combined focus on vision, purpose, values, and creative conflict management.

Now, as Mercy learned, this is hard work—to be on purpose no matter what you're doing. But if you are, you won't get involved in petty conflicts and you'll go through the work that you need to go through to embrace and value the big conflicts.

OUR PERSONAL MISSION AND VALUES

Why do I bother to get up in the morning to go to work? To get on airplanes and speak? What is my purpose in life? How is what I'm doing today serving my larger purpose? These are the questions I ask myself every day in order to stay on purpose. Staying "on" our personal purpose helps us to constructively use conflict.

I would suggest to you that you need to have a purpose that is big enough to serve you in both your work life and in your home life so there's no conflict of values between who you are at work and who you are at home. Now I'm not suggesting that you should go to your boss tomorrow morning and start sobbing about your personal problems. But we need to have a goal that's important enough that we are on purpose no matter where we are.

I'm clear that my life's purpose is to limit the distance between you and me. If I'm involved in a conflict with you, my purpose is to close the space between us; to see us both in relationship. I ask: How can we use this conflict to enhance our relationship? My purpose, if I'm working with a group, is to look at how we can all come together as a community. How can we create more community at work and at home? How can we make the conflict work for the organization to create more innovation and creativity?

My eight-year-old twins are going to be around in 2050. I want them to have a planet where people can talk to each other; where people can close the space in relationships; where people can have a real community at home and at work; where people realize that conflict can be embraced and managed and need not tear groups and nations apart. And if we practice conflict management and consensus building skills, we can create more connection and community and find more creative solutions to our deepest problems. We can learn to value conflict.

How do you find your own purpose and learn to stay on it consistent with your goals and values? Let's consider some ways that work.

LOOK FOR MODELS

To help you stay on purpose, it's important to look for models. Models help us realize what we can do. Certainly, there are the famous models of conflict transformation—people like Gandhi and Martin Luther King Jr.—who were faced with enormous conflicts, but were so clear about their purpose that they never forgot what they were doing no matter where they were. They were able to embrace the creative potential in conflict.

Consider Queen Elizabeth I, for example. She ascended the throne in 1558 when England was in shambles. Impoverished, shackled by runaway inflation, and lacking both an army and a navy while facing rebellion in Ireland and enemies in Scotland, the English found a woman on the throne to be just about the last straw. They presumed that, as a woman, Elizabeth was unsuited for leadership and intellectually inferior to men.

Despite the widespread doubts about Elizabeth, she proved more than capable. Enemies and power hungry lords regularly sought to overthrow her. She surrounded herself with extremely competent advisors, retaining some from the past and adding some of her own choosing. Elizabeth transformed crises into opportunities.

Her approach to conflict was unique in a time when many rulers were nothing less than dictators. In contrast, Elizabeth invited dissent. She was not afraid to fuel the fires of creative conflict.

Another famous example of creatively managing conflict by staying on purpose is, of course, Mahatma Gandhi, the leader in the Indian struggle for independence in the 1930s. He pioneered the notion of passive resistance (successfully used again by Martin Luther King Jr. in the 1960s) and organized a campaign of noncooperation. Because of his efforts, India's public officers resigned, government agencies were boycotted, Indian children were withdrawn from governmental schools, and he orchestrated a complete boycott of all British goods. He called upon Indians to refuse to pay taxes, particularly on salt. (He chose salt because it was used as the basic commodity at the time and was controlled by the British.) Gandhi led a historic protest march from Ahmadabad to the Arabian Sea and made salt by evaporating seawater.

Due to Gandhi's relentless and creative management of the conflict that crippled India, the Indian people gained independence in 1947.

All of these historical examples can help keep us on purpose during our own quest through conflict.

One of my personal favorite models is someone who might not be as well known—a woman named Elizabeth Glaser. In the 1980s she found out she was HIV positive. She received the virus through a blood transfusion. Glaser passed it along in the womb to her two children before she knew she had the virus.

Although it was a devastating blow, Glaser took on AIDS as a cause. Not many people knew at that time that children could be HIV positive and that kids could get AIDS. So Glaser found that doctors, hospitals, and schools discriminated against her precious children. She sought out the discriminators and started forums where they could meet, share their fears and creatively resolve their conflicts. She went on the road and started speaking about AIDS. Glaser brought the term "pediatric AIDS" into our vocabulary and raised millions of dollars for this particular cause.

It's interesting because she was a tiny person—under five feet and less than 100 pounds—a shy wife and mother who never worked outside the home. Yet she learned how to speak publicly because she was on purpose and believed in her cause. In fact, Glaser was asked to speak at the 1992 Democratic Convention. I'm told that before she spoke, she looked out—there were 20,000 people in the live audience, 20 million more watching on TV—and was absolutely petrified. Glaser was afraid that she wouldn't be able to talk. They had to put a step behind the big podium because she was so tiny that she couldn't see over it without one.

Glaser wrote that just before she stepped up she thought she might not be able to find her voice, but she felt someone grab her hand and help her up the steps. She was able to give a powerful speech and influence many lives. Glaser realized later that it was the hand of her daughter who had died two years earlier.

If you're on purpose, I promise you—no matter what conflict you're in, no matter what challenge you're facing—someone will step up to hold your hand and help you do whatever you need to do.

So what's your purpose? Please get clear about it if you haven't already.

One of the most useful tools for conflict transformation is for us to clearly hold a purpose to build partnerships, alliances, and communities. If that goal is a part of our purpose, both as individuals and organizations, we will be able to stay more committed to embracing the conflict instead of running away or seeking to flatten the opposition.

A SUGGESTED PURPOSE: COMMUNITY BUILDING

Is anyone else sick of the word *networking?* I am! When I meet a new person that I want to get to know, personally or professionally, the specter of networking rears its ugly head. If I'm interested in them, I wonder if they're wondering about my motives, especially if I know they're well connected in business.

If someone acts extremely interested in me, I face the same suspicions. Why do they care? I sometimes wonder. Do they want to be friends or do they want to add me to their Rolodex—or, more recently, their "contact management" computer program?

Stop "managing your contacts." I know this is contrary to every bit of career advice you've received in the new millennium, but trust me. The future does not belong to networking; it belongs to partnerships, alliances, and communities. Building these kinds of relationships is a skill that successful leaders naturally have.

Let the difference in those words sink in. *Network* has a cold, metallic ring. *Networking* has acquired a superficial meaning. It's the word linked to using people; it's the word of takers. I know many bright, capable people whose careers have stalled because—even though they believe they should engage in networking—something in their soul rebels. These are caring, connecting kind of people. The idea of networking leaves them cold.

The future, I believe, will not reward superficial connections. If you want to thrive in your industry or profession, think deep, think long-term, think partnerships, alliances, and communities. Think giving, not taking.

Creating more opportunities for people to get to know one another will automatically create more productive dialogue and fewer uncreative arguments. Unfortunately, in our high-tech culture, when many of us spend both our work and our private time staring at computer or TV screens, we are moving in the opposite direction.

Partnerships, alliances, and communities imply equality—especially equal initiation and participation—as opposed to *networking*, which implies one person latching onto or using another. These words symbolize long-term, deep commitments to other people and organizations.

I don't mean to suggest that you must stay with your present employer, boss or co-workers for life. But even if you leave, would it serve you and them to leave on the best terms with a commitment to maintain your relationship, to continue to include them in your community?

I must confess that my bias on this issue comes from a philosophical perspective. I believe that we have a responsibility to respect and serve and assist others in our pathway through life. We are all connected in a fragile web—whether we like it or not. I view the Internet as a wonderful (if flawed) reminder of this truth. If we don't take care of our connections with others, these precious, connecting strands tend to tangle or break. When we disconnect from someone—because of uncreative conflicts or lack of attention—we are both lessened. Ironically, one of the best ways to connect is to work through a conflict with someone.

Creating connection and community isn't just a "touchy-feely" idea; there's hard evidence that it creates real productivity gains.

Researchers William Judge, Gerald Fryxell and Robert Dooley conducted extensive interviews at eight U.S. biotech firms. They assessed innovation through an analysis of the "cycle times" of the companies' patents—the shorter the cycle time, the faster the new technology is brought to market. They divided the companies into fast and slow groups. They found striking differences between the cultures of the two groups. The "ability of management to create a sense of community in the workplace was the key differentiating factor. Highly innovative units behaved as focused communities, while less innovative units behaved more like traditional bureaucratic departments."[6]

In the innovative companies, leaders provided overarching goals, but allowed the scientists autonomy in reaching them. In the less innovative firms, leaders granted either too much or too little autonomy.

I'm convinced that the most powerful need we share as human beings is the need to move from *conflict* to *connection*, and then from connection to creativity. If you can make it a part of your individual purpose as well as your organization's purpose to constantly look for ways to create *connections*, many conflicts will evaporate and those you do have will be embraced and creatively transformed more quickly. Consider including *connecting* through partnerships, alliances, and communities in your own purpose.

HOW DO WE DEVELOP PARTNERSHIPS, ALLIANCES, AND COMMUNITIES?

When you meet someone new and interesting, or when you hear about a great team or organization, think: How can I help this person or group? What do I have to offer that could help their long-term needs and mission? What kind of partnership could we create together? How can we work together to contribute to the larger local and world community? How can we embrace and transform our inevitable conflicts in order to build more creativity? How can we have more good fights and fewer bad ones?

One way is to examine our own attitudes. Luckily, I have learned to view life as a cultural anthropologist, appreciating many diverse thinking and working styles and most people interest me—even when their values and personalities differ from mine—more than they irritate me. This attitude helps me stay on purpose and use the energy of conflict creatively.

A kind of detached amusement at the flaws and personality quirks we all share as fellow humans, bumbling along this strange path called life, is an attribute we can all develop, I've discovered.

People today in our mobile, disconnected, distracted society are hungry for community. If you lead with your heart—and have cultivated the heart of a warrior so that you're not injured by every slight— you'll see opportunities to build community everywhere. Do it, even if you can't see any immediate pay off for your career.

Thirty years in the world of work in many different kinds of jobs, professions, and businesses has convinced me that *soul leaders*—those who build deep connections with people no matter what their skin color or their position, and regardless of whether they walk or wheel themselves into a room, come out winners—both personally and professionally—in the long run.

And really, what do you want on your tombstone: "She Was a Great Networker" or "She Was a Great Community Builder"?

Having this kind of attitude toward life will make your job of embracing and valuing both every day and more difficult conflicts much easier. It will help propel you and your organization through the hard work of transforming conflicts into creativity and building innovative consensuses.

PART 2

The Power of Styles: How to Understand and Use Different Conflict Styles to Release Your Creative Potential

CHAPTER 4

FIVE BEASTLY CONFLICT COPING STYLES: HOW TO RETRAIN YOUR ANIMAL INSTINCTS

The reptilian brain is hidebound by precedent.

—Paul MacLean

Kathleen Hamilton is under enormous pressure. A successful manager of a posh women's clothier, she's flown to Denver to oversee the company's newest store opening at the Flatiron Crossing Shopping Center. The company has staked their success on her. She's responded by working 14 hours a day, attending to every detail, and catching fast food on the fly. Alison, the store manager Kathleen is training, has matched her hour for hour, but Alison's now starting to bark at the rest of the staff—giving orders and yelling when trainees make mistakes. One of the new employees runs to the back room to escape the tirade. Another pacifies Alison, her new boss, agreeing with her and mollifying her while a third one quietly seethes. Kathleen sees the turmoil and doesn't flinch. She calmly sends Alison on a break and then meets with her 30 minutes later.

Kathleen and the rest of the crew typify five basic coping styles that people use when faced with a conflict. Some choose to respond like a pit bull that's been taunted or dash away like a roadrunner. Others will wag their tails like happy golden retrievers, lay in wait like cobras going for the kill, or respond gracefully and swiftly like eagles. Each style has significant advantages and disadvantages.

While each of us is naturally inclined to a particular style, with practice we can adapt our style according to the situation and improve the outcome. In addition, with an awareness of the styles others use, we can learn how best to respond to them.

A key to embracing conflict and harnessing its creative power is to understand these different styles. Once you identify your own and others' style, you'll be able to acknowledge and utilize differences to your advantage. You will also be able to value conflict as an opportunity to explore those differences and welcome diverse views as a key to creativity. You'll also be able to choose the style that assists you best in using the energy of the conflict. If we don't understand these style differences, we'll tend to personalize conflict or avoid it.

Most of us, however, have not thought about how style influences our approach to conflict. In fact, the first time a pit bull attacked my friend Emily, she was totally unprepared. She had no idea how to deal with other styles of conflict resolution.

THE PIT BULL ATTACK

The year was 1979 and Emily was starting a new job. She was excited to have this job. She'd worked her way through college and law school and had no other source of income. She was also thrilled because she was going to be working at a prestigious downtown Denver law firm. The partner who had hired her had a national reputation and she was going to be practicing the kind of complex litigation she wanted to do.

Like most women attorneys in the late 1970s, Emily dressed in her John Malloy *Dress for Success* suits in dark blue, brown, or black. She wore her long hair up in a conservative bun. Women tried to fit in.

Two or three months after she started, Emily was walking down the hall one day—minding her own business—when all of a sudden someone started screaming at her that she had forgotten to do something for a client. In fact, he was screaming obscenities at her! Emily turned around to discover that the screamer was the partner who had hired her. (I'll call him Claude.) Standing beside Claude was another senior partner she barely knew, as well as two clients Emily didn't know at all.

She was so shocked that, for once, she had nothing to say. She just looked at him in shock, crept down the hall, and hid out in her office, trying to decide what to do. That night, she went out with me to discuss her options. We sat there drinking Johnnie Walker Red and came up with three possibilities: (1) Emily could pretend the conflict never happened and hope it never happened again, (2) she could leave, or (3) she could confront him.

Confronting him was the scariest option to Emily: This was a powerful man, one many people in the firm were afraid of then and still are today. Leaving would create serious problems, too; Emily *needed* this job. Just pretending it never happened was equally dangerous because it risked setting a precedent of allowing him to continue the abuse.

What would you tell Emily to do if you were sitting across from her? In fact, what would you do? Run away? Confront him? Or would you stay and pretend nothing had happened?

Is the advice you would give her different from what you know you would do? (Sometimes we're braver in our advice to others than we are in taking risky action ourselves.)

HOW AND WHEN DO WE RAISE CONFLICT?

The answer to the question of how and when we raise conflict will tell us many things. One thing it will reveal is how much you value conflict as reflected by your conflict resolution style, and how skillfully you deal with conflict management styles that are different from your own. The answer will also tell us how likely the conflict is to be embraced and creatively used.

It's a delicate balance, I've learned. If we raise dispute too often, we run the risk of generating unnecessary emergencies or of seeming petty. If we don't raise issues soon enough—if we're a classic conflict avoider—we may spin into the *negative spiral of conflict*, which means conflicts are less likely to be embraced.

When Emily faced the issue with her new law firm, we hadn't studied conflict management and negotiation. We didn't really know how to value conflict. That's not a subject most law schools teach. Rather by accident, I managed to advise her to follow many of the rules in this book. Her run-in with Claude started her on the road to learning more about different styles and skillful conflict management.

Because even then, at that early stage of my career, I realized that conflict—skillfully embraced—builds trust, builds relationships, and builds our reputations as leaders in the organization.

WHAT IS "A GOOD FIGHT"?

After the "Johnnie Walker Red" session with me, Emily went home to bed, only to toss and turn. None of her options seemed easy or risk-free and she kept wrestling with the consequences of each choice. She slept very little. Emily awoke the next morning assaulted with that queasy stomach you have when you haven't had enough sleep. She applied her makeup with a shaky hand, adding an extra layer of concealer to cover the dark circles. She squirmed into panty hose and a dark suit and drove to the office on automatic pilot.

She sat in her office drinking coffee and trying to work up her nerve to approach Claude. Then Emily paced the hall for a while. Finally, she took a deep breath and approached the lion's den.

Claude sat alone at his desk working on some papers. He didn't look up. She sat down on the couch in his office because her knees felt shaky.

"Claude, I need to talk to you about what happened yesterday," Emily said.

He looked up from his desk and grunted. He wasn't breathing fire, but he didn't look pleased to hear from her.

She took another deep breath and continued. "Claude, you're my boss. You have a right to give me feedback. In fact, I welcome feedback. But I need to have criticism conducted privately, without yelling or profanities, and I need to have a chance to have a dialogue about it because, Claude, that mistake you were yelling at me about, wasn't my fault. The client forgot to send me the form and I'd been calling him for days trying to get it and they hadn't returned my phone calls." There! She'd said it, all in a breathless rush. She sat back on the couch, exhausted.

Well. This was a person who had a pit bull style approach to conflict. You know the type?

Claude wasn't going to take this sitting down, say "okay" and apologize. He leapt up from his chair and started trotting around the room, ranting and barking: "Well, if you don't want anyone to yell at you, the way to avoid that is to not make any mistakes and if you hadn't screwed up, I wouldn't have been yelling at you and I'm just going to have to talk to that *&^% hiring committee about how they keep hiring incompetent new associates and ...."

He was getting more and more agitated as he talked, stalking around the room in circles, talking, yelling, barking "rrrup, rrup, RRRUP!" Finally, he was so worked up, Claude yanked his phone out of the wall and threw it across the room at Emily.

Luckily, he missed. She jerked back in her seat, took a deep breath and repeated what she'd said earlier, using what I call the *broken record technique*. Claude just stared at Emily, frowning so deeply his eyebrows were practically touching, and then he started shouting and trotting again.

"You will never make it at this firm or any other if you have that kind of attitude! This is a tough business and you have to toughen up! We sometimes yell! This isn't a charm school ... bark, bark, rrup, rrrrup, RRRUUP!"

Emily sat glued to the couch, eyes wide, trying to breathe and calmly repeat what she'd said before. This time Emily added, "You know, Claude, if I have to wait tables again I will, but I need to be treated with respect at work."

They went through several more rounds like this: Claude yelling, barking, and trotting around the room; Emily calmly repeating how she wanted and needed to be treated. Finally, he ran out of steam—as pit bulls usually do. He sat down at his desk and they were able to have a real conversation.

From that day on, he treated Emily with respect. They had disagreements, conflicts, and many discussions, but he never again yelled or swore at her. They developed a highly creative and successful approach to their cases. He became a wonderful mentor to Emily, both at the firm and after she left. In fact, he remains a mentor to her today.

Many people, when they hear the title of this book, *The Power of A Good Fight*, say, "What do you mean a *good* fight, Lynne? I've had many fights in my life, but I've never had a *good* fight?"

Emily's discussion with Claude was what I call a good fight because she didn't avoid the conflict, flee, or pretend it never happened. She decided to value the conflict by embracing the issue. She managed to confront a pit bull without backing down, allow him to vent until he ran out of steam, and gain his respect in the process. The fight actually improved their relationship and led to a more creative working partnership. Emily negotiated the tricky terrain of handling a pit bull and managed to embrace the conflict by following most of the 10 steps to conflict management you're going to read about in this book.

CONFLICT AND THINKING STYLE PREFERENCES

The five basic conflict management styles represent simplified versions of other social style systems such as Myers-Briggs. These social style indicators are *thinking-style preferences*, closely related to how we handle conflict. In my experience, these differences in thinking styles lead directly to differences in how we handle conflict. Through a combination of genetics and our personal history, these thinking styles seem to be "hard wired" and then reinforced by years of working. Just as we instinctively seem to prefer certain food or clothes, we have habitual ways of thinking and reacting that we don't often analyze.

These so-called cognitive differences lead to diverse approaches to perceiving and assimilating data, making decisions, solving problems, and relating to other people—including how we relate to other people during conflict. The most widely recognized distinction between different thinking styles is between left-brained and right-brained thinkers. Current brain researchers tell us that this popular distinction doesn't really correlate: not all so-called "creative functions" are located on the right side of the cortex and not all so-called "left-brained" functions are located on the left. Still, the description does serve as a short-handed way of describing differences in thinking styles that we all recognize.

Thinking styles influence work styles, and particularly relevant to conflict is their influence on decision-making activities. Some people, for example, prefer to work cooperatively on solving problems, yet others need time alone to process information. Forcing an introverted thinker—who may also appear to be a conflict-avoider—to think on his or her feet during a contentious meeting can lead to disaster. Conversely, some extroverts like to think out loud and discuss options endlessly with others while they decide what they think.

Different thinking styles also produce differences in thinking as opposed to feeling. Some of us evaluate evidence and decide issues though a structured, logical process. Others "go with their gut," relying on their values and emotions to help them decide.

During conflict or decision-making, abstract thinkers want information from a variety of sources—books, reports, videos, and conversations. They prefer learning from those sources, instead of direct experience. Others want information from interacting directly with people and things. Differences abound during conflict. Some people decide issues quickly, others want to mull over the options. Some of us focus on details, whereas others look at the big picture.

We also tend to pick professions that support out different thinking styles. Most so-called right-brained creative types, for example, don't end up as engineers, even though some kinds of engineering requires a great deal of creativity. A poet may rely more on feelings and intuition when solving problems rather than numbers or diagrams.

Why is understanding these differences in styles so important to harnessing conflict to drive creativity, innovation, and productivity? Because the most creative groups contain a mix of diverse people. One of the best ways to ensure that mix is by making sure that we combine people with different thinking styles.

Instead, most of us want to hire and work with people who are like us. As Dorothy Leonard suggests, this limits our creative options as an organization. She cites the example of two different managers.[1] One, John, was a rising star in a large, diversified instrument company who damaged his career by failing to create a diverse team.

The CEO gave John, as the new manager of a new-product development group, a free hand in finding radical and innovative ideas, products, and services. John scurried to hire three of the brightest MBAs available. He completed the team with engineers who also had strong quantitative skills. The group busily analyzed exiting products, sorting through data and numbers. While advised to hire some right-brained creative types to spark new ideas, John stuck with his left-brained friends. After 18 months, the group rejected all new product ideas with exhaustively researched reports on the technical and financial risks but came up with no new products. The disgruntled CEO disbanded the group.

In contrast, Leonard cites Bob, a successful entrepreneur who embarked on his latest adventure with the knowledge that his own highly analytical style clashed with his most creative people. Yet even with this self-awareness, Bob almost fired Wally, his experienced director of human resources. Bob found Wally "a quart and a half low." During budget meetings Wally ignored the financial data and instead raised "people" issues of day care, flextime, and benefits. Although irritated, Bob managed to yank himself back from the abyss of a mistake by realizing that Wally brought a missing element to the management team. Wally helped avoid employee problems by focusing on human needs. As Bob told Leonard in describing how he learned to work with Wally, "You would have been proud of me. I started our meetings with five minutes of dogs, kids, and station wagons." Bob's realization helped minimize labor's antagonism toward management and assisted in employee dispute resolution.[2]

THE FIVE BASIC CONFLICT STYLES

As I've mentioned, the five basic conflict styles are simplified versions of the dozens of diagnostic instruments managers use as thinking style assessment tools, such as Myers-Briggs or Herrmann Brain Dominance Instrument. The problem with these more complex systems, however, is that they are difficult for most people to remember and use effectively. Most of us have enough trouble remembering our own four letters in the Myers Briggs system, for example. We're hopeless when we're asked to recall and respond to the letters of all of our teammates.

By contrast, these "beastly" conflict resolution style symbols are vivid and easy to remember. Most users find that they become like icons that readily pop up on our computer screens, reminding us how to respond to someone who is using a different style. They also assist us in being more self-reflective about our own style.

While some people use more than one style and some a mixture of several, most of us fall into one style, especially when we're under stress and our backs are against the wall. Each style has advantages and disadvantages. Each has a different level of ability to truly value and embrace conflict. Each style brings different skills to the creation of a diverse team.

The five styles are described as follows:

- **Pit bull:** Attacks conflict, likes to argue and debate, threaten, and intimidate; highly competitive; avoids concessions. Can be useful in all-out wars.

- **Golden retriever:** Usually accommodates; can be extremely loyal and has a need to please people and to be liked. Can be useful for team building and raising morale.

- **Roadrunner:** Avoids conflict; can be difficult to pin down to determine interests. Can be useful in avoiding unimportant disputes or petty disagreements.

- **Cobra:** Triangulates conflict, talks to other people rather than the person or persons directly involved. Can be useful in building consensus among groups with little power.

- **Eagle:** Approaches conflict with skill and balance; uses other approaches only when necessary after much thought; truly understands the value of conflict. Constantly applies the 10 steps of conflict management (see Chapter 11).

We have to be careful to remember that we all use all of these styles at different times and in different situations. It's not useful or productive to use these styles as new ways to label or harass others. No style is completely good or bad; each one has pros and cons. We will discuss each individual style in the chapters that follow.

We use unproductive styles when we're responding to conflict in an automatic, emotional way. Why do we do this? The answer lies in what physical anthropologists, who study the development of our brains, call the "reptilian brain."

OUR REPTILIAN NATURE

What these anthropologists tell us is that we all have an old part of our brain that resembles that of a reptile. When reptiles are stressed, they respond in "flight or fight" mode. A large part of our brain is still based upon this emotional section. To understand how large, imagine an avocado.

The fleshy part of the avocado is this emotional, reptilian brain. The skin is that small part of our brain that serves as a manual override. The pit represents the unconscious part of our brain—basically, we have no idea what's going on there. Our task is to try to develop and access the thinking part of our brain, to override the emotional part and react with thought during conflict.

When we are similarly reacting emotionally during conflict, we're frequently generating and sustaining personality conflicts instead of productive conflicts over ideas, theories, and programs. In addition, as discussed in Chapter 2, intense emotions interfere with our ability to process our thoughts during conflict, increase the emotional charge for others, and lead to bad fights.

The styles of conflict management that avoid conflict—roadrunners, golden retrievers, and cobras—are simply accessing the flight mode of their reptilian brain. Those styles that tend toward aggression during conflict—pit bulls, especially—are simply reacting to stress with a fight mode. None of these extreme styles truly value and embrace conflict. Aggressive styles simply steamroll over others' needs and interests, while conflict avoiders do not understand or utilize the creative potential in conflict.

Most of us primarily use one style in conflict situations. We use this style when considering new ideas and problems of conflict within ourselves as well as when we interact with others.

For example, because of my training as an attorney and my innate personality (it's no accident that I became an attorney), I tend to use an analytical, argumentative, and critical conflict resolution style. If someone presents a new idea to me, I imagine all the reasons why it won't work. I will argue. I am a pit bull.

If I don't guard against this tendency, without thinking, I go into what I call my "debate mode." Although this is a useful skill when engaged in an actual debate, courtroom battle, or a dispute with the plumber, this style creates disadvantages in personal and most professional relationships. I'm not seeking the creative spark in conflict, I'm simply running over the needs and ideas of others.

When we use this conflict resolution style, it's akin to having a black belt in karate. Just because we have the skill to cut someone down with our hands doesn't mean it's appropriate to go around karate chopping at the least provocation. I've had to learn to rein in my pit bull tendency when it's inappropriate and to instead use other conflict styles.

Changing our conflict resolution style takes three things:

1. Developing an awareness of the style we primarily use.
2. Consciously choosing to use a different style when appropriate.
3. Finding the discipline to practice.

Most of us have not really thought about developing or using conflict styles other than our habitual mode.

STEP 1: DEVELOPING AN AWARENESS OF THE STYLE WE PRIMARILY USE

We need to start with ourselves. Once we identify our own style, we'll gain insight into the ways our style unconsciously shapes our own leadership and communication during conflict. If you want to use conflict to encourage creativity, you need to understand that your own style may be interfering with the very innovation you seek. Consider, for example, the experience of two different managers from two highly creative organizations.[3] Both learned the hard way to recognize how his own style limited the very creativity they sought.

Jim Shaw, for example, the executive vice president of MTV Networks, learned that he squelched productive conflicts and stifled creativity by his responses to new ideas. By attacking anything new as a critical pit bull, he sent the conflict-avoiders scurrying to their corners instead of engaging in a constructive conversation.

Jerry Hirshberg, president of Nissan Design International, faced the opposite problem in understanding how his own style impacted his team. At first he threw information at his people and expected instant creativity in return. Following the Golden Rule, he managed people the way he wanted to be managed. Yet instead of generating the creative abrasion he wanted, his tactic made people react to every suggestion with a "yes, but ..." Frustrated, he initially assumed that such hesitation to engage was an anti-innovative bias. What he finally realized was that some of the thinkers in the group wanted time to digest the problem and construct logical approaches. After he initially threw down the gauntlet, he would allow them the time to formulate their own responses. They would then return to the discussion with helpful and insightful plans for implementation. Instead of continuing to avoid the conflict and creativity Hirshberg was trying to generate, they simply needed the time and space to gather their own thoughts.

We all need to step back from the fray and look at our own style first in order to understand how we impact others. So how do you determine your own style? Look at the different styles back in the section, "The Five Basic Conflict Management Styles." The following sections contain questions that will help you assess your usual approach, the first step in changing our conflict resolution style.

ARE YOU A PIT BULL?

The following questions will help you assess the approach of a pit bull:

- Do you enjoy the give and take of a good argument?
- Are you competitive—even in situations where the results aren't very important to you?
- Do co-workers frequently give in to you because it's too much trouble to work things out?

- Are there some people in the organization who avoid you or fear interacting with you?

If you answered yes to two or more of these questions, your habitual conflict management style is that of a pit bull.

ARE YOU A GOLDEN RETRIEVER?

The following questions will help you assess the approach of a golden retriever:

- Is loyalty one of your highest values?
- Is it important to you to have your co-workers like you?
- Do you give in during disagreements—even when you think you have a better idea—because you believe it's best for your team or organization?
- Are you constantly trying to take care of the feelings of others or to make them feel better?

If you answered "yes" to two or more of these questions, your habitual conflict management style is that of a golden retriever.

ARE YOU A ROADRUNNER?

The following questions will help you assess the approach of a road-runner:

- Do you generally avoid conflict even when the issue is important to you?
- Are you frequently unsure about where you stand on a particular issue that others seem to feel strongly about?
- Do you avoid certain people in your organization who have an abrasive or competitive style?
- Do you prefer to have time to think before you speak or answer questions?

If you answered "yes" to two or more of these questions, your habitual conflict management style is that of a roadrunner.

ARE YOU A COBRA?

The following questions will help you assess the approach of a cobra:

- When you're upset with a co-worker, do you feel a need to talk to someone else about the issue?
- Does the idea of confronting someone directly with your issues intimidate you?
- Do others at your level of the organization come to you to talk about their problems with their co-workers?
- Do you need to talk extensively about your feelings with someone before you're sure what you think and feel?

If you answered "yes" to two or more of these questions, your habitual conflict management style is that of a cobra.

ARE YOU AN EAGLE?

The following questions will help you assess the approach of a eagle:

- Do others frequently ask you to mediate their disputes?
- Do you consistently step back from the emotion of a conflict and think before responding?
- Are you able to see the big picture during disagreements?
- Are you able to remember and consider your own goals as well as your organization's goals during an argument?
- Do others tell you you're a good listener?
- Do you understand how to use and value conflict?

If you answered "yes" to two or more of these questions, your habitual conflict management style is that of an eagle.

STEP 2: CONSCIOUSLY CHOOSING TO USE A DIFFERENT STYLE WHEN APPROPRIATE

This is the second step to changing our conflict resolution style. This requires us to develop the "manual override" thinking part of our brains. We need to learn to practice stepping back from the emotion of a dispute and to react with the most skillful response.

I'm not suggesting that we should "stuff" or ignore our feelings—emotions must be acknowledged and released—but we need to learn the proper time and place for that release. Frequently, it's not appropriate to dump our feelings during the heat of a debate. Perhaps we need to talk with a trusted advisor instead of the person we're upset with, write out our anger, or go for a walk around the block to cool off.

The five chapters that follow will help you decide when and how to use a style different from the one you normally use.

STEP 3: FINDING THE DISCIPLINE TO PRACTICE

This is the third step to changing our conflict resolution style. Contrary to what may be a popular belief, a skillful conflict approach, one that values conflict, is a skill that can be learned, just as you practice a new computer program, your golf swing, or a new cooking technique.

The key is to find nonthreatening situations to practice your new skills so that you'll be able to draw upon them during a more emotionally charged situation.

Some people naturally use different styles in different settings. A working mom, for example, may be a roadrunner in the office while dealing with a difficult boss, yet act like a pit bull drill sergeant at home when trying to organize her family for dinner.

My natural style, for example, and that of many attorneys, tends toward the pit bull type. We have had to train our inner canine to think before launching an assault. When Emily's boss attacked her, for example, she practiced with me over Scotch the night before in order to determine the best approach. While Scotch helps in any role-play, simply asking a friend to coach you in responding more thoughtfully to a pit bull can help you gain some emotional traction in a situation with the real dog. Because Emily had practiced before talking with Claude, she was able to utilize an eagle response instead of her natural knee-jerk reaction.

Similarly, I've practiced in lower stress situations where, for example, I'm not receiving the best service from a store clerk or bank teller by stepping back from my natural inclination to bark at them and instead, asking assertively but without emotion for what I want. If we try using these skills in less charged situations, we'll be more able to use them in the midst of a real conflict.

In addition, by observing roadrunners, I've learned that there are some conflicts worth avoiding. I've found that we don't have to swing at every pitch. We can step back, think, manage our own emotions, and decide if the conflict is really worth our creative energy. Since I tend to react emotionally to disagreements and start barking like a pit bull, I've had to consciously practice using a different style when appropriate.

There is also nothing wrong with using different styles in different situations. The key is to examine whether the style we're using for a particular situation is the one that serves our goals as well as the goals of our organization.

HOW DO YOU THINK AND APPROACH CONFLICT?

Do you use only one style? If so, you may be limiting your future success. Looking at the way we think and react, and learning how to approach conflict more creatively and effectively will be one of the most important skills you can learn.

If we recognize which conflict resolution style we're using at any given time, we can help improve our conflict management mode and clarify both the problem and the solution. We can consciously choose the appropriate style. Also, if we recognize that someone else primarily uses or reacts under stress with a specific conflict style (which may be different from our own), this insight can help us step back from personality clashes and creatively move toward solving the problem.

It's important to realize that none of these styles are right or wrong, better or worse. They are simply examples of style. The key is to try to increase the different styles we use to skillfully resolve conflict, solve problems more creatively, and prepare more effectively for the future.

If we open ourselves to the idea of thinking about style—of reflecting on how we think, react, and negotiate—we'll develop the ability to face whatever challenges we have in conflict with renewed vigor and with new and more powerful tools. This system also helps us depersonalize our conflicts with others by helping us detach from their personality and conflict style instead of judging them as "right" or "wrong" on any particular issue.

Understanding that another person's style is "hard-wired" helps us take their actions less personally. It helps us use the energy of the conflict to spark creativity and innovations instead of sinking into the murky waters of a destructive dispute.

In the chapters that follow, you will learn ways to deal with pit bulls, roadrunners, golden retrievers, cobras, and eagles.

CHAPTER 5

WHEN THE PIT BULL ATTACKS: HOW TO STOP THE FUR FROM FLYING

You must watch your fear. Fear is the path to the dark side. Fear leads to anger, anger leads to hate, hate leads to suffering.

—Yoda

Steve Jansen is sitting in his cubicle, fingers flying across the keyboard as he pounds out a dynamite proposal for a client. He's thrilled with how it's shaping up and excited about the prospect of landing "the big one." Just then his boss, Joyce Clarkson, roars into the entryway of his cubicle. Despite her petite frame, she fills up the space with her screaming. Humiliated, Steve's face reddens. It doesn't matter that the rest of Steve's colleagues know that this is just another ridiculous tirade by a tyrant of a boss. The exhilaration about his proposal and what it could mean for this small company evaporates and his excitement is replaced with his own unspoken outrage as Joyce yells about the overuse of office supplies. The proposal Steve was working on is due at 10 tomorrow morning and he has completely lost interest.

It's a dog-eat-dog world when a pit bull attacks. The fur flies, the growling turns deep, the fangs come out, and the intensity stirs up the adrenaline of everyone within hearing range. When it's over, the devastation takes its toll. This is the era of the aggressive, confrontational style of management that leaves in its wake a victor and the vanquished and disguises organizational dysfunction. There are no sustainable spoils for the victor. In today's diverse workplace and global business environment, successful organizations are built from collaborative teams who value conflict, manage it creatively, and actively build a consensus. Pit bulls need to be understood and tamed.

WORKING WITH PIT BULLS

Pit bulls appear angry. The number one tool to cope with a pit bull and move from conflict to creativity is to *look for the fear, hurt, or loss beneath the anger*. To do this, you need to remember a bit about how our brains work.

Remember the emotional part of our brain that physical anthropologists call the reptilian brain? What this means is that when a threatening stimulus comes at us—through what we see, hear, or feel—we immediately react as a reptile would: flight or fight.

This is our knee jerk reaction to fear. So what's most important to know when you're facing an angry, attacking, debating pit bull is that underneath the anger is fear. Fear usually leads to hurt or stirs up memories of past hurts. Frequently the fear involves the fear of loss, especially a loss of status, power, or image.

Ask yourself of what this person might be afraid. Are they afraid of change? The perception that they're facing someone potentially more powerful? Do they fear losing face or their own power? If you can identify a potential fear or fears, you can answer that question and it will help you measure your own response.

One of the best ways to cope with a pit bull is to allow them to vent, to talk themselves down from their fear and anger high. Pit bulls are like a balloon full of hot air. If you can provide the space for them to talk, they will simply run down.

Psychotherapists call this trying to talk the person *through* his or her emotions, rather than trying to talk him or her *out* of them. You do this by paraphrasing back what someone has said to confirm, clarify, and pursue his or her train of thought.

A psychotherapist tries to help people explore how they feel. They accomplish this feat by mirroring what's said rather than minimizing it. What this means is that even if the anger and fear seems petty or insignificant to you, you must validate the other person's feelings. (Not as though the anger or fear is justified, but that it is real to them.)

For example, in the case of a boss who is mad that his work hasn't been completed, the assistant might say: "You're angry because your work didn't get priority. Is that correct?"

The surprised boss, expecting an argument, rather than snapping back, may respond: "Yes, I thought we agreed that you would do my work first rather than Bill's. If I don't get this to *my* boss today, I'm really going to be in hot water." Or he might engage in a host of other explanations below the feelings. This way you can find out what is really going on. It may take several rounds of questions and mirroring before you get to the crux of the fear.

By paraphrasing what people say without trying to talk them out of it, cheer them up, or immediately solve their problems, psychotherapists help clients become conscious of what's really bothering them.

It's important to learn to "paraphrase" rather than "parrot." Called "reflexive" or "active" listening, rather than just repeating what someone says, you search for the meaning underneath his or her angry words and ask if you *understand* what is being said. This sincere effort will help you to defuse tension and anger and use the energy of the conflict to creatively solve issues.

Usually, when people are upset, they have a legitimate reason to be so. Try to acknowledge what they've said and move on to the creative solution to the underlying cause.

In cases where it's not appropriate to agree with someone, at least acknowledge his or her emotions and be willing to take helpful action by asking, "How can I help?" "What can I do?" "How can I make the situation better?" "I think I understand your *complaint* now, do you have a *request* of me?" Sometimes people fall into the habit of complaining about things without really asking for what they need to improve the situation.

Such gracious behavior defuses the complainer's emotions and prevents the situation from becoming explosive. By focusing on what can be done *now*—instead of what should have been done and wasn't—you can often remedy a problem or a mistake before it gets blown out of proportion.

This is skillful conflict management. This is the way an eagle would approach the problem.

The worst thing to do with a pit bull is to argue, attack back, defend, and debate. This just continues to pump up their already overstimulated adrenal glands and leads to intractable conflicts. One of you needs to stay in your sane mind. By looking for the fear underneath the anger, you may be able to generate compassion for the pit bull rather than anger or fear.

You might also try humor. This often works with a pit bull if you're skillful. Be careful, the best humor to use is not something that pokes fun at the other party. Instead, use self-deprecating humor: Poke fun at yourself or the organization. (Unless you're dealing with the CEO!)

Mainly, you need to be patient. If you allow pit bulls to vent, they will—like a balloon full of hot air—wear down. As a last ditch effort when nothing else is working, try *emphatically* agreeing with them. For example, when the angry boss starts yelling at his assistant, she might try saying: "You're right Mr. Smith! I am a complete idiot and should be fired immediately!"

When said with the right tone of voice and a Mona Lisa smile, this will stop most pit bulls in their tracks. Usually, they will get so confused they will switch sides and argue your side of the issue.

Be mindful of the effect of our communication habits. Some pit bulls are so used to defending, debating, and arguing that they will launch into attack mode without even thinking about whether the issue merits a vigorous debate. They may even believe that they like arguing or find that it is the only way they know how to attract people's attention and connect with them.

WORKING FOR A PIT BULL

If you work for a pit bull, in addition to the ideas mentioned previously, you'll need to develop a thick skin and the ability not to take things personally. It helps to constantly remind yourself that they're behaving the way they are because that's the way they're "hard wired," not because they want to irritate you. This doesn't mean that you should become a doormat or tolerate abusive behavior—no one has a right to treat you with disrespect. But if you can gain some perspective on the problem, you can learn to *respond*, rather than *react*.

Let them know specifically how you want to be treated; focus on their behavior, not their assumed intention or their attitude. If, for example, your boss yells at you for a mistake that you know you didn't commit, for example, take a deep breath, and calmly respond that it wasn't your mistake, and ask for feedback in a normal voice. Use the broken record technique until they wear down.

Most of all, in working for a pit bull, you must continually practice managing your own emotions first before you respond. You may need to take a time out before you do, or talk with someone else about the issue before you go back to your boss. If the problem persists despite all your efforts and you're being subjected to truly abusive behavior, you may need to talk with your boss's boss, request a transfer, or leave the situation. No one needs to repeatedly tolerate abuse in exchange for any job.

MANAGING A PIT BULL

Pit bulls usually behave better with bosses than with subordinates, so your task is somewhat easier in this role. Focus on the behavior that you want them to exhibit and their accountability for the behavior you want. Many people are under the mistaken impression that they do not need to cooperate and act respectfully with their co-workers, yet you have both a legal and ethical right to demand acceptable and professional behavior in the workplace. Chapter 13 provides more specific suggestions on feedback and behavior management.

Many times a disgruntled worker will respond that "being nice" is not in their job description. If they do, simply tell them that "now it is." Work to make everyone in your organization understand that skillful and creative conflict management is in everyone's job description.

WHAT TO DO IF YOU'RE A PIT BULL

When you find yourself launching into an unproductive attack, stop, breathe, count to 10, and ask yourself: What am I afraid of here? Especially ask: What am I afraid of losing or what loss have I already suffered? Am I feeling hurt or is what's happening reminding me of past pain? Is there a more skillful way to handle grief? If you can't think of anything, spend some time by yourself or with a trusted friend, mentor or counselor, trying to understand the underlying fear or hurt feelings. You might try writing down all of your thoughts about the issue. Keep asking yourself: What am I afraid of here? What hurt am I feeling here? Then just write, keeping the pen moving on the page until something comes up.

Once you've identified the fear or hurt, ask yourself: Is this the best way to solve the underlying problem? Am I willing to use this conflict to spark creativity instead of indulging in my need to run over others' interests? Can I learn to engage in a creative dialogue instead of a win or lose debate? Will what I'm doing alleviate my fear? Usually, the answer is no. Yelling, attacking, and arguing work only in the short run. You may win the battle, but you'll lose the war. The other problem is the harm this response does to your own body and health. When the adrenals work overtime, the stress response in our bodies leads to high blood pressure, ulcers, clinical depression, and heart attacks.

Pit bulls often consider themselves courageous. If you really are courageous, ask yourself the following: Am I courageous enough to reveal the underlying fear or hurt to the person with whom I feel angry? Usually, the very idea of doing this is enough to make strong men weak at the knees. You may be amazed to find, however, that if you do this, a miracle will occur in your communication.

For example, I coached an attorney, Joe, who was a powerful partner in a major law firm. All of the associates and many of his partners were afraid of him. Yet, when I talked with Joe I sensed a great sadness. After many probing questions, he finally admitted: "None of the associates like me; they won't even talk with me. They call me the 'prince of f---- darkness'!"

This powerful person, like most of us, had a deep need to connect. For some reason, Joe had it wired that even arguments created some sort of attention and connection with people. He needed to learn another way: basically, being vulnerable and revealing his fears.

Do you think this was easy for him? No way! He resisted and persisted in arguing that to do what I was asking would be tantamount to professional suicide. I'm familiar with this fear. Again, it's our animal brain taking over and telling us that to reveal the soft underbelly of our emotions is to leave ourselves open to wounding. What these people don't realize is that they already wound themselves in small ways every day by failing to connect with other people. The failure to connect can lead to a nagging sense of isolation, the loneliness I sensed in Joe. They also injure their organizations by failing to harness the creative power of conflict because they simply run over the ideas of others or inhibit their co-workers from even offering a new suggestion.

I kept suggesting that Joe try responding by revealing more of his own weaknesses and vulnerabilities in some conversations, starting with small, perhaps unimportant interactions, and then that he notice what happens. The next time an associate was brave enough to say good morning and ask how he was in the coffee room, for example, instead of snapping "Fine" and stomping off, Joe responded that he was worried about how to respond to a motion he had just received from an opposing attorney. The surprised associate asked him to explain, and after Joe did, Joe asked his associate for his suggestions, really listened to his response, then thanked him for his ideas. Taking small risks and small steps like this is a good way to move along this path.

Joe continued to reveal small worries and insecurities to his colleagues. He was amazed at the results. Rifts with partners that went back years were healed. He went on to learn how to embrace conflict instead of attacking it. He was able to use his energy to work with others to manage his cases innovatively instead of spending his time in destructive disputes. He became a mentor to young attorneys at the firm. Rather than reducing his real power and strength, he increased his influence in ways Joe could not have imagined. This is the power of transforming conflict into creativity.

CHAPTER 6

WHEN THE ROADRUNNER REVS UP: HOW TO STOP OTHERS FROM FLEEING THE SCENE

Were we to fully understand the reasons for other people's behavior, it would all make sense.

—Sigmund Freud

At the request of her boss, Maria Rodriguez takes on additional responsibilities in the marketing department and is given the title of senior marketing manager. She oversees the creation and production of the entire scope of collateral materials for three lines of business, along with a host of other miscellaneous duties. She has weekly meetings with her boss who is the vice president of marketing. Maria comes to every meeting prepared with a written agenda that always includes the issues of her compensation and workspace. She wants the same perks that every other senior marketing manager receives. Without fail, when these issues are raised, her boss finds an excuse to take a phone call, talk with his secretary, or simply end the meeting with excuses about other commitments. Three months go by and Maria quits to work for a competitor.

Maria's boss is a typical roadrunner. While a pit bull invites conflict, the roadrunner bolts at the first sign of trouble. Not only does every workplace have its share of roadrunners, just about every family has one. When a potentially controversial topic comes up for conversation at the dinner table—grades, in-laws, curfew, family, finances—the roadrunner slips away to do something that suddenly can't wait. Like the pit bull, the roadrunner responds to conflict with one of the most basic survival instincts known—fight or flight. However, the roadrunner prefers to take wing instead of taking heat.

The problem with the roadrunner's strategy is that the conflict can't ever be creatively managed. The user of this style doesn't value conflict or know how to harness its power to innovate. Since the roadrunner refuses to acknowledge the disagreement, there is no way to move beyond it. The conflict festers and frustrates colleagues, enmeshing them even more.

WORKING WITH ROADRUNNERS

When I conduct workshops on conflict, a question frequently asked is: "Which style causes the most problems in workplaces?"

My participants are surprised to learn that roadrunners cause as many (if not more) problems than pit bulls. Avoidance and denial of conflict can be just as detrimental to using the creative spark of conflict as is the attacking, argumentative style of a pit bull.

Why do roadrunners run from conflict? The surface reasons are many, but the underlying reason (surprisingly) is the same as pit bulls: fear, hurt, or loss. Roadrunners are just demonstrating the flip side of our leftover reptilian brain: flight or fight. Instead of fighting, they choose to flee. Somehow, they have it wired that escape is easier than facing the issue head on.

The problem with this response is that problems do not get embraced and creatively addressed with this strategy. When people avoid conflict, it festers; it doesn't disappear, and relationships deteriorate. At some point, when the conflict can no longer be avoided, the other people involved will become more and more frustrated and exhibit more unproductive confrontational behavior and more emotions. In a kind of weird conflict symbiosis, what some avoid will be demonstrated by others in the group. In fact, the pit bulls usually become even more pit bullish out of sheer frustration and the road-runners flee faster. Instead of generating creative discussions about ideas, the entire conflict becomes even more unproductive and personal.

WORKING FOR A ROADRUNNER

First of all, never chase a roadrunner. Chasing simply leads to even more frustration. Instead, you must tell them directly that you know they do not want to talk about the conflict. Do not speculate with them about why they are avoiding conflict or accuse them of hiding. Instead, the best approach is to ask them what you can do to make it easier to come to you directly. The first time you ask a roadrunner this question it is unlikely they will give you a response. But if you keep asking every time this conflict avoidance behavior happens, eventually they will give you some valuable information about how to work with them.

If they refuse to discuss the real issues with you, simply accept your lot, remind them that you're ready to talk whenever they are and go about your business. It's important to act happy and productive when you do this so that you don't give them the impression that you're reacting to what they're doing. In addition, you should periodically circle back into their orbit and ask them if they're ready to talk about the issue.

I was hired by Bob, a CEO who always seemed to have several messy, unproductive personality conflicts brewing with his executive team and upper managers. Before I knew him well, I could not understand why such a nice, fair, and reasonable man kept creating so many conflicts around him. I did a lot of work mediating among the various warring factions below him. He seemed to be relieved to hand over the continuing problems to someone else. Finally, I discovered what was happening.

Bob avoided conflict, avoided making the difficult decisions his executive team needed him to make about people and policies. He tried to wait out conflicts, hoping that they would blow over. He did not understand the power of embracing the creative potential in conflict.

At times this works. In fact, one of the things I learned in living with my ex-husband for 20 years—he also likes to avoid conflict—is that, sometimes you *can* just wait the issue out and the problem will disappear. One thing about roadrunners, they are never petty; they do not make a big deal out of small matters.

This kind of attitude with a CEO, however, does not work. Decisions need to be made. Consensus management can be effective in the right situations, but this style can lead to an endless delay in what gets accomplished. Creativity is stymied. And continual avoidance can also leave the people affected by the conflict steaming with hostility. They want problems solved and they want them solved now. At the very least, they want someone to communicate with them on a regular basis about how the conflict is going to be managed. This, however, is not something that a conflict avoider is willing to do since, by definition, they want to have the conflict disappear and not have to face the issue.

Bob spent a small fortune on my services, hiring me to come in to manage conflict among his executive team. Along the way, I tried to coach the CEO on what I thought was the underlying problem, but that did not seem to be effective. Bob wasn't open to my gentle prodding about how his style might be causing the continual issues.

Finally, the head of their global conglomerate made an interesting suggestion: He sent Bob to a week long leadership school at the Center for Creative Leadership, one of the country's premier leadership training programs. One of the hallmarks of the program is that they require feedback from each member of the leader's staff before they go. That way, they have that data and can present the results to the executive during the week. They also have structured exercises that help them understand their own style by having psychologists watch them during interactions and then give them feedback on their style.

After that week, Bob came back and told me that the sessions had helped him tremendously. "What did you learn?" I asked. "I learned that people don't know who I am. I learned I needed to be more vulnerable with people and let them know who I am and what I *need* and want. I learned that people think I'm indecisive, avoid conflict, and fail to deal directly with issues."

This was an amazing leap of honesty from this man. What does a fear of our vulnerability have to do with conflict avoidance? you may be asking. Everything!

What's important to understand is that roadrunners run from conflict for the same reason that pit bulls start fighting: fear. One of everyone's major fears is that someone will find out who he or she really is and what he or she needs. Most of us, as children, have been given messages from the world in some way that who we are and what we need is not okay. When we become adults, it's understandable that this hiding has become so much a part of who we are—even those of us who are successful CEOs—that we don't even realize what we're doing.

Learning to value conflict, however, requires that we reveal ourselves and let others know what we need and think about the issues. If we don't, it's simply impossible to creatively work with the spark of conflict.

Bob's admission to me and his team was a major step forward in helping embrace the issues that constantly swirled around them.

MANAGING A ROADRUNNER

Many of the general techniques for working with a roadrunner will also work well if you have a subordinate who is this type. First, look at your own behavior. Are you confrontable? If not, review the material in Chapter 15. Talk directly to them about how you can make it easier for them to come to you. If their behavior persists, make them understand that skillful and creative conflict management is in their job description. Offer a class in conflict management or refer them to a coach. Monitor their behavior, offer feedback, and follow up with them to make sure that their behavior changes.

WHAT TO DO IF YOU'RE A ROADRUNNER

First admit that this is your style and ask yourself whether this style is really working for you. Most people find the answer is no, at least if they use this style too often. It may seem easier in some ways to avoid conflict, but avoidance can wreck havoc with your relationships. All of the emotions you're avoiding expressing—that you are *repressing*—will be acted out in spades by the people around you.

You may constantly wonder how you manage to attract so many angry, resentful, sad, or worried people. Here's why: They're simply expressing the emotions that you don't own. And they will continue to do so until you start appropriately revealing and owning your own feelings.

Every human being has emotions. There's no escape from this. Feelings pass through our bodies like changes in the weather. We can learn to appreciate all of them just as we welcome a change of seasons. The trick is not to deny that we have them, but to acknowledge them and find ways to appropriately express them. This is *Emotional Intelligence*, as brilliantly described in the book by Daniel Goleman. Goleman argues that people succeed, not because of their intellectual I.Q., but because of their emotional intelligence or E.Q. He provides a very important look at how to go about accessing and improving your own E.Q.

Until you're willing to take this step of owning and thoughtfully expressing your emotions and needs, you'll find it difficult to harness the power of conflict.

Next, learn to value conflict. As we explored in Part 1, the conflicts we need to encourage, value, and use creatively are all about ideas, not personalities. Learn to appreciate different styles and embrace their contribution to the creative fuel of conflict. Learn to manage your own emotions so you can sustain your own participation in the messy process of working through a disagreement. If you can do that, you'll be able to use conflict creatively instead of feeling abused by its very existence.

CHAPTER 7

WHEN THE GOLDEN RETRIEVER WAGS ITS TAIL: HOW TO TEACH "JUST SAY NO!"

What's important in communication is to listen for what's not being said.

—Peter Drucker

The vice president of a Fortune 500 company conducts a performance appraisal with a key member of her management team over a wonderful lunch at an avant-garde restaurant near the office. She gives the employee a nice raise, catches up with the latest news about their respective families, and talks about future career plans. The lunch meeting is productive, upbeat, and enjoyable. A month later the vice president is stunned when she opens a letter of resignation from that employee. The vice president thought she had a great relationship with the manager. The resignation letter stings. The fact that the employee chose not to tell her, but instead leaves her a letter, adds salt to a big wound.

Golden retrievers bounce around the office with an infinite supply of loyalty, innocent eyes, and energy. They seem happy, easygoing, trustworthy, and supportive of every decision. That's a great pet—not a great worker. Obedient dogs are to be treasured—no one wants a dog testing its creativity in the living room. However, an employee who always marches cheerfully to the corporate drum can be an ambush waiting to happen.

Golden retrievers tend to say yes to everything—they take on extra assignments, they come in early, they agree with you *all the time*. Success is stymied because the golden retriever doesn't give honest feedback, explore creative alternatives, or challenge the status quo. This contributes to organizational stagnation, stifling innovation.

Furthermore, in an effort to please, retrievers can burn out because they take on too much. Because they abhor disagreement, they can become passive/aggressive when the strain becomes too great.

When an individual is described as passive/aggressive, it means that they say one thing and do another. A subordinate may agree to take on a project, for example, even though she doesn't like it, and then drag out completing the work.

WORKING WITH GOLDEN RETRIEVERS

You might ask what could be wrong with working with a golden retriever? Loyal, trustworthy, cheerful—aren't these the characteristics of an ideal worker? Yes, but ....

The problem is that golden retrievers—like roadrunners—have a problem revealing who they really are and what they're thinking and feeling. The first time you may learn that a golden retriever is unhappy and is leaving, for example, is when his or her resignation letter appears on your desk.

The other problem with golden retrievers it that they tend to say yes. Yes, I agree with you. Yes, I'll take on the extra assignment. Yes, I'll be there early. Agreeing with you all the time might seem like a gift, but the problem in this style doesn't give a leader or co-worker the creative feedback he or she needs to be successful. What this leads to is a problem for organizations: They stagnate and can't keep up in a global market that constantly demands a proactive stance and new, creative ideas. Many old, slow organizations tend to be full of people who can't tell their leaders what they really think. This organizational dysfunction inhibits invention and growth.

A *Fortune* magazine study, "Why CEOs Fail," found that leaders don't stumble for lack of smarts or vision. Most unsuccessful CEOs stumble because of one simple, fatal shortcoming: the failure to put the right person in the right job and the related failure to fix people problems in time. *Fortune* found that the failure is one of "emotional strength," usually a mechanism for conflict avoidance and a misguided sense of loyalty.[1]

Golden retrievers are also highly susceptible to burnout. They may start engaging in passive/aggressive tendencies—saying one thing and doing another—as a way to be able to get some rest from the constant demands of work.

WORKING FOR A GOLDEN RETRIEVER

If you work for a golden retriever your work life may be pleasant on the surface but swirling with dangerous currents below. You may not discover what your boss really thinks about your work until it's too late. You will have to actively seek feedback, including asking specifically for areas that you need to improve.

Request periodic reviews from your boss. If such reviews tend to be "all smiles," specifically ask for what they see as any weaknesses. If you, like Bob's group, are faced with an indecisive leader, you will have to tell him or her directly that "we need you to make a decision about this issue by next week in order to get our own jobs done. Not having this decided is affecting the productivity of the group."

MANAGING A GOLDEN RETRIEVER

If golden retrievers work for you, you need to constantly be asking them how things are going and what they need from you. I recommend weekly one-on-ones where you ask two questions:

1. What do you need from me (or from anyone else in our organization) in order to be more successful at work?

2. Is there anything I'm doing or that anyone else here is doing that is interfering with your success?

Now, the first time you ask these questions, I doubt you will receive any useful answers. Most golden retriever types will simply stare at you like a deer frozen in headlights and insist that everything is fine. If you keep asking these questions week after week, however, you will eventually receive answers. Once you do, you can start giving this person what they really need. If you can't give them what they need, you must find a way to manage their expectations and directly address their disappointment.

WHAT TO DO IF YOU ARE A GOLDEN RETRIEVER

You need to take care of yourself. You will find that you are highly susceptible to burnout. You need to constantly monitor your reactions to make sure that you are doing what you want to do and what you're capable of doing.

You need to learn to reveal who you are and to ask for what you really need. If you can't do that, you won't be able to creatively embrace the conflict. While using this style some of the time is fine—some disputes are not worth taking a lot of our time and energy to manage— if we use it too often, we will deplete our energy and ultimately fail to achieve what we want.

If you're protesting that you really are a golden retriever— constantly cheerful, loyal, etc.—beware! No one is. It's great to have those qualities as a part of your natural tendencies, but you need to recognize and admit your humanness.

Most golden retrievers have some fear they haven't faced that keeps them from revealing what they need and want. Sometimes, their behavior has become so habitual that they aren't even aware of their own needs and want. They tend to focus instead on pleasing those around them. If you have this pattern, it may require that you dig through the archaeology of your own psyche to determine what your true needs and interests are.

All of us have unmet needs and interests that are different from the interests of those with whom we live and work. Learn to explore, identify, and creatively honor yours. Learn to value conflict as a creative fire for you and your organization and to actively participate in the process of innovative dialogs.

CHAPTER 8

WHEN THE COBRA STRIKES: HOW TO TANGLE WITH A TRIANGULATOR

When dealing with people, remember you are not dealing with creatures of logic, but with creatures of emotion, creatures bristling with prejudice and motivated by pride and vanity.

—Aristotle

Janet Olafson is responsible for producing a quarterly newsletter for the division. Along with Janet, a number of other team members are involved in determining the editorial content and reviewing the final document, including Janet's boss. She regularly employs the services of a small business-writing firm to draft and edit the copy. They meet to discuss the upcoming issue. The firm completes the project without a hitch. Moreover, Janet praises their work and thanks them for the additional assistance they rendered under adverse circumstances. Shortly thereafter, the writing team meets with one of Janet's colleagues to discuss a new project. In the course of the meeting, the colleague reveals that Janet told him that she is planning to find a new writing team for future newsletters because Janet has a problem with their work.

Janet is a cobra. Cobras have the perception—which may or may not be factual—that they lack power in the organization or with specific individuals. Consequently, they typically opt to circumvent customary channels because they feel those avenues are closed. They go around the person with whom they have a conflict to a third party. Cobras triangulate because they are *afraid* to talk candidly with others. Triangulation is a particularly insidious problem because it can impact numerous staff members, promote rumor-mongering, cause a host of repercussions, and divert time, energy, and productivity. For these reasons, cobras can be deadly.

Powerful people who command attention in the corporate jungle are unlikely to be cobras. However, groups of people who have historically been unempowered at work frequently use the cobra style to deal with conflict.

WORKING WITH COBRAS

Why don't they just talk to me face to face? Why is he always going behind my back?

These are the questions I'm frequently asked about triangulators. The answer? In a word: power. It takes some kind of power—either because you're a member of the dominant group, have your own sense of personal self-confidence, are viewed as a superstar, or some other reason—to give you the confidence to talk to people directly.

Cobras—the term I use for people who do not resolve conflicts directly with others—do so because they're *afraid* to talk directly.

Once you understand this dynamic, it may make it easier for you to deal with them. Remember the discussion about our reptilian flight or fight response in Chapter 4? Cobras are in the flight category; their behavior is a way of avoiding the direct resolution of the conflict because they can't manage the emotional intensity.

Once you understand what drives a triangulator, you can take constructive action. And you must act. If you just allow this kind of behavior to go on, the conflict becomes strangled—what I call *triangulation strangulation*—and becomes unresolvable. Triangle patterns can be complex and confusing. Once they form, they can be difficult to dismantle.

Interestingly, triangles tend to persist because they're stable. If people deal with conflict directly, yet lack a creative approach, the relationship may become too intense and perish. With a triangle, the third leg creates stability. The three can endlessly circle around each other. The conflict isn't managed creatively, but the relationship remains in place although stagnant.

Psychologists believe that we use triangles to manage our own anxiety in a two-party relationship. If we bring a third person into the system, it serves as a kind of "safety valve" to release pressure that can build when two people have a difficult relationship. You see this in dysfunctional families when two parents disagree and lack sufficient skills and courage to resolve the matter directly. They bring their child into the argument as a third player in the dispute.

Cobra behavior lurks around the kitchen table, the conference table, and even in the boardroom. I work with an organization that was founded by two old friends, Rose and Paul. They've been in business together a long time. Rose is the head of the clinical team, and Paul is the company president. Several years into the venture the two had a serious disagreement about the direction the business should take. After weeks of loud and long arguments, Rose had ultimately backed down and acquiesced to Paul. Yet in truth, she never bought into Paul's strategy and continued to whine about the decision to her own staff. Of course, her complaints ultimately reached Paul's ears. He tried to talk to her directly about the problems, but she avoided his attempts at discussions. Paul recognized that Rose's actions were devastating to morale and the bottom line, so I was asked to mediate the dispute.

Rose felt very conflicted about what was happening at work. Her relationship with Paul had deep historical roots and was important to her. Yet her behavior was actually damaging the relationship instead of strengthening it. Because Rose couldn't manage the emotional intensity of talking with Paul directly, she had used the classic triangulation tactic to try to get her message out. This indirect approach only sabotaged the relationship.

Thankfully, Rose valued her relationship with Paul enough to be willing to do some hard work to salvage both her relationship and the business. I did some executive coaching with Rose so she could explore why she was managing with a triangulation strategy. Until Rose was able to work with her own emotions around the issue, she couldn't talk with Paul directly. She didn't know how to step back from the emotion of the situation and become more neutral. Once she acquired the skills to grapple with her own emotions, she was able to discuss the issue with Paul directly. Both she and Paul needed to understand that by talking to others, Rose was actually seeking to *preserve* the relationship, not torpedo it. Both Paul and Rose were able to come together and discuss the issue in a respectful, honest way. Rose discovered that when she stopped using her staff to triangulate, the staff's productivity and morale rose significantly.

When we understand why others triangulate, it makes it easier for us to work with them. It also heightens our own awareness of how often we use triangles in our own life. We may innocently ask a third person to settle a disagreement, complain to our sister about our mother, or engineer a new assignment by asking a supporter to talk to our boss. Examining our own behavior provides a window that enables us to see why others may also lack the courage to approach us directly.

Triangles in organizations tend to rise when anxiety is more intense. When the system is calmer, triangles are less noticeable. Managing oneself in a triangle takes considerable mental effort. Basically we need to step back from the emotion of the situation and become more neutral.

It is important to become aware of all the forms that triangles take. In everyday life, they turn up in innocent activities, such as asking a third person to settle a disagreement between two others. In churches, workplaces, or social groups, triangles are ever-present, but they are more apparent and intense when anxiety is running higher.

WORKING FOR A COBRA

Working for a cobra is a dangerous pursuit. Knowing where you stand and trusting the feedback you receive will be difficult. You will have to develop a Machiavellian-like mastery of forming alliances in order to ferret out what your boss is saying about you. Take every opportunity to spend time alone with your boss and get to know him or her on a personal basis. Think of small ways to gain their trust. Continually ask for feedback on your strengths and weaknesses.

As you develop productive alliances with others in your organization, seek similar feedback from them.

MANAGING A COBRA

If you are the leader or manager of a triangulator, you must make it clear to them that you will not tolerate that kind of behavior. Make talking directly to the person who can solve the problem a part of *their* job description. Otherwise, you will find yourself leading a group full of personality conflicts, politics, backbiting, and unproductive gossip.

If you work with people who triangulate conflict, first understand why they are doing what they do. It's not because they are sneaky, malicious, or untrustworthy—although they may also be all of these things—it's because they are *afraid* to talk with you directly. Somehow, their relationship with you has become too intense. In fact, triangulating is the chief strategy of women and people of color who tend to have the least amount of power in most organizations. Historically, they have banded together in groups such as civil rights movements or women's groups before they've talked with anyone directly.

And history has proved that they were correct in their approach. Most people in these groups have not had the power to talk honestly with anyone. Labor unions are another example. Historically, workers have had less power than owners and, therefore, it has made sense for them to talk with each other first, organize, and then face management as a collective.

The best approach is to ask to talk to the person in private and state the problem directly and empathetically. Take some responsibility in the conversation that acknowledges their fear. Consider what might be increasing the emotional intensity in the organization as a whole. Is there some threatening change taking place, for example? Is the business suffering through financial problems or reorganization? You might ask, for example, what it is that you have done to make it difficult for him or her to talk with you directly and what you can do to make it easier to talk with you.

Expect that it will take some time to gain this person's trust. You may have to have several sessions or several incidents before he or she will work with you to resolve the problem.

Be sure you name the game. Say, for example, "I heard you talked to Mary about 'X.' In the future, if you have a concern about 'X' and me, I'd like for you to talk with me directly. What can I do to make that easier for you? What can we do to resolve 'X' right now? If you need some time to think about possible solutions, when can we get together to talk about it?"

When you do persuade cobras to talk to you, you will need to make sure you practice all the skills in this book to embrace the conflict: Be sure you listen to their point of view, restate, and look for creative solutions that meet everyone's needs. You will gain trust with this person by embracing a number of conflicts with them—not by avoiding the conflicts. Strengthen your own resolve by learning to value conflict.

You may also need to clear up misunderstandings with others that the triangulator has already talked to about you. Don't hesitate to say directly to them, "What Joe said about me is mistaken. Here is what really happened ...."

WHAT TO DO IF YOU'RE A COBRA

Once you realize you're in a triangle, ask yourself questions such as the following:

- What is my contribution to this pattern?
- How am I triangulating?
- How do I go about changing my part of the triangle?
- What do I have to do to get emotionally more neutral and still communicate with both other parts of the triangle?

After you've considered your own part in the triangle, you're ready to approach the other person.

You need to work to develop courage. You need to utilize all of the strategies in this book to learn how to talk to people directly. You may even need to have a coach to help you work through matters. What you cannot do is continue to avoid these issues. The gossip train in most organizations is faster than the intranet. People will hear what you say about them—and you may be quoted incorrectly or out of context. A more effective strategy is to find a way to talk with the person or persons involved in the issue.

I was hired to coach a woman named Lilly who learned this lesson the hard way. She worked for a large corporation and had long-standing conflicts with two men—very powerful people in the organization—that she had never resolved. She had managed to work her way up to a vice presidency, and these two men also ended up being vice presidents in this organization.

Lilly didn't like them. In fact, she couldn't stand them, but believed she was hiding her feelings. Even though she discreetly expressed her disapproval to others in the organization, Lilly thought these men wouldn't hear.

I kept saying to her, "You know, you really need to work with them because I know the CEO expects all the VPs to work together as a team." And she would reply, "Oh, they don't know how I feel. I'm sure they don't know how I feel." Well, eventually, unbeknownst to Lilly, they started organizing a kind of conspiracy to force her out of the organization. They succeeded.

Lilly was shocked. When the CEO asked her to leave, the reason he cited was that she was not nice enough. Now, since when is "niceness" a requirement for success in most corporations? The reality was the two VPs knew that she didn't like them. We really do telegraph how we feel to people in the workplace.

One of my favorite quotes is from Emerson, who said, "Who you are speaks so loudly, I can't hear a word you're saying."

I'm not suggesting that you become stupid about the power imbalances found in most organizations. I'm also not suggesting that you reveal your inner most feelings and fears during every workplace conversation; that strategy isn't skillful or smart. There is no doubt that most organizations have people who have more power than others and that there are those who sometimes abuse authority. It is also true that women and minorities still tend to have less power in most companies. But you need to recognize that differential and still find a way to skillfully communicate your needs and interests.

If you refuse to do so, you're failing to value the conflict and ignoring its creative potential.

CHAPTER 9

WHEN EAGLES TAKE FLIGHT: HOW TO DEVELOP THE SIGHT AND SKILLS TO SOAR

Eagle: *any of several large, diurnal, accipitrine birds of prey noted for their size, strength, and powers of flight and vision.*

—*Random House Dictionary* (1979)

Some 200,000 miles above the earth's atmosphere an explosion rips through an oxygen tank and within three hours, the Apollo 13 *spacecraft loses all oxygen stores, water, electrical power, and the use of the service module propulsion system. Adrift in space with only a glimmer of hope for survival, it would have been easy for hysteria or a bad fight to take over. Instead, command module pilot Jack Swigert calmly utters his famous understatement, "Houston, we've had a problem here." With lives hanging in the balance and an international audience watching the rescue efforts, NASA departments could start blaming each other for the catastrophe. However, calmer heads prevail. Mission control assembles in a room to find creative solutions before time runs out. Ultimately, ingenuity, collaboration, and good fortune create the most dramatic and successful space rescue mission in history. Using tape, cardboard, plastic bags, and parts of a lunar suit, the crew fixes the life support system responsible for removing carbon dioxide from the spacecraft's air system. Navigating by the stars, they use the moon's gravity to slingshot back toward earth.*

None of these brainstorms would have happened if not for the superior leadership and creative conflict management skills essential to success. Not your everyday office dilemma, that's for sure.

We've all experienced death knells of a project or a budget request, but barring extraordinary circumstances, we've never had to put our creative conflict management skills to the supreme test. The lesson of *Apollo 13* is that with the eagle style, and that bird's powers of flight and vision, performance and results can soar far beyond the ordinary. Eagle behavior is courageous, creative, disciplined, and highly functional. Using the eagle style, you will be able to take command of any situation with exemplary leadership.

WORKING WITH EAGLES

If you doubt that successful leaders with eagle style welcome conflict, consider the case of Jack Welch, the legendary former CEO of GE. When he took over GE in 1980, the stock had lost half its value over the previous 10 years. Welch told his managers that he wanted "a revolution."

He burned the "blue books," the five volumes of guidance for every GE manager that discouraged innovative practices. Welch created the famous workout process, in which employees at all levels would gather for "town meetings" with their bosses and ask questions or make proposals about how the place could run better. He committed to answering 80 percent of the questions on the spot. During his tenure, Welch created a cultural revolution. As an electrician put it: "When you've been told to shut up for 20 years, and someone tells you to speak up—you're going to let them have it."[1]

Welch also created a lot of good fights. The workout sessions took huge chunks of waste and bureaucracy out of GE's processes, but their most important accomplishment was to teach people they had a right to speak up and be taken seriously. Welch rewarded those who created new ideas as well as those who implemented them.

Welch also encouraged good fights in his behind the scenes people practices. According to *Fortune* magazine: "When a manager meets with Welch, the exchange is candid, not scripted. There may be shouting. The manager will almost certainly have to stretch his mind and do new thinking on the spot."[2]

The results of Welch's revolutionary style were startling. He transformed GE and multiplied its value beyond anyone's exceptions:

from a market capitalization of $14 billion to more than $400 billion today. Now GE is the second most valuable company on earth, behind Microsoft. And Welch is the most admired, copied, and studied CEO.

Many less recognized eagles soar in other institutions. Consider, for example, a vice president of a large regional health care system. The organization was at war with its nursing staff in its home health division. Tensions escalated to the point that the nurses mobilized to unionize. Fanning the flames toward an unproductive conflict, one middle manager strangled the dispute by triangulating: She gave the nurses misinformation while concealing her acts from her own supervisor. The vice president successfully intervened.

She went directly to the nurses, called a meeting, laid out the ground rules for a productive discussion and turned the situation around. She used many of the skills in Part 3. She listened to their concerns, acknowledged the errors the organization had made, addressed the unfair pay scales, and made commitments about the future. The group brainstormed to create innovative solutions for the issues, the inequities that had simmered below the surface for many years, but that would never have been resolved without the conflict being directly and creatively addressed.

Two years later, the organization underwent a survey by Gallup and the vice president had the highest level of employee satisfaction in the entire hospital system. Moreover, Gallup said their rating put them at the top of all industries.

Eagles like Jack Welch also instinctively embrace differing opinions. Heretics are welcomed into the fold as harbingers of change, virtual "canaries in the mine" who warn miners that they're low on air by dying before them.

It can take enormous courage to listen to controversial opinions or complaints, yet failure to do so can lead to disaster. Consider, for example, the managing partner of a large Midwestern law firm, Lewis, who sought my advice after a young associate complained of sexual harassment by one of their most prominent, successful, and politically connected partners. Because the young woman had a reputation of being "emotionally volatile," as well as "a bit seductive," the other partners and associates refused to believe her claims. In addition, the firm was proud of its record of hiring and promoting women, so they were loath to admit that there might be any problems.

Lewis brought me in and allowed interviews of all the women associates, despite intense criticism from his partners, who insisted that he was overreacting and stirring up a stew of problems. His partners felt so strongly about the issue that Lewis faced a near mutiny.

In true eagle style, Lewis held endless meetings with his partners and me, explaining to them why we needed to do a through investigation, despite their belief that the associate's claims were incredible and that the accused partner couldn't possibly have acted the way she claimed. He listened patiently to all his partners who stomped into his office, taking apart their lawyerly arguments one by one.

After I talked to the other women in the firm, three of them revealed that they also had been sexually harassed by the same man—claims that never would have seen the light of day if Lewis had not been willing to listen to one brave and unpopular woman. Because he tolerated the one "canary in the mine" he averted an entire negative chain of events—including lawsuits. Lewis also adopted my suggestion that we conduct meetings with all the associates to explain what we were doing and why, in order to hold down the rumors and gossip. This move also raised his partners hackles, because they were convinced that we should try to hide the process from the associates. Based on my advice, Lewis finally convinced them that whatever rumors the other employees were hearing were more inflammatory than the truth.

After the sexual harassment claim was resolved, Lewis led the firm through a painful self-examination. They were forced to consider whether their own perception of themselves as a great place for women to work and thrive was consistent with reality. After Lewis began the dialog, the floodgates opened, and the women partners and associates detailed other, more subtle problems of unequal treatment. We held a series of workshops on gender issues for all employees where their underlying beliefs and prejudices could be explored. Although sometimes painful and contentious, the process ultimately resulted in a better working relationship for all employees. None of this could have occurred for the firm without Lewis's willingness to embrace the conflict and see the ultimate value in working through the process.

Can you view heretics with interest instead of irritation? If so, you are on your way to developing an eagle style. You are learning to do what you need to do to foster creative sparks.

WORKING FOR AN EAGLE

If you're lucky enough to work for an eagle, count your blessings! Take every opportunity to observe them, ask questions and consider how they manage various interactions. Ask for feedback on what they observe about your own style of managing conflict. Ask them for coaching on what to do in various situations. Don't be afraid to ask specifically how they handle group decision-making, feedback, specific conflicts, or any other issues. Most leaders are happy to answer such questions and provide mentoring and support. Don't make the mistake of failing to ask for such help because you believe that you should already know it all. Good leaders understand that we all need to constantly grow and develop our own skills.

Consider, for example, the eagle-style of one of my clients, the CEO of a manufacturing company. Bill inherited a management team riddled with conflict. He hired me to facilitate an executive retreat with his team. We did an exercise that I frequently use with groups where we draw a time line for the organization and have each person chart their own high and low on the time table. Bill was astounded to hear that many of the low points on the others' time table involved descriptions of his associates suffering through one of his blistering attacks. As the head of his operations department put it, "Listening to feedback from Bill about the Casey project was not only the lowest day at the firm, it was the lowest day of my entire life."

Before my eyes, Bill grew wings in an instant. After a moment of silence while he dealt with his shock, he jumped up and announced that they were going to do another exercise. He ripped out pieces of flip chart paper and started plastering them around the room. "Okay, guys, here's what I want you to do. I want you to give me three things that you think I do well and three things where I need to improve. Don't hold back. I want to hear the best and the worse of it. The rules are that I can't say anything in response, and I need to write down what you say right here so that I won't ever forget it. Then I'm going to have it typed up, framed, and hung in my office so I can focus on what you've said on a daily basis."

The quiet in the room was deafening. Finally, Linda, the VP of PR found her voice and started listening his strengths: He was decisive, visionary, and good with bottom-line issues. Weaknesses she saw were that she and others frequently didn't feel as if he heard what they said, he was impatient, and he didn't really seem to want to get to know people on a personal level, limiting, she thought, his ability to harness their strengths and weaknesses.

The other 11 subordinates followed Linda. Bill listened and wrote, saying nothing. When they were finished he thanked them, sat down, and said nothing. The team squirmed in the silence. Finally, the head of their global marketing team asked if he could go next. Bill agreed, and that lead to the entire team moving through the spontaneous feedback process.

Bill made good on his promise to frame his feedback in his office, and the others followed suit. The lists became a proud company tradition and—far from avoiding feedback—led to a practice of executives welcoming suggestions and input and actually feeling left out of the process if they had yet to receive their lists.

Asking for feedback will also help you develop your own creative eagle conflict skills.

MANAGING AN EAGLE

If you're managing an eagle, promote them! That's a joke but the reality is that they are rare birds. Be humble enough to realize that you can learn, even from your own subordinates. Ask, as Bill did, for their feedback, advice and suggestions for improvement. Encourage them to serve as coaches, facilitators and mediators for the others in your group. Study Chapter 17 with them to help them develop those skills.

Interestingly, studies show that most managers spend 80 percent of their time dealing with the 20 percent of their people who are unproductive and create problems for the organization. In order to increase the productivity and innovation of your group, however, you should spend most of your time encouraging the upper 20 percent to be even more creative. The most successful CEOs in the world have realized this secret.

Les Welch, CEO of the retail clothing store The Limited, realized this after the stock of his company plunged during the 1990s.[3] Determined to uncover where he was making mistakes, he decided to study the most successful CEOs. He shadowed director Stephen Spielberg, Jack Welch, CEO of General Electric, and Jack Callaway, the CEO of Pepsi. Les Welch found, to his astonishment, that they all spent their time very differently from the way he used up his days. While he reviewed budgets, approved deals, and put out fires, Jack Welch told him that he didn't do those things. Instead, Welch and the others he studied spent most of their time encouraging their best people in doing their best work. With good teams working under them, these CEOs simply let their people do the things that Les Welch found himself mired in. He changed his focus and The Limited stock rebounded.

As a manager of eagles, you should spend most of your time learning how you can help them do their own jobs better. If you help make your best people even more productive and innovative, the effort will rebound to the entire organization.

WHAT TO DO IF YOU'RE AN EAGLE

If you are an eagle, ask for a promotion! Obviously, that's also a joke but the truth is, you need to recognize your own strengths. Use your skills to influence your organization and to mentor and grow others.

Study the tactics and suggestions in Chapter 17 to learn how to expand your own natural conflict management style by offering your skills as a mediator and facilitator to your organization. Offering to serve as a facilitator for groups outside your own hemisphere of influence is a good way to showcase your talents.

You may not have realized how unique and valuable your style is. Honing these skills and taking the opportunities to use them with others can both propel your career forward and help your organization grow.

CHAPTER 10

A CREATIVE MENAGERIE: HOW TO HARNESS THE UNIQUE STYLES

The opposite of a correct statement is a false statement. But the opposite of a profound truth may well be another profound truth.

—Neils Bohr

Michael Johansson sits on the train headed to work, examining his Palm Pilot with a sigh. He is scheduled to run his weekly staff meeting today. Sometimes he feels as if he might as well be at home, mediating squabbles among his three kids; his technically talented team seems to have the social skills of a bunch of seven-year-olds. They have to discuss resource planning for next year's budget and he can already predict how the meeting will come down: Linda will charge in armed for combat with stacks of papers to buttress her department's extra funds requests; Manny will say nothing, but whine to Joe afterward that his department never got a fair shake; and Tom will smile and agree to whatever anyone proposes, yet will strike back later by procrastinating about requests from anyone he feels abused him in the budget process. What a mess! And Michael is somehow supposed to create order and teamwork out of this chaos. Why couldn't they address their differences openly and fairly, the way he wanted them to?

Michael is struggling with a classic leadership dilemma: how to encourage different styles to utilize each other's strengths during conflict instead of pouncing on their weaknesses.

Let's just admit it right up front: Most of us think the way we operate is best. We think the world would run better, be better, even resolve conflict more creatively if others thought and felt the way we do. We don't really want to understand and work with the styles of people who behave differently. We just want them to conform to our expectations. Stubbornly, they refuse.

So we are left with a dilemma: We need to find a way to harness the creative strengths of others, respect their styles, and believe in their creative potential. Not an easy task for most of us. One way to begin is to understand that diversity actually creates more vibrant, creative, stronger organizations and to educate your co-workers to value diversity. A plethora of research points in that direction.

THE CREATIVE VALUE OF DIVERSITY

Academic researchers have identified three primary reasons to value diversity in the workplace:

1. Diverse workplaces are more interesting places to work and help attract and keep the best people.

2. Workplaces whose members reflect the broader community can better understand and meet the needs of increasingly diverse potential customers in a competitive environment.

3. Diverse workers bring a variety of opinions and ideas that enhance creativity and innovation.

Laboratory research has also consistently demonstrated that groups that are diverse with respect to abilities, skills, and knowledge perform more creatively than groups that are more alike.[1]

To verify this finding in work groups, researcher Susan Jackson contacted the CEOs of 199 banks and asked them to assess the level of innovation in their organizations and to identify up to eight people who are key players in their top management teams. Jackson found a significant relationship between the extent of innovation (in products, programs, and services) and the degree of diversity in "functional background" in the top management teams. That is, teams made up of people with different professional backgrounds, experiences, and thinking styles were more creative than those made up of only engineers, for example.[2]

Diversity in the workplace comes in many guises: cultural, generational, professional, thinking, and conflict styles. A mix of all these diverse elements tends to make group dynamics more effective and creative—as long as the members have been encouraged to value differences and work well with those who are different.

Diverse groups are more likely to avoid "groupthink," a dynamic identified by Irving Janis.[3] If loyalty to the group becomes too strong, members will quickly agree to decisions that the rest of the group seems to support. As Janis explains, the unspoken norm in groupthink is, "Preserve group harmony by going along uncritically with whatever consensus seems to be emerging."[4]

As previously mentioned in Part 1, Janis found groupthink to be responsible for foreign policy fiascoes like the Kennedy administration's Bay of Pigs invasion. A handful of people with similar views were isolated from diverse thinkers and were discouraged from voicing dissenting opinions. Their decisions led to tragic outcomes.

To avoid these results and harness a group's creative power, we must think about how we build teams. Researcher and professor Teresa Amabile found that if you want to build creative teams, you must pay careful attention to the design of such teams. That is, you must create mutually supportive groups with a diversity of perspectives and backgrounds. Why? Because when teams comprise people with various intellectual foundations and work styles and experiences, as well as different expertise and creative thinking styles, ideas often combine and combust in exciting and useful ways.[5]

How do we translate this academic research into practical ideas for leaders who want to build diverse teams that can embrace conflict to fuel creativity? First, the organization must make a conscious and committed effort to cultivate diversity. Leaders must "walk the talk" by publicly recognizing and appreciating diverse working styles as well as modeling their own different ways of approaching problems.

Second, leaders cannot assume that staff members know how to deal with diversity, let alone appreciate it. Many groups have hopped on the diversity bandwagon without investing in broadening the attitudes and skill sets that people need to work effectively with people who are different than they are in thinking styles, attitudes, and perhaps religious or ethnic differences. Staff members must be given ample development opportunities if they are going to successfully work with all kinds of people. In an ever-expanding global economy, these skills are crucial. A 58-year-old career company man may have no idea how to relate to a snowboarding, 23-year-old woman who sees this job as a stop along a winding career path that may take her to 6 or 7 employers throughout her life.

You need to think creatively to change this dynamic. For example, I know a manager who works for a large mutual fund company. She has more than 200 employees on her staff. On the first Monday of every month she e-mails a brainteaser or problem of some kind to her staff. Within two weeks the staff must turn in a list of possible solutions to the problem. The catch? Along with the brainteaser comes a list of "Brain Trusts." Every person is assigned to a Brain Trust comprised of five to six people from various departments. People stay with the same Brain Trust for a quarter, and then everyone is reassigned. The prize? The group that turns in the greatest number of solutions gets to go out to lunch together on the company's time and dime. The bonus? Employees get the opportunity to work with a wide range of employees, forge new friendships, and learn to respect other staff members who are different from themselves. The organizational rewards can be huge.

You might be surprised by how powerful something like the Brain Trust project can be. It knocks down all kinds of barriers, prejudices, and assumptions people make about each other. It increases morale, adds levity, and makes creativity go through the roof. You wouldn't believe the zany ideas these teams think of that open up all kinds of possibilities.

Organizations also have to invest resources and actively support an environment that welcomes differences. Clients of mine who have invested in significant informal discussions or more formal training on these issues have reaped substantial productivity gains and a wealth of creative energy that has vaulted their businesses to new levels. Harnessing the power of diverse styles also requires that we create environments where people exchange ideas and data by working together. Those kinds of environments lead to greater knowledge and more creative thinking. Sometimes this may require a change in the physical environment as well as encouraging more formal discussions.

Many of my high-tech clients, for example, have intentionally designed spaces that are more fluid than separate offices or sterile cubes. They have changed the architecture to include open conference rooms, break rooms, and coffee shops to fuel informal discussions and information sharing.

My former law firm maintained two bars in conference rooms on separate floors of the firm where many productive and enjoyable after-work conversations about cases and projects occurred spontaneously. The environment allowed people to "blow off steam," and seek new ideas to tough problems while encouraging more informal bonding between people whose paths might not otherwise cross. The convenience of it was an important dimension. The same people who would wind up sitting together over a beer at the firm bar would never have organized a formal jaunt outside the building after hours.

Creating opportunities that expose people to different models of problem-solving also fuel creative thinking and usually increase people's enjoyment of work. Structured brainstorming exercises and roundtable discussions, in tandem with more formal presentations by various groups and individuals detailing their own successes or failures, can spark dynamic creative discussions.

Most organizations don't follow these paths, unfortunately. They tend to sacrifice creativity to the gods of productivity and control. Creativity researchers such as Amabile have proven that it's possible to have "both worlds: organizations in which business imperatives are attended to and creativity flourishes."[6]

HOW TO AVOID SQUELCHING WORKGROUP CREATIVITY

The academic research on creativity points to creative solutions for workgroups. If an expert is comfortable disagreeing with others—and, in my experience, part of that comfort comes from appreciating different styles—she will be more creative. People who can learn to examine problems in different ways as well as combine knowledge from different fields have also been found to be more creative. Such individuals can be aided by an organization that supports and encourages the creative ferment of having diverse experts from different fields clashing and creating together.

Workgroups that are the most creative are those who have the most diverse professional and ethnic backgrounds. Although without training and knowledgeable leaders who model valuing diversity, such diversity can lead to significant communication problems. However, with assistance and development, teams can be more insightful and attain higher goals.

In workplaces that lack both creativity and conflict, managers frequently squelch innovation by ripping apart any new ideas. One of my clients in the high-tech medical field was looking to add some innovative zing to the organization and decided to hire a new product development manager. They selected Vince, who had an impressive academic background. Underneath the veneer, Vince was a classic pit bull. He gleefully critiqued each new idea with such relish and academic finesse that his researchers stopped bringing their projects to him. Instead of valuing new ideas and embracing the conflict they might create, Vince simply rolled over his subordinates, leading them to retreat, withdraw, and refuse to share their own creative potential.

How can you avoid squelching the very creativity you want to foster? Three things are required: building diverse teams, harnessing their unique style, and allowing enough time for them to clash and hash through the conflict to creative breakthroughs.

BUILDING DIVERSE TEAMS

In terms of the first issue, you can imagine the chaos created by a team full of pit bulls! Many law firms are stacked with these types, creating endless personality conflicts and turf battles instead of the creative tensions that more diverse styles may bring. The opposite extreme, however—a group full of golden retrievers and roadrunners—is also uncreative since people are afraid to express their issues and ideas openly and skillfully. The ideal? Teams and organizations with a balance of styles to foster the creative abrasion of success.

What works is to emphasize that leaders and others must be willing to openly discuss the differences in style, ideas, and opinions that team members use to consider conflict.

What's especially useful is to encourage your team members to consider the advantages and disadvantages of different styles. Once they do, that will help them embrace the value in working with those who are different from them.

CONSIDER THE PIT BULL

Ask your team what might be the advantage of working with a competitive, abrasive pit bull and they're likely to come up blank. Yet clearly, there are advantages. If you're engaged in an all out war, for example, where you've tried everything else and you're quite convinced that nothing else will help you resolve the issues, that's when you *want* a pit bull on your side.

Certain kinds of lawsuits, for instance, that you're convinced will have to be tried, not settled, require a pit bull approach. Or consider World War II, which has been described as "The Last Good War"; this is another situation where creative conflict-solving had been tried and it failed. At that point, you want someone who is geared for all out combat. The problem, of course, as we've previously explored, is that people who operate in this mode tend to do so all of the time without considering the long-term consequences of their actions. You'll have to constantly remind the pit bulls on your team that most instances don't call for armed combat, and that they need to cultivate an eagle style in order to utilize the creativity inherent in conflict.

Pit bulls also make good devil's advocates, a technique that assists groups in avoiding the pit falls of groupthink. A devil's advocate is someone that intentionally takes a contrary view during a group discussion in order to make sure that the group has carefully and fully considered all of the issues and options. In addition, one reason many organizations put up with pit bulls is that they are sometimes some of the brightest members of the group. They can, in fact, be true geniuses who need your careful guidance in order to fit into the team. Although pit bulls can be notoriously prickly, impatient, appear fiercely individualistic, and refuse to participate as team players, their inner lives can be surprisingly fragile and vulnerable. Consider the advice of one of the world's most gifted choreographers, Mark Morris, director of the Mark Morris Dance Group, widely considered to be the most exciting company in the business.[7]

In advising others about how to work with geniuses, he emphasises that "the important thing about me is that I work very, very fast":

> I think fast; I choreograph quickly. Sometimes I choreograph as I am going along and because I'm so fast, I can be impatient. I say things sooner than maybe I should. So I can hurt people's feelings, though I don't think I'm mean for meanness' sake.[8]

With the pressure of creating innovative work, Morris says he sometimes will "scream and chase people around." Yet like many pit bulls, he denies that he's angry, just caught up in the moment of trying to make things perfect.

Because everyone needs the true geniuses to survive in the competitive world of the twenty-first century, Morris believes that managers should spend time bolstering the fragile egos of their exceptional pit bull people, yet not in an obvious way:

> You've got to guide these very talented individuals without actually intruding. In addition, you can't be fake … real artists or geniuses or whatever you want to call them especially need the truth. They're not fooled by false praise and empty encouragement. Only honest recognition of their real accomplishment means anything to them at all.[9]

Morris emphasizes that his own ambition is not about his individual career, but that "I am totally ambitious in getting something right: I must have excellence." Managing such a creative genius on your team requires you to both respect their unique contribution and help them interact more successfully with other team members.

You may wonder what to do about the pit bull who is just a fearful spoiled baby instead of a creative genius, like Morris. The truth is, we're sometimes better off without such people on our team. In fact, one thing we'll discuss in Part 4 is the issue of accountability. If leaders have tried unsuccessfully to encourage a pit bull to change, sometimes the only solution for an organization is to part company with the spoiled pup. Investing more time and energy with a talentless brat only drains a leader's time that could be spent more productively on encouraging the really useful people on your team to be even more productive.

CONSIDER THE ROADRUNNER

The obvious advantage of roadrunners and others who avoid conflict is that you don't have to worry about them creating unnecessary and destructive disputes. They are not the members of your team who will plague you with pettiness, raising issues that are not worth the team's time and energy. Discussing this style openly can help them and others see that a certain hesitance in rushing into the fray can sometimes be an advantage. These are the thinkers, the philosophers, and careful engineers among us. We can learn to appreciate and use their ability to research and mull through an issue. The problem, of course, is that these team members need to be encouraged to speak up when it's clearly necessary for them to do so.

One way to do this is to consistently ask for their opinion on important issues—especially about areas within their expertise. It also helps to use a facilitator for meetings so that everyone's opinion is solicited and valued. Realize, however, that they will often not want to issue an opinion on the spot but may need to think about it before answering. You need to structure requests for information and meetings in a way that allows them the time to do this.

CONSIDER THE GOLDEN RETRIEVER

These friendly critters are so lovely to have around that it's easy to see why everyone wants to welcome them on their team. They will consistently want to volunteer, to help out, and to be there when you need them. The advantage of this style is obvious; who wouldn't want to have someone on their team with such a loyal way about them? Again, openly talking about the value of loyalty and obedience can help these members be more appreciated by the entire team. As a leader, however, you need to foster an atmosphere where they feel comfortable speaking up and offering their feedback, advice, and even criticism. Otherwise, you'll be leaping off the cliff before you realize that the golden retriever failed to bark about the dragons lurking below.

You may also need to protect them from themselves since they're frequently susceptible to burnout. Be sure you monitor their workload and ask pointed questions to make sure that they haven't taken on too much. Continue to ask their opinions about important issues and encourage them to disagree with you when appropriate.

CONSIDER THE COBRA

Hard to think of an advantage to having cobras on your team? Consider this: They serve as an early warning device that something is wrong with the balance of power in your organization and it needs to be addressed. Remember, cobras triangulate because they feel they lack the power to address the issues directly and because triangles are stable.

Talking openly about how and why individuals triangulate can help both those who constantly use this technique to become more conscious about what they're doing as well as helping others be more open to hearing about what's happening. Cobras also signal that the intensity in the group is increasing. You need to help people to manage their own intensity so that direct relationships feel more stable and they don't have to rely on the "third leg" of the triangle. Leaders can also educate people that triangles are ubiquitous—we all triangulate when we feel weak or unable to face the fire of a particular interaction. Asking others to mark when they triangulate can help them appreciate those who use this technique more habitually. They can remind all of us to notice and correct unproductive power differentials.

You will need to constantly challenge the cobras among your group to speak directly about their issues to the people most able to solve their problems, instead of to those who are not involved in the issue. As a leader, you can model the openness and willingness to accept criticism that you would like others to exhibit. Let them know that it's healthy to talk to you directly about their problems and provide as many opportunities as possible for them to do so.

CONSIDER THE EAGLE

Encourage the group to notice the eagles among them. These people can be useful coaches, mediators, and mentors for others. If you're their manager, it can be useful to talk to them individually about their skills and brainstorm creative ways to use their talents with the entire group. Use the material in Chapter 17 on mediation and facilitation in order to expand the talents of your eagles. Consider using them to facilitate meetings with other groups in addition to your own.

HARNESSING UNIQUE STYLES—EMBRACING THE DRAGON

The next issue for fostering creativity is to harness the unique styles of the individuals that make up the group. Working skillfully with these different styles, then, requires that you recognize the necessary diversity up front, discuss your differences openly and talk about the ways in which various styles would be useful to the team.

In fact, it's useful to begin the process of appreciating different styles at the hiring stage. When Jerry Hirshberg first set up the Nissan Design International studios in San Diego, he designed the organization for creativity. Resisting the temptation to hire only people in his own image—intuitive, big-picture, visually oriented right-brained individuals—he instead also deliberately hired a few left-brained individuals who sought structure and always questioned "why" before proceeding. These thinkers frequently avoid conflict. Initially, these "different" individuals annoyed him. They seemed to be "anticreative" and threatened by novelty. He soon realized that instead, "They simply come to the table with a different set of preparations and expectations."[10] He needed such individuals to complement his own inclination to leap first and ask why and how later. Hirshberg describes himself as:

Somebody who is likely to leap off a cliff with a joyous intuition and halfway down, scream up to the rest of the group, "Hey, let's build a parachute—*now!*" and thanks God, the [left-brained] people were there. I might have told them beforehand that I was having this impulse, and I thought we were going to jump off a cliff tomorrow morning about seven. If I did that, they would say "thank you, Jerry," and they would go home that night and think about it and come in with some ideas about how to make it work.[11]

Under Hirshberg's leadership designed to facilitate *creative abrasion*, he hired designers in complementary *pairs*—as unalike as possible "so we keep from becoming a harmonious choir, all singing the same tune."[12] So, for example, they hired a "breathtakingly pure artist who is passionate about colors" the same year that they hired a "Bauhaus, Tectonic, rational, clear-headed" designer with a "function-form orientation," who is "passionate about clarity and logic." He invited dissent, but also guaranteed conflict. Hirshberg did so deliberately, believing that conflict would generate energy that could be channeled into creativity instead of destructive anger.

If we can appreciate the value of other styles of thinking and conflict management, we can construct more creative solutions to problems. For example, when Fisher-Price moved to a cross-functional team structure, a thinking-style preference diagnostic was part of the training. The director of marketing, Lisa Mancuso, found understanding others' preferences enlightening. "One man on the team had been driving me nuts," she said.

"He wanted to give me every little detail about why a schedule had slipped or what was going on in the factory—all I wanted was the bottom line ... it turned out that he had thought me really rude because I wasn't interested in all the details, and just wanted him to get to the point. It really helped us to communicate to understand that we just approached things differently."[13]

Harnessing diversity may require an organization to think creatively about the needs of different kinds of people in order to build and keep creative teams. The opportunity for generational conflict is abundant in the food service industry, for example. A restaurant's success is highly dependent upon the teens and twentysomethings. Management, however, is rife with baby boomers and older. Harnessing the creative power of these different generations has required some organizations to do things differently. Yet the generational conflict has sparked solutions that have made some organizations high performers.

For example, Chevy's Fresh Mex, a full-service restaurant chain with rapid growth found that traditionally to climb the restaurant ladder to management required working endless nights, every weekend and major holidays. Yet to fuel its growth, Chevy's needed the Gen-Xers. These young people weren't willing to abandon the idea of having a life outside of work. The turnover caused Chevy's to hire six to eight managers per store instead of the three or four it had been hiring. The change allowed the stores to cut down on the managers' hours and rotate weekend and holiday duty while retaining young talent with new ideas.

Founded in 1965 in New York City as a private, family-owned casual dining chain, T.G.I. Friday's also wanted to put an end to the revolving door. Recognizing that the potential cultural conflict between management and Gen-Xers was significant as was the opportunity for disastrous outcomes, the chain looked for a creative solution. They realized that the Gen X work force loves mobility and the freedom to roam, and often has post-college wanderlust. In response, they designed the Passport Program. Any full-time employee (whether server, dishwasher, host, etc.) who's been with the company for six months and who has passed the TGI Friday's training program can get a Passport. The Passport is valid for six months and allows workers to travel around the country and work at any Friday's restaurant they wish along the way. The employee gives the passport to the general manager of the store he's visiting along with an address to which his paycheck will be mailed. At the end of the stay—whether it's a single shift, a few days, a week, or longer—the manager stamps the passport and gives it back. The employee is off to a new destination with tips in hand, a paycheck coming in a couple of weeks and a new destination ahead.

These generational examples illustrate ways to harness—rather than resist—unique styles. While your diversity conflicts may be different, creative thinking about the strengths that differences in personality and backgrounds bring to your group can help you see your way through conflict to innovation.

ALLOWING CLASH AND HASH TIME

In encouraging groups to appreciate diversity, it helps to remind them that creativity involves different types of intelligences. Psychologist Robert Sternberg considers intelligence a balance of three types:

- *Creative intelligence* is the ability to generate new and unique ideas.

- *Analytical intelligence* is the ability to analyze those ideas and make decisions based on that analysis.

- *Practical intelligence* is the ability to see the connections between the ideas and real-life situations.

It is possible, but not likely, that one person might have all three. Therefore, the best way to ensure a creative group capable of elaborating novel ideas and seeing them through is to have all three types.[14]

The key for a leader is to encourage the group to appreciate these different styles of intelligence, which inevitably result in different conflict resolution styles. Hirshberg calls this process of honoring different thinking and conflict styles "Embracing the Dragon." For the individual, it requires "a willingness to adopt an alien, even threatening viewpoint to gain a fresh, reorienting take on an entrenched position. This process is specifically involved with 'the other hand,' as opposed to the interaction between two of them."[15]

Hirshberg recalls the first time he realized the value of this process when he was trying to persuade the president of Nissan, Takashi Ishihara, that they should integrate a group of engineers into the design team. This was considered a radical approach because of the long-standing tension between architects and builders. "From the viewpoint of traditional engineers, designers are decorative artists with little grasp of what it takes to build a car or make it work. To the designers, engineers are technicians so lost in the parts and pieces they are blind to the expressive power of the fully integrated whole."[16]

Ishihara was concerned that integrating the two would interfere with the pure design center he had envisioned, asking at one point: "But why would you want the enemy with you?"

Hirshberg responded: "They're *not* the enemy …. And even if they were, *with us* is exactly where we'd want them!" In that moment of dialog, Hirshberg discovered that he didn't want the typical engineer, but engineers of "the concept, engineers whose responsibility it would be to find a hundred ways we might be able to do something new rather than a thousand reasons why we couldn't."[17]

HARNESSING DIVERSITY

Most of all, harnessing diversity requires that you continually remind your co-workers of the value of dialog instead of debate. This means helping them understand that several points of view, instead of just opposing points of view, creates the richest soil for the best ideas to generate. As linguist Deborah Tannen has observed in *The Argument Culture*, "opposition does not lead to truth when an issue is not composed of two opposing sides but is a crystal of many sides. Often the truth is in the complex middle, not the oversimplified extremes."[18]

Forming diverse teams whose members have different styles promises to help us avoid the debates of two polar opposites that Tannen finds clouds the truth in modern culture. Tannen suggests that we avoid metaphors that focus on sports and wars and instead encourage the exchange of more ideas by introducing a plural form. "Instead of asking "What's the other side?' we might ask instead, "What are the other sides?" Instead of insisting on hearing 'both sides,' we might insist on hearing 'all sides'"[19]

When leaders are working with diverse groups, it helps to expand our thinking from debate to dialog. Instead of two sides clashing and attacking, dialog assumes that one person's comments will build upon another's until the group as a whole creates a more complex and layered solution.

For example, I was facilitating a community group where a team of developers was trying to build a new shopping center in the midst of an old, culturally rich neighborhood. When we started meeting, the developers brought in their slides and studies to show how the economic impact of the shopping center would ultimately benefit the neighborhood and the community. Although the neighborhood did not want the center, they had to admit that their own economic options were limited, especially for young people wanting new jobs.

The community group presented their own passionate and emotional defense of their ethnic way of life, the value of their historic homes, and the peace and quiet of the neighborhood. The two groups were completely polarized with two proposals: The developers wanted the shopping center as they had envisioned it, and the community members remained convinced that any encroachment would be a violation of their way of life.

The first thing I did was to break the 30 representatives into 6 groups of 5 each. Each group was a mix of developers and community members. Their assignment? To come up with six different proposals that considered the needs and interests of both camps. Instead of "either/or," their mission was to propose a solution that represented the truths of both sides.

Everyone groaned, moaned, and protested that it was impossible. They had nothing in common, they couldn't possibly compromise their positions, and on and on. I just listened until all the objections subsided and then repeated the assignment. "Pretend," I suggested, "that you are advising a different group in another city. You are to come up with *hypothetical* suggestions and solutions, not ones that you are actually endorsing for this situation."

Sometimes there's something about the authority of being designated the facilitator that tames even the most savage beast in these meetings, I've noticed. For some reason, that's what finally happened here. The groups gathered their colorful magic markers and buckled down to work, filling pages of flip chart paper with ideas and drawings.

We met for three sessions before all six groups could come up with their proposals. Remarkably, each one had a slightly different slant and different elements. While viewing the other proposals, I kept encouraging the members by broadening their field of vision. We then had six more meetings in which the entire group was encouraged to dialog about the unique features, benefits and limitations of each proposal. Ultimately, the group came up with a solution that they could live with that incorporated elements of each.

The shopping center was built, but it was a radically different structure than the one the developers had originally envisioned. The buildings were shorter and constructed of a more natural material to blend in rather than stand out. The entire facility was surrounded by an earth mound with extensive trees and plantings to minimize noise and visual distractions. Traffic was routed around rather than through the neighborhood, as originally drawn.

The final proposal reflected the needs and interests of both groups but was far from the original model of either camp.

Harnessing the strengths of diverse styles requires that you move your co-workers from debate to dialog so that they realize that there are more than one or two sides to any issue. Convincing them of this distinction is an important first step toward using the power of diverse styles.

Encourage team members to value the strengths of different styles and to even try them on, when appropriate. Harnessing diversity also requires those of you who are leaders to harness the different styles and use different people for different projects, as appropriate. If you have a situation where you know that only open warfare is possible, or you need a devil's advocate, for example, it's good to have a pit bull on your team. If you already have a bunch of warring pit bulls, sprinkle the mix with a few golden retrievers to cool things down and prevent unproductive meltdowns. If you've created a team full of brilliant prima donnas who seem to leap destructively into the unknown, inserting some thoughtful roadrunners into the fray will force the group to consider the implications of their actions. Finally, holding the concept of an eagle style out there as a model will give the entire group something to work toward. Most of all: Model eagle style yourself; the vision and strength are catching.

Now that we've considered the power of styles and demonstrated how to harness the unique styles of your group, in Part 3, we'll discuss specific skills you can employ to help transform yourself or your team from a pit bull, roadrunner, cobra, or golden retriever to an eagle.

PART 3

The Power of Skills: How to Harness the Strategic Value of Conflict

CHAPTER 11

THE TOP TEN STEPS: HOW TO USE CONFLICT TO YOUR ADVANTAGE

In a culture that tends to leave the resolution of conflict to lawyers and law enforcement officers, few people have experienced the rewards that can come from working openly and skillfully with disagreements.

—Carolyn R. Shaffer and Kristin Anudsen

A software development team files into a conference room, laptops in hand, for its weekly meeting. They are designing a new program that was supposed to hit the streets three months ago. Over budget and behind schedule, the manager has no idea when the product will be ready. The meeting starts and the attendees have their laptops fired up. However, they aren't taking notes or checking schedules. When a team member presents an idea or offers a comment, the other people in the meeting shoot off instant messages that disparage the idea and the person. One message says, "Dog breath! That is the stupidest thing anyone's ever said." Unbelievable, but true.

In this case, the conflicts were so deep that I pulled out all the stops. That meant using the entire "Top Ten" list of conflict management steps. It also required confiscating the laptops for a while. Following these steps provides a logical road map to navigate through a tense situation to use conflict creatively.

In Parts 1 and 2, we talked about the "what" of conflict: what it is, what makes it valuable, what we need to do to assume leadership. In Part 3, we need to focus on how we go about using conflict to fuel innovation. Changing our attitude about conflict will take us a long way, but we also need the power of skills.

In this chapter, you'll learn these 10 steps:

1. Don't Despair, Prepare!
2. Follow the Yellow Brick Road
3. Reveal, Don't Conceal

4. Tackle the Problem, Not the Person
5. Play Within the Bounds
6. Stir Up a Storm
7. Take a Time Out
8. Talk Until You Drop
9. Circle the Wagons
10. Write to Avoid New Fights

Remember the first key to assuming leadership: plan for conflict. Don't be surprised when it comes up. As a part of planning, educate yourself about the elements of conflict and the types of conflict.

Every conflict has two elements: the content (the facts of a disagreement) and the process (the patterns and style of dealing with the disagreement). The content is "what" the argument appears to be about. The process is "how" we deal with it.

The content is often easier to focus on and deal with than the process problems. As explored in more detail in the next chapter, learning to have good fights requires us to learn to map conflict and to think about both content and process. We also need to teach ourselves and educate our organizations to recognize the difference.

Moving from conflict to creativity requires learning new skills. While we're learning, it's helpful to focus on the 10 steps that encapsulate many skills. Although you'll seldom use all of these in every conflict, understanding all of them will help you when you need a more innovative approach.

STEP ONE: DON'T DESPAIR, PREPARE!

Perhaps the most important part of your preparation is understanding and using the concepts in Parts 1 and 2. Learning to *value* the creative spark of conflict, assuming *leadership* in conflict, and appreciating the *diverse styles* of others will take you far in your preparation.

How many different ways can you prepare to manage a conflict? Certainly, thinking through the 10 steps, especially Step 2, is important. The other way is to do as much research as possible on the other party's needs and interests. Perhaps you can interview their associates or clients. Find out what style of conflict management they practice and what is most important to them about the issue.

Review whether this is a substantive conflict or a process conflict and map the conflict as outlined in the next chapter: Is it data, relationship, or structural? As explored in detail in the Chapter 12, a substantive conflict concerns a true difference in the needs and interests of the parties involved and the perception that all of the parties can't meet all of those needs and interests at the same time. A process conflict involves the way the conflict is being resolved; something about the process of managing the conflict itself is fueling the dispute. One party may not feel that they're being heard, for example, or the thinkers in the group need more time to process the options before they can decide what they think.

The other important step is to think clearly and completely about your own needs and interests. Why do you care about this issue? How important is it? Is the problem the type of conflict that can fuel creative sparks? Is the issue really something you want to spend your time on? Conversely, are you intervening soon enough or is it something that you've let spiral into a negative?

Identify your own "exit point." This is the point at which it makes more sense to walk away from the conflict than it does to work creatively to manage the issue. Ask yourself, what will happen if you don't resolve the conflict amicably? What will you do? What will the other party do? The answers to these questions are helpful, but often not even considered. Some people simply go into a negotiation or try to talk to someone without wondering *why* it's important. Sometimes, your best option *is* to walk away, especially if you've already made skilled and extensive attempts to resolve the issue, or if you can come to a better solution on your own.

Finally, rehearse. Find a trusted friend, coach, or other advisor. Ask them to role play various scenarios with you and brainstorm ways to talk through the problem. Explain to them what the other person's style is likely to be, the impact you believe this will have on the negotiation, and then ask them to role play that style. This practice is an invaluable and often ignored step.

STEP TWO: FOLLOW THE YELLOW BRICK ROAD

As part of your preparation, identify goals for yourself. Then, when you actually sit down with the person or parties to manage the issue, start here. If you can agree upon a *common goal*—to creatively solve a problem, to generate a new idea, to sell more product, or to achieve the goals of the organization—you will have a clearer chance of harnessing the conflict. Many times, in fact, the root of a conflict may be that you do not even agree upon what the problem is or that you are struggling to address different issues.

Sometimes, there are many difficulties to address. This step can help you identify and sort those issues. Try to list them in order of importance. You may want to start, however, with the one that you feel you have the best chance of managing or the one that addresses a relatively minor issue. Successful conflict management breeds success and builds trust. If you creatively solve a small issue, you'll build the energy to move forward.

Another useful approach to identifying goals is to sort problems into historical, current, and beyond issues. Historical issues are those that are no longer relevant but may need an airing just to clear the slate. Current issues are those still on the table. "Beyond" issues are those beyond the ability of those present to solve the problem. Structural problems, for example, may be beyond issues when you need input or a decision from a higher up.

For example, I was hired by a large law firm to mediate a dispute between two associates. The firm valued both women for their hard work and intelligence, but the two constantly tangled instead of working as a team.

Bill, the managing partner who hired me, had brought in Carol, an associate in her seventh year of practice, to support Debra, an associate in her sixth year of practice. Debra worked directly with Bill to help him with his successful, but hectic, legal work. Both Debra and Bill thought they had clearly explained to Carol that she would need to take some direction and supervision from Debra since Debra had been with the firm longer and knew Bill's clients and work. When

I spoke with Carol, however, she held an entirely different view of her role. She whined that it was "inappropriate" for a sixth year associate to supervise a seventh year associate and that she took the job to work with Bill, not Carol. Debra complained that she rarely even saw Bill and that Carol "micromanaged" her in a way that was "insulting" for a seventh year associate.

After meeting with the women individually, I talked to Bill to deliver the common, but unpopular news: I could mediate between the two associates forever, yet the issues wouldn't disappear. The real issue was a "beyond" issue, one that was beyond the two parties in the room and that Bill needed to solve it by delineating the roles and working relationship of the two parties. Bill was then able to see how he had contributed to the continuation of the conflict and was able to solve the problem by scheduling regular meetings among the three of them to delineate duties and responsibilities.

STEP THREE: REVEAL, DON'T CONCEAL

Step 3 requires that we identify our own needs and interests and avoid positions. This is the most important step in so-called *interest-based* conflict management and negotiation. The whole premise of this system is that it is possible for people to gain most or all of what the disputants want if they are willing to continue talking until they come up with a creative solution. This is the most powerful tool in your ability to use the conflict.

Other kinds of negotiation systems focus on helping you win the most for your side. Those systems tend to focus on short-term gain for one party rather than long-term gains for both parties and for the relationship or the entire organization. In a workplace, it is best to assume that you will be there for the duration and, that, therefore, creating a good working relationship is an important goal. Although you can leave a job where you can't creatively manage the conflict, this is an expensive solution—both in terms of emotion and money.

In addition, even if you exit a job because of destructive conflict, in many industries, you may meet again. The world is becoming a very small place.

A need or interest is the underlying reason why we think we must have our way in any dispute. It is the reason why we think our solution is the best. In this form of conflict management, you must agree—to at least some extent—to be vulnerable, to *reveal* why you want something and to declare what's really important to you about an issue. Many people are afraid to do this, especially at work. We're fearful that if we acknowledge an underlying need or interest, the issue will be used against us.

Could this happen in a creative conflict management or negotiation? Absolutely! I don't want to suggest that other people will always play fair or show sympathy. What I do know, however, is that it is difficult to formulate sustainable agreements if we are unwilling to reveal our underlying needs.

What happens instead is that one party wins and the other feels cheated, plotting revenge against the winner at some future point during the implementation of the agreement through foot dragging, sabotage or other forms of passive/aggressive behavior. If we don't stop to understand the real needs of the parties, the solution may not be the best or most creative for all over the long haul. In addition, we may not be considering the needs of the customers, clients, co-workers or shareholders that the parties represent, which could lead to a fatal flaw in any suggested solution.

The other reason to reveal our own needs and interests is because people at work usually know how we feel even if we don't tell them.

Certainly, we don't need to reveal everything at work or in any negotiation: that's never smart. Yet, if we can be the first to open the door and be just a little bit vulnerable, we will witness miracles in our negotiations.

In contrast, if we stay stuck on arguing for our positions, the conflict may never be managed creatively. The classic story used to illustrate this difference is about two sisters and an orange. Two sisters lived in an isolated house, far from any convenience store. They had only one orange in the house and they both believed they needed and wanted the orange. If they stay stuck on their position, "I want the orange," the conflict is unlikely to be managed creatively.

They may decide to compromise—an idea that's considered enlightened by many in our society. If they compromise in this situation, they might decide to cut the orange in half. Compromise frequently results in a very interesting situation: both parties end up with half of what they thought they wanted!

In contrast, if the sisters are willing to reveal their underlying *needs* and *interests*, they may be able to find a creative way to meet all of them. For example, why might someone need an orange? They might need one for cooking, juggling, making a pompadour, painting a still life of fruit or for one of many other reasons.

In this situation, if one sister wants the juice of an orange to bake a cake and the other wants to use the peel (the zest of the orange) to bake a muffin, they are both able to receive what they want—if they're willing to be vulnerable enough to say *why* they want it.

Revealing our underlying needs frequently sparks creative solutions. If we're concealing our true interests, it's hard to fuel an innovative solution. In addition to being unwilling to be vulnerable, we may also fail to reveal our needs and interests because we fall in love with our solution; we become attached to our conclusion as the best or only way. Sometimes we even choose our friends based on our solutions. We favor only those who agree with us.

The following table shows some additional examples of *positions, needs, and interests* that may help you understand the difference.

POSITIONS, NEEDS, AND INTERESTS

Position	Need or Interest
I must have a raise or I'll leave.	I need to have more recognition of my work.
You need to transfer to a different department.	We need to find a better way to match your skills with the needs of this department.
I'm quitting to work some place closer to home.	I need to find a way to spend more time with my children.

continues

POSITIONS, NEEDS, AND INTERESTS *(continued)*

Position	Need or Interest
We have to ship this new product before July 4.	We need to find a way to show headquarters we've been productive and are making progress.

What if the other party stonewalls and refuses to reveal his or her interests? What if the other party's only real interest is to win? Then you need to ask some skillful questions. The following probes may help you find the underlying cause of stonewalling or a "winner takes all" attitude.

- What's important to you about this issue?
- What's most important to you about this issue?
- What's least important to you about this issue?
- I'm wondering about why you want _____ (the proposed solution).
- I'm puzzled about why you want _____ (the proposed solution).
- I'm curious about your reasons for proposing _____ (the proposed solution).
- Explain to me how this solution might work for both of us.
- Well, that's an interesting idea. What other ideas do you have that might work for both of us?
- What do you think will happen if we don't find a creative solution that meets both our needs and interests?
- What would you suggest I tell my team (group, organization, etc.) if we don't create a solution that meets all of our needs and interests?
- What standards do you think we should use to resolve this issue?
- What might be an innovative idea that would allow us all to get what we want?

Identifying the other parties' needs and interests when they're trying to stonewall or win at all costs requires that you engage in detective work. What's most important is that you listen and try to understand the other person's story.

When we're in conflict, we always have a story—usually one that justifies our proposed solution. If we focus on listening and ask open-ended questions, eventually the other person or parties will reveal a clue that will lead us to their underlying need or interest. For a "winner," for example, we may discover they need a way to save face. They may need to take a "time out" to consider their real options. You may be able to find a small point or give them an unimportant win that will help them save face.

STEP FOUR: TACKLE THE PROBLEM, NOT THE PERSON

Try to focus on identifying the problem and persuading the other party to join you in solving the problem. If you can make the *problem* your common enemy rather than blaming the other *person* for causing the problem, creative solutions may arise.

Research clearly shows that destructive conflict is mired in personality clashes. To harness the creative power of conflict, we need to nurture conflict about ideas, but discourage conflicts from becoming personal. Part of what drives conflict into negative spirals of personal attacks is not assuming leadership and stepping in early enough to manage the conflict.

If the other person insists on blaming you for the problem, keep *reframing*. Reframing is a way of changing someone's statement to reflect a potential solution to the problem rather than as a simple constant restatement of the same issue. One way of reframing, for example, is to restate general complaints into specific requests. If they say, for example: "We wouldn't have this project disaster if you could get your part of the job finished on time." You could respond: "It sounds as if you're concerned about deadlines. Perhaps we could discuss how to establish reasonable timetables that work for everyone and allow us to succeed on this project."

Continue to reframe and to ask for their innovative ideas about transforming your *joint* problem rather than blaming each other for causing the problem.

PERSONALITY CLASHES

Creatively working through a conflict requires the individuals involved to share a high degree of trust in each other as well as in the process of conflict management. If there are interpersonal issues as well as substantive issues, you must sort out the interpersonal issues first. This may require the use of an unbiased mediator (see Chapter 17). If used skillfully, people can trust the process until they are able to trust each other. Whether working directly with someone or with a mediator, it's important to acknowledge the relationship issue up front and then work through it systematically.

How do you know if it's a relationship issue? If most problems you're trying to solve degenerates into personal attacks, name-calling, slugfests, or walk outs, the underlying issue may be personal.

First, try going through an analysis of the conflict styles in Part 2. Sometimes this step alone can assist people in sorting through relationship issues by helping them realize that people approach conflicts differently because their brain and personality are "hardwired" uniquely, not because they're trying to annoy the other party.

If this step fails to work, try charting the relationship history. Often people who did work well together experience an event that changes their relationship. They may perceive this event differently or one party may not even be aware that the other party felt so strongly about the issue.

For example, I was mediating a dispute between Bob, a CEO, and Joanne, one of his vice presidents. They had reached the point in the *negative spiral of conflict* where almost everything they did irritated each other.

I led them back to the beginning of their relationship. Both of their facial expressions softened and smiles and grins emerged as they described the early days of building the company together. As we traveled through their joint history, however, things changed radically when they spoke of a sexual harassment case that had dramatically altered their relationship. Joanne still felt that Bob had handled the entire incident incorrectly, something she had argued at the time. Bob had responded then, and repeated in our session, that he was just following the advice of their attorney. Joanne thought they were both wrong and they were off and running again on the substantive argument.

This sexual harassment case had happened three years before, but Joanne had never released her personal anger about the situation. Nothing about their relationship had been the same since.

Bob—a very busy CEO with a host of other vice presidents under his management—had not realized this was when the relationship had unraveled. We were finally able to clear the air over this issue, go on to manage current conflicts, and agree on how they would work together in the future.

A tool I have used effectively in this process is to ask the participants to individually fill out the following relationship chart before we meet.

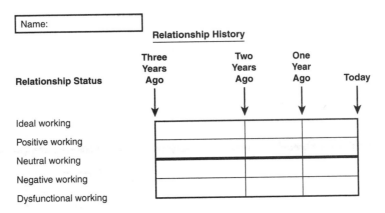

Relationship history. (Adapted with permission from John Wiley and Sons, Inc. [Landau, Sy, Barbara Landau, and Daryl Landau. From Conflict to Creativity. *San Francisco: John Wiley and Sons, Inc., 2001])*

When the parties come together, I invite them to share their results. This analysis frequently allows them to step back and become more objective about their feelings and understand the role played by their own personal perceptions and approaches. Once the parties understand how the other party may have misinterpreted their behavior, they are usually able to make commitments to reduce the negative fall-out.

If the parties are still stuck, a helpful process I have used at this stage is to have the participants fill out another chart as a pair or group. It is especially useful if everyone is blaming someone else for the problem. This chart tracks all the ways the participants must change in order to make the relationships work.

Using this technique in a meeting with all the blamers, draw a large chart with all their names across the top and along the side in the same order. Tell the group that each column represents that person's opinions and each row represents changes the group would like to see in one person's behavior. Ask each participant to fill in each of his or her squares.

	Anne says:	Bob says:	Carl says:	Doug says:
Anne change:	?	stop seeing Bob as enemy	stop being paranoid	cut out power struggle with Doug
Bob change:	end male chauvinism, end animosity toward Anne, move his office	?		end animosity toward Anne
Carl change:	end male chauvinism, take more initiative		?	wake up and look beyond organization chart
Doug change:	end male chauvinism		stop usurping authority	cut out power struggle with Anne

Who changes what? (Reprinted with permission from Kaye, Kenneth. Workplace Wars and How to End Them. *New York: Amacon, 1994)*

It is common for each party to leave one significant space blank: the one indicating what *they* must change in order to make the relationships work. After the group fills out all of the other squares, I often engage in a bit of creative manipulation, saying something like, "Oh well, it looks like I can't help resolve this then because you've left the most important space blank. I guess there's no hope and we might as well close." I sigh deeply, cross my arms, and sit silently. One party usually comes to his senses when I say this and fills in his missing square and we break the deadlock.

When we believe a problem is a personality conflict, we need to focus on specific behavior, not personality. Sometimes people annoy us for no rational reason: the proverbial oil and water. Sometimes it's chemistry; sometimes it's something from our past that we can't release. The best solution is to focus on the future and the specific.

What exact behavior do we want from the other person? This approach is particularly useful in relationship conflicts that continue despite other attempts to resolve the conflict.

In my experience in trying to resolve workplace conflicts, people frequently focus on vague personality characteristics rather than on what they specifically want. Someone might insist, for example, that the other person is a rude jerk who shouldn't be allowed to walk the planet and doesn't respect him.

The problem with words like "respect" is that we all have different ideas about what we mean by respect. If I'm a person who just likes to come in, do my work as quickly and quietly as possible, and leave the office early, for example, I might not even notice if my co-workers acknowledge my presence in the hallway. For some people, however, acknowledging their presence and making polite conversation is an essential part of their ability to work with other members of the team and to trust them. If you fail, on a regular basis, to say hello in the hall, they may see that as a deliberate snub.

I worked with a team with exactly this problem. A group of male utility construction workers kept clashing with their new manager, Rudy. When I asked them what they wanted, they said that Rudy didn't like them. When I forced them to be specific, all they could come up with was that he never said "hello" to them in the halls and that he was "stuck up." When I brought him their request, he was floored! "That's it?" Rudy couldn't believe it. "What is this," he fumed, "high school?"

As one of the characters—an elderly priest—in one of Graham Green's novels responded when he was asked what he had learned from a lifetime of hearing confessions, "I've learned that there are no real grown ups."

So rather than making vague statements such as: "I want you to respect me," you need to make a specific request. You should ask for exactly the behavior that you want. Say, for example, "I want you to talk with me in a normal tone of voice and I don't want you to use obscenities when you talk to me," or "I want you to focus on creatively solving our problems instead of constantly telling me why my ideas *won't* work."

When we're focusing on behavior, we talk about things we can objectively see or hear rather than our conclusions, assumptions, or biases. The examples in the following table may help you understand.

PERSONALITY VS. BEHAVIOR

Personality	Behavior
You're not a good listener.	I need you to stop talking and listen.
You lack leadership ability.	I need you to make decisions faster.
You're not a good choice for the job because you're an introvert.	If you want to be considered for this position, you need to spend more time talking to the team members and getting to know them.
You're lazy.	I need you to meet deadlines.
Your ideas are stupid.	Let's brainstorm some ways we can create more innovation in our department.

If the *other* person insists on using vague terms, telling you, for example, that "you need to change your attitude," ask them to explain exactly what they want. Ask what they mean by "attitude." You might say: "When I hear people use the word 'attitude,' I know they mean many different things. When you say that I need to have a different attitude, can you give me an example of what specific behavior would indicate to you that I have a different attitude?" My experience is that this kind of dialogue leads to creative conflict management.

STEP FIVE: PLAY WITHIN THE BOUNDS

Standards can lift you out of an intractable conflict. If the other party remains difficult, start talking more about standards and procedures than about the problem. This can help you creatively manage a conflict that seems like an immovable object.

For example, if you want to take every Friday off to be with your children and you're willing to make up the time on other days, but your boss insists everyone work the same hours, ask your boss what standards he or she is using to solve the problem. Does he or she believe that retaining good people is a priority? Does he or she believe that people who are more relaxed make better workers? Or does your boss think that everyone has to be treated the same in all situations? If so, how does that work with his or her other standards? Is he or she interested in getting the work done or in "face time"? Also, review the material on conflict mapping in Chapter 12. Intractable conflicts are sometimes caused by process problems rather than substantive issues.

STEP SIX: STIR UP A STORM

Brainstorming is vital to successful conflict management and a step many miss. Make sure all sides, as a part of their preparation, discuss many possible solutions, not just one. We need to understand that the best resolution for all concerned may not be the one we had previously discussed. Many of us fall in love with our solutions and decide that our idea is the only possibility.

Brainstorming was invented by Alex Osborn in 1938 for his advertising firm. He believed that of all the requirements for imaginative thinking, "the most important is to guard against being both critical and creative at one and the same time."[1]

To achieve this goal, a facilitator, participant, or leader needs to enforce a few basic rules such as:

- No discussion of the ideas until after the brainstorming process.
- Generate as many ideas as possible.
- All ideas are welcome.
- Separate the process of generating ideas from the process of evaluating ideas.

In order to discuss more creative possibilities, use *brainstorming*—have everyone list possible solutions as quickly as possible—no criticism or cynicism allowed. Welcome all suggestions to get the brainpower flowing. After that, you can spend more time sorting suggestions and determining which ones merit further study.

This is a good way to move people off their positions.

In order to make brainstorming effective—especially in a group setting—you'll need to establish both the process and the purpose. Unless skillfully managed, brainstorms can merely promote the illusion that the group is being creative. Laboratory research actually shows that people generate more and better ideas working alone if you don't carefully attend to process and purpose.[2]

People fear appearing stupid in a group. Therefore, it's useful to submit the issues ahead of time and ask people to come with several ideas. Alternatively, during the session you can have individuals generate their ideas on sticky notes. The facilitator or mediator can then collect and arrange them according to some theme or let the group develop the arrangements. Once the stickies are arranged, the group can then expound on them using the same brainstorming rules.

A newer and sometimes useful variant on traditional brainstorming designed to eliminate idea blocking is called *electronic brainstorming*. Participants type their ideas while the ideas of other members appear in a separate window on the screen. The virtual brainstormers are encouraged to read others' contributions and elaborate on them. Evidence suggests that because people are free to focus on their own idea production, more ideas are generated than in traditional brainstorming.

Again, it may be a matter of diverse styles, as we discussed in Part 2. Some people need to think through both the problem and the solution before they offer any of their own thoughts. Others are stimulated by the group and prefer to work with others.

I have also used *visual brainstorming* with groups to break entrenched conflicts. When a group is stuck, for example, I'll frequently give them large pieces of paper and crayons and have them work on the floor. After dividing them into small teams, I'll ask them to come up with a visual image of how they want things to be, kind of a thematic purpose they then use to steer the group toward a creative solution. Although most people groan at first and may suggest firing the facilitator, they usually sink into the task and the resulting creative and colorful work can spur a breakthrough. I've also brought in an artist to quickly sketch the ideas of various blocked parties. Sometimes a visual representation of a solution to a conflict can move people beyond their positions into new ground.

Role-plays and skits can also help break through a deadlock with a group if used skillfully. Either the facilitator can put something together or ask separate groups to generate ideas and then act them out.

Sometimes the issues are important enough to bring in the professionals. One of my clients hired a talented troop of improvisation actors to participate with me in giving a keynote address to their sales conference. After conducting extensive interviews with the attendees ahead of the meeting, we came up with several typical conflict scenarios that the sales staff faced when they interacted with the operations staff.

At various points as my presentation on the value of conflict proceeded, I would stop and set up a scenario and the actors would act out the workplace situation. I'd then ask the audience to brainstorm and coach the actors through the scene again. This time, however, they'd ask the actors to play the scene in a way that valued the conflict and used the energy of the situation creatively. When a salesperson seemed to be especially invested in a particular scene, we would ask him to jump up onto the stage, switch places with one of the actors, and role-play the scenario with a different outcome. Usually, the enthusiasm was infectious and others would volunteer to join in the fray.

The opportunity to see their own work life acted out before their eyes and to imagine alternative realities moved the sales group in ways that would not have been possible without the improvisation. Many creative solutions to the sales/operations conflicts emerged from this session.

I've also placed various toys around the room and on the tables to help the group come up with creative solutions during a conflict. Modeling clay, Silly Putty, Tinker Toys, or Legos all help people move through the session with a more creative and playful spirit and may even help them actually "construct" a solution they had never before imagined.

It's especially important during the brainstorming process for the leader or an enlightened participant to model a noncommitment to a point of view and urge others to do the same. Because we live in a society built on frontier values, we tend to favor John Wayne types as leaders who are quite sure of what they want, where they're going, and the correct answer to any idea.

Brainstorming creative solutions, however, requires that we set aside our preconceived ideas and make way for something new. Remember the three bowls from the introduction? If our mind is already filled up with a point of view, nothing new and innovative can enter.

Instead, we have to be willing to try to hold ourselves in a "beginner's mind," a kind of open spaciousness, beyond what we think we know. That space is where the potential for the most creative thought exists.

Sometimes the most useful step for a leader or facilitator is to stop the brainstorming meeting just when everyone begins to question their underlying assumptions. The quality of the questions themselves may tell you when it's time to take this step. Halting the process before it reaches closure allows something new to percolate up in the participant's underlying assumptions.

One way to know if you've reached this stage is by the quality of the questions. If the questions themselves are open and contain a sense that suggests people really don't know the answer to what they're asking, innovation is possible. The more such inquires you're creating during any given session, the more creative potential you've generated in the room. Most people, however, don't ask real questions in these sessions, but make speeches instead, shutting down true inquiry and creative potential.

STEP SEVEN: TAKE A TIME-OUT

When you're really mired in a conflict and unable to fashion a creative response, it's time to go out for a beer, coffee, ice cream, or a movie. Classic advocates of creative conflict management have used a more restrained version of this move. Martin Luther King Jr., for example, suggested that we "go to the mountain" during conflict to gain the higher ground and a better perspective on the problem. Gandhi retreated to meditation and fasting during the most intense periods of his struggle to free the Indian people.

Every parent or teacher knows the value of sending quarreling kids into time-out. A chance to cool off and rest frequently solves the problem so that the kids return with renewed enthusiasm to work things out or a creative idea about how to share a toy that they had claimed was theirs alone.

In my own mediation and conflict management practice, I've developed a keen awareness of when individual combatants or groups need a "time-out" from the process. If you're feeling overwhelmed and stuck, or if you can't seem to prod the other side into thinking creatively rather than only of their own positions, it's time for a break. Sometimes, it's best to allow people their own time away from the process, but at other times, it's my sense that forcing them to take a break together—going out for ice cream or coffee—with no talking about the issues allowed, can forge a breakthrough.

Most leaders, however, hesitate to take this step when a group is stuck. They seem to be reluctant to lose momentum and believe that keeping the pressure on will solve the problem instead. They rely on motivational talks or threats to move people. Pep talks can inspire people, as well as give participants a break from trying to solve their own problems.

As a mediator, I frequently interrupt the process to encourage people to keep talking, remind them how much work managing conflict creatively can be, and urge them to keep going. Although this can sometimes keep a group working temporarily, sometimes a break is a better idea.

In my experience, threats works equally poorly as a motivator when groups stall. One VP of advertising I worked with, for example, constantly threatened his team with firing if they didn't come up with better ideas. While the tactic generated a lot of nervous energy, and a slew of designs, none of them really were able to do their best work under that kind of pressure. Most of the new work was ultimately scrapped as below standard. Instead, when your group is stuck, consider going out for a beer!

STEP EIGHT: TALK UNTIL YOU DROP

The truth is, most of us do not allow enough time for creative conflict management. William Ury, in his book, *Getting to Peace*, studied conflict resolution techniques from around the world. As he spent time with the Bushmen of Africa—who have an extremely sophisticated conflict resolution system—he learned why their methods are so successful. First, they spend 40 percent of their time visiting with other community members building strong ties so they have a deep foundation when a conflict does break out.

Then, when two members of the community do fight, the entire community drops everything and sits with them until they come up with a solution that serves the community as well as the individuals. If it takes hours, they sit. If it takes all night, they sit. If it takes days, they sit. The community stands ready to serve as what Ury calls the "third side" in the conflict.

In our modern world, where we scream at the microwave because it's too slow, where we expect everything to come to us through a drive through and where instant gratification takes too long, we believe that we just don't have time for this.

Yet look at the costs of unproductive conflict: simmering resentments, lack of innovation, passive/aggressive behavior, open warfare, delay, and sabotage. If we don't creatively and thoroughly manage problems as they arise, the long-term costs are far greater than the short-term conflict management time.

Now, I'm not advocating that you go back to your workplace tomorrow and inform your co-workers that you're going to use the Bushmen technique for resolving conflict. Clearly, that's not practical. In fact, one thing I hope you will learn through studying the methods outlined in this book is that some conflicts truly are not worth our time and energy. We need to be much more discerning about what is and what isn't a conflict.

Yet when we do realize we have an issue, we need to make sure we allow sufficient time for management. You may object to using many of the techniques in this book because they seem to be time consuming. Yet things like conflict mapping as described in the next chapter, going through the 10 steps and the other ideas of this book will save time in the long run. Talking about these ideas with those with whom you have a conflict can pay off. Realize that it may take more than one session, as well as frequent time-outs to manage a conflict creatively. My own experience is that it usually takes longer than we think to produce good fights instead of bad ones.

STEP NINE: CIRCLE THE WAGONS

When you reach an agreement or a creative solution, you need to go through some sort of closure process. Perhaps you need to arrange to meet some time in the future to review how the agreed upon solution is working. Also agree on an action plan to accomplish the goals of an agreement. Decide who does what, when, and where.

In this step, an agreement is also more likely to be sustainable by closing with a review to learn from the conflict. The intention is to provide closure and to improve your conflict management skills for the future as well as to strengthen your relationships. Try to discourage discussion; just ask each party to speak and listen.

Option One (for close colleagues or partners):

- What worked during the conflict management session?
- What didn't work?

- Who do we need to forgive and for what?
- Who do we need to thank and for what?
- What do we need to say to feel complete?
- In the future, how could we use this conflict or one like it to be more creative, innovative, or productive?

Option Two (other workplace situations):
- What was effective about the way we managed this conflict?
- What was ineffective?
- What can we say by way of compassion for others' shortcomings or incompetence?
- What can we say by way of respect for the others, their competence, their conduct in this situation, and their commitment to resolving this case?
- Assuming we might not speak again about this matter, what else do we need to say?
- In the future, how could we use this conflict or one like it to be more creative, innovative, or productive?

"Circling the wagons" by paying attention to closing the conflict can help people learn to value the conflict and be more creative in the future.

STEP TEN: WRITE TO AVOID NEW FIGHTS

As an attorney and former litigator, I have scant faith in the ability of written contracts to protect our individual rights. If you have to sue to enforce an agreement, you've all lost because lawsuits take too long and cost too much. Even if you win, you lose.

I do have great faith, however, in the ability of written contracts to facilitate the possibility of creative conflict management. If you write down what you think you've agreed upon at various stages, the process helps clarify your own thinking as well as the agreement. We all tend to assume the meaning we ascribe to a certain word or discussion is the same for everyone. This causes more conflict. In fact, we all use words differently. As Lewis Carroll said in *Alice in Wonderland*, "A word means just exactly what I say it means, no more, no less."

If you find that some words or phrases are controversial, you may even need to include a "definitions section" in your written document. The written document can be as formal or as informal as you need, depending upon the conflict involved. Both parties should keep a copy of the document and agree upon a specific time to review how well the agreement is working.

Welcome the process of clarifying your agreement by committing the details to writing. That act will save you a world of hurt down the road.

SUMMARY TO THE TEN STEPS

The 10 steps can provide a roadmap to lead you skillfully through using the conflict to generate creativity. While you may not need to use all 10 for every situation, it's useful to review them before you try to resolve any specific issue. If you do, you'll be able to see where you're stuck and what step needs more emphasis. For complex disputes, working your way through all 10 steps with all the parties will serve you well.

The 10 steps in this chapter will guide us through the stickiest disputes, but as we will discover in the next chapter, what we do before the dispute is joined can be even more crucial.

CHAPTER 12

PREPARE FOR CONFLICT: HOW TO MOVE FROM DESPAIRING TO PREPARING

Suffering is a part of our reality, a natural fact of our existence. It is something that we have to undergo, whether we like it or not. We might as well adopt an attitude that enables us to tolerate it so that we are not so intensely affected by it mentally.

—The Dalai Lama

Scott Fitzpatrick is a rising star at a high-tech company in Boulder, Colorado. The last thing Scott does before he calls it a day is flip open his Palm Pilot and review his schedule for the next day. He prides himself on being prepared. He's got an important meeting tomorrow so he decides to wear his new suit. He's also got an impossible schedule with competing priorities so he writes a "to-do" list. The justification for his budget is due in four days so he stays late to plot a strategy and draft some talking points. Last, he's scheduled to talk with a staff member who's not performing well. He's certain the conversation will be difficult. He sighs and shuts down his computer—he'll cross that bridge tomorrow.

The one thing that stands in the way of Scott's meteoric rise to greatness is his reluctance to deal with conflict. It doesn't have to be that hard. The steps to successful management of a conflict begin with preparation. Conflict is a predictable and valuable part of every day life and there are numerous ways to pave the way for innovative success instead of frustration. Yet, most of us, including Scott, spend more time organizing our "to-do lists" than doing the legwork essential to managing a conflict.

Every conflict has two elements: the content (the facts of the disagreement) and the process and the pattern and style of dealing with the disagreement. Working with both is what facilitates creative conflict management. Great diplomats, negotiators, and famous military strategists aren't noted for their luck; they are revered for their strategies and tactics. It's their fastidious preparation undertaken to understand the terrain and their parties—their viewpoints, priorities, passions, unspoken issues, points of compromise, strengths, weaknesses—and the cultural and political landscape. Preparation leads to good fights that harness the power of conflict.

PREPARE BY UNDERSTANDING PROCESS VERSUS CONTENT

First on your preparation list should be to consider whether you're dealing with a process problem or a content problem. For example, a CEO and his Chief Financial Officer came to me complaining about their long running battles. The CFO—younger and female—liked to debate the finer points of every financial statement and quarrel about how things should be reported. She relished arguments and details. The CEO often reacted quickly and intensely to her. He didn't have time for all those details, he told me. He just wanted *her* to handle their problems.

She carped that he didn't take her seriously. They both whined that the other drove him or her nuts. The CEO said the CFO never gave up and always had to be right. "She tells me what to do," he complained. The CFO said the CEO treated her as if she had nothing valid to say. "He won't listen to me and avoids our meetings," was her rebuttal.

I got the picture: The conflict was all about process and style— the way they handled issues. I worked out a plan with the two of them: They agreed to specific times and time limits they would discuss the company's financial matters and came up with a specific agenda about what the CEO did and did not want to discuss.

When they came back for a follow up session with me, they agreed that they had a much more peaceful month. In the car coming to my office, however, an argument had erupted.

The CEO had been musing about a recent meeting they'd had with the board of directors and some things he felt he hadn't done as well as he should have. He just wanted to ventilate and have a sympathetic ear. The CFO jumped at the chance to critique his performance and inform him of all the ways she believed he hadn't presented her numbers as well as he could have, all the details they should have included, and so on. They were off to the races and the conflict spiraled downward from there.

Of course, the argument started all over again in my office. I let them fuss for a while so I could observe their process. I finally stopped them and reminded them they had agreed to work on not always thinking it's the other's fault—our project for the week.

"What were you each doing wrong in the argument?" I asked them, shifting our attention from an argument over the facts to a discussion about process.

After I persisted for a while, the CEO admitted he had overreacted, yelled, and been too caught up in countering the CFO's argumentative points. The CFO admitted that she was telling him what to do rather than asking what, if any, feedback he wanted, and that she had been judging him as well as being overly critical. Then she added, "And I have another point to make ...," and she started yapping again about how he had misrepresented her numbers at the board meeting.

This was a great chance for me to point out that their respective views of the CEO presentation was the content (a fleeing, resolvable topic), and we were not trying to resolve the content or we would have to convene every day for every new issue. I was not a judge charged with determining right and wrong, fault or blame. We'd agreed to work on what was really bothering the executive team: *the habitual dysfunctional process*.

Once the two finally began to consider what they were doing wrong, they did a pretty good job of self-criticizing. The lesson didn't take hold immediately, but over time they learned and improved.

Distinguishing between *process* and *content* is similar to determining, "What are you really angry at?" Many times what really drives a conflict is a process issue; it becomes the real substantive "what."

All organizations have a process for managing conflict—some are healthy, creative, and skillful processes and some are not. Your job in planning and assuming leadership in conflict management is to see the process behind the current feud and to model and teach the best way. In order to use the conflict as fuel for creative energy, you must be able to reflect upon process.

PREPARE BY PICKING YOUR TIME, PLACE, AND MOOD

Timing is everything in creative conflict management. You won't be likely to manage a conflict if you try when you or the person with whom you're entangled is hungry, angry, tired, or distracted.

We need to calm ourselves down and warm up the person with whom we're in conflict in whatever way works for them. Both our moods and the other's need to be considered. If we're too light, silly, tentative, nonchalant, or pleading, the other person(s) may not take us seriously. On the other hand, if we're stern, stubbornly authoritative, intense, or irritable, we're also not likely to successfully manage the conflict. And we're probably likely to provoke more resistance and resentment than cooperation and creativity. Be prepared to be upbeat and positive. We're probably not ready to manage the conflict if what comes to mind to say first is, "I'm sick of this problem with your temper and you're going to learn this way to fix it." We need to soften our "tee-up" to the problem.

We're more likely to succeed if we genuinely feel like saying, "Wouldn't it be productive if we learned a new way ...." Our mood leads to our tone. Our tone—the aura we create around us as we step up to assume leadership in conflict resolution—largely determines whether the other person will be defensive or not.

PREPARE BY UNDERSTANDING THE CIRCLE OF CONFLICT

The classic *circle of conflict* in the diagram that follows outlines some of the major sources of conflict, whether interpersonal, intra- or inter-organizational, communal or societal, and regardless of setting. As explained by C. Moore in *The Mediation Process: Practical Strategies for Resolving Conflict*, there are five central causes of conflict:

- Relationship conflicts: problems with the people's relationships
- Data conflicts: problems with data
- Interest conflicts: perceived or actual incompatible interests
- Structural conflicts: structural forces
- Value conflicts: differing values

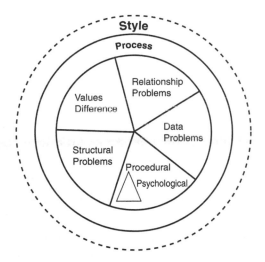

Circle of conflict. (Adapted with permission from John Wiley and Sons, Inc. [Moore, C. The Mediation Process. San Francisco: Jossey-Bass, 1996])

To Moore's model I would add the issue of style (see Chapter 4) as well as the issue of process as described in the previous section, "Prepare by Understanding Process Versus Content." Both of these issues are overarching concerns in any conflict. Moore describes the various kinds of conflicts as follows.

Relationship conflicts happen when we carry baggage from our past interactions forward into our current relationships. We may be holding onto strong negative emotions, stereotypes, previous miscommunications, or misperceptions about someone or we believe they engage in destructive behaviors or they are against us. When we do this, the result is unnecessary conflict since we may have relationship conflicts even when other reasons for conflict such as limited resources or different goals or values are not an issue. Relationship problems often fuel disputes and lead to the negative spiral of destructive conflict. When we're stuck in a relationship conflict at work, we're unable to separate the person from the problem. Creative conflicts are not fueled by relationship problems. As suggested in the last chapter, if we find we're mired in a relationship problem, we need to resolve it first.

Data conflicts happen when we lack accurate information to make an informed decision, or when different people or groups advocate conflicting information or interpret the same data differently. Poor communication can also drive data conflict. Other data conflicts may be genuine because the way people collect or view the information is frequently different.

Interest conflicts involve competition between perceived or actual needs and interests. If we believe that in order to satisfy our own needs and interests, the other party must give up his or hers, we have an interest conflict. We can carry these over substantive issues, such as money or space, as well as procedural issues, such as the way the dispute is resolved. We can also create interest conflicts over psychological issues, such as perceptions of trust or fairness. In order to creatively manage a true conflict of interest, all parties must find a way to have a significant number of their interests acknowledged or met on (psychological, procedural, and substantive) issues.

The *satisfaction triangle* in the following diagram shows the relationship of these three kinds of needs. A creative conflict management is not sustainable (meaning it will not last) until all three sides of the triangle are complete. For example, even if you satisfy the parties' substantive needs, if you don't address their procedural and psychological satisfaction, you will not produce a lasting agreement.

Satisfaction triangle.

Often, what causes a conflict is when one or more of the parties insists only one solution will meet their needs. Usually, if the parties work hard enough to solve the problem, there's a variety of creative ways to meet everyone's needs. The key is to urge everyone involved to bring all of their creative potential to the table to brainstorm the best solutions for all concerned. Bringing these underlying needs to the table fuels creativity and productivity.

Structural conflicts result from organizational issues. The organization may have limited resources, space, time, poor role definition, or conflicting agendas. These structural issues may cause conflicts and be beyond the control of the involved parties. Simply identifying a structural conflict, however, can help the parties begin to see what parts are within their control.

Value conflicts are created when perceived or actual belief systems clash. We use values to explain what we believe is good or bad, right or wrong, just or unjust. Values often cause conflict yet need not. People can work together with strikingly different value systems as long as they accept their differences and do not try to force their own values on anyone else. It's also helpful if the organization itself has clear values and goals. You may need to remind the parties of these organizational priorities when they're in the midst of a conflict.

HOW TO USE THE CIRCLE OF CONFLICT AND CONFLICT MAPPING

To prepare for conflict, use the circle of conflict and conflict mapping tools to create value and assume leadership in creative conflict management. These tools can help you gain perspective on the dispute, detach from the emotions involved, and reveal the root cause of the conflict behavior.

If we examine the dispute according to the five categories—relationship, data, interest, structure, and value—and if we consider the overarching issues of style and process, we can begin to determine what the primary and secondary causes of the dispute are (there may be more than one) and determine if the cause is a genuine incompatibility of interests or some other issue. If we stop to do this analysis before jumping in to resolve the dispute, our chances of success will be much greater. We will be better able to harness the conflict to drive innovation and productivity.

For example, I recently worked with a financial institution that wanted to revamp its process for loan approval. Committees had met for months without success, trying to understand why the process took so long, engendered so many disagreements, and created so much customer dissatisfaction. After interviewing several members of the team individually to determine what they thought the problem might be, I brought the group together to work on the issue. One of the first steps was to ask them to map the various conflicts that had emerged. This activity helped de-personalize the issues and help everyone see what was contributing to their inability to work through the issues. Hidden structural and values conflicts quickly emerged when they were able to step back from the problem and see the problem diagramed in this way.

When we prepare for conflict by gaining this broader perspective, we're more able to use the other skills outlined in the chapters that follow, including the next chapter about skillful confrontation. Diagramming the conflict helps us harness the contention to use it for productivity and creativity. Launching into an attack *without preparation*—a common practice—can lead to many bad fights.

CHAPTER 13

GRACE UNDER FIRE: HOW TO SKILLFULLY CONFRONT OTHERS

Facts do not cease to exist because they are ignored.

—Aldous Huxley

Denise Everhardt is an operations manager for a large insurance carrier. An endless stream of e-mail from her boss dogs her. He chooses to communicate exclusively electronically. He gives her all her assignments, holds virtual discussions, and even does her performance appraisal via e-mail—despite the fact that their offices are next door to one other. Denise finally has enough; she slaps her boss with a complaint for harassment for his relentless electronic feedback.

According to *Webster's Ninth New Collegiate Dictionary*, feedback is "the return of information about the results of a process." It sounds pretty innocuous. Yet it is the bane of many a manager's or co-worker's existence. Feedback, by definition, is not meant to be personal. Yet, often the way it's given and received causes people to take such umbrage that they feel assaulted, maligned, misunderstood, or personally criticized. Constructive feedback and skillful confrontation is an elemental part of almost anyone's job in these days of interdependent teams.

You must frequently evaluate the performance of others. If you want productivity, profits, and goal achievement to increase, then individual performance improvement is a must. Logically, then, that entails finding ways to improve processes. It means using tact and motivation to assist co-workers in garnering new skills, being more creative, and seeking "personal bests" on the job. It means skillful confrontation and feedback.

An essential skill then is to learn when and how to raise conflict, especially how to skillfully confront and criticize someone else's behaviors. Yet sometimes, in working in today's diverse workforce, we become so confused or paranoid about making mistakes that we withhold positive or negative criticism or fail to confront someone about their performance or behavior.

Our withholding denies the person the opportunity to grow, and fails to fulfill our duty and the organization's responsibility to give employees feedback on their performance. In addition, leaders and managers have a legal—not to mention ethical and moral—obligation to intervene when they see or hear behavior in the workplace that is harassing, discriminating, unproductive, noninclusive, or disrespectful. Many of us, however, feel uncomfortable addressing these issues and don't know how to constructively confront someone. With awareness and practice, skillful confrontation is possible.

When we provide constructive feedback with the motive of giving support and encouraging growth, learning begins. If we're afraid to confront someone, we also won't be able to use the conflict to drive creativity, innovation, or productivity.

WHY WE DON'T CONFRONT

Why don't we talk more directly to people about our conflicts? We may be concerned about one or more of the following:

- We lack the skills to manage the confrontation and fear making the situation worse.
- We've had a history of negative experience with conflict or come from a family with violence, alcoholism, abuse, or other serious dysfunctions.
- We fear they will list our shortcomings and confront us back.
- We fear losing an otherwise good employee, client and/or friend.
- We fear retaliation in some way, or even violence.
- We fear making the other person angry and the loss of their respect or approval.

We've all seen these things happen, so our fears are not totally groundless. Most of these problems can be avoided by following the tips outlined in this chapter. Failure to act doesn't lead to the kind of positive learning environment most of us want to create in our workplace.

POSITIVE CRITICISM AND CONFRONTATION

When we avoid talking to someone because we fear creating conflict, we don't avoid the underlying problem, and we may create even worse issues by waiting. We also miss opportunities to use the conflict creatively.

In order to skillfully confront someone, follow these guidelines:

- Just do it! Intervene early and often. The biggest mistake leaders, managers, and co-workers make is looking the other way when they see poor performance or inappropriate behavior. We are not doing co-workers or our companies any favors by taking a passive stance.

- Be prepared. Be clear about what it is that concerns you—have specific examples and know how you want the other person to change. You may need to prepare by first role-playing the interaction with someone else.

- Talk privately to the co-worker, unless there's a specific need to stop an entire group from engaging in inappropriate behavior.

- Come to the point quickly; don't keep the other person guessing.

- Talk about specific performance or behavior—not the person, their personality, or attitude. Describe the details of what you saw and heard. Don't speculate on their motivation. You want them to behave differently.

- Make "I" statements; own the conflict as yours or the company's. Let the other person know how his or her behavior affects you. "When you're late for our meetings, we can't get our work done." "When you called Susan a sexpot, it violated our company policy on harassment." "When we were brainstorming in that meeting, you dismissed all my ideas." Focus on the results and impact of the person's behavior, not your opinions about it.

- Listen to the other person's story. Conflicts are frequently the result of poor communication and/or misunderstandings.

- Once you're clear there is no misunderstanding or miscommunication, be specific about the behavior change you seek. Explain what was wrong with the behavior: that it doesn't contribute to creative conflict management, that it violates the company policy, affects the ability of the team or you to do your work, is inconsistent with the team's goals and objectives, is uncreative, unproductive, harassing, disrespectful, discriminatory, or noninclusive. Clarify any confusion your co-worker has about what behavior is unacceptable.

- Directly ask the co-worker to stop engaging in the behavior and obtain a commitment to stop. If you're their manager or leader, let them know you expect compliance as a part of the requirements of the job.

- If the situation is serious, or this is something you've talked with them about before, be specific about the consequences if the behavior continues, and then follow through. For example: "If you continue to miss deadlines, I will need to put a letter in your file or bring it up with your boss."

- Monitor the workplace to make sure the behavior stops and/or improves.

These guidelines may not make the process painless, but they will give you a roadmap to guide you through a skillful confrontation. If you follow these suggestions, your chances of success are much greater.

INCLUDE POSITIVE STATEMENTS

Many organizations value only negative criticism. It's often easy to find things that are wrong, yet it seems unimportant or difficult to identify positive aspects. Your co-workers will respond much more positively to your confrontation or criticism if you also regularly include positive comments. Reinforcing creative or innovative behavior also leads to more of the same. People need to know exactly what they have done well.

Identify specific behaviors, what the person said and did. For example, to say, "Bob, you did a nice job," or "Mary, I feel good about your work" is not as useful as saying, "Mary, when we were trying to generate new ideas and you told Bob you wanted him to listen to Jim and stop interrupting him, the communication really started working well." This kind of information lets people know what tools, skills, and behavior work effectively. It also helps drive more creative and productive interactions.

NEGATIVE CRITICISM AND CONFRONTATION

Negative criticism shouldn't be used as a weapon, for example, for revenge when someone criticizes your work or to hurt someone because they did an ineffective job.

Example of unhelpful feedback: "Jane, your report was bad. How could you do such terrible work?"

This criticism doesn't help the co-worker learn because it doesn't specifically describe what Jane did wrong, nor does it identify what behavior would be acceptable, creatively manage conflicts, or foster long-term relationships. This type of criticism leaves the receiver feeling bad and doesn't foster learning or correction. Ask yourself why you would offer such a critique. If you're not allowing someone to change his or her behavior or skills so the work can improve, why are you saying it?

Example of helpful feedback: "John, I noticed when you typed this report you didn't use the margins I specified. We need to stay within a certain page count to fit the form. Also, when you answered the phone just now, you didn't ask how you could help the caller. Please do that in the future."

This criticism improves the learner because it lets John know what he did, when, and how the other party was affected. This criticism is also helpful because it lets John know what he can do correctly in the future.

CURIOSITY OR CONFRONTATION

When you feel the need to confront someone about an issue, consider changing your own attitude before you talk to the person. Can you find a way to be curious about the other person's behavior? If you come from a place of curiosity and wonder, the interaction will have a much better chance of succeeding. Consider reframing your confrontation to use the following statements:

I'm puzzled by "x" behavior. Can you explain to me how it would help our team meet our goals?

I was curious about why you did "y." Can you explain it to me?

The statement you made yesterday about "z" confuses me. Can you explain to me how you believe it will help us finish this job?

Genuine interest in the other person's point of view and their behavior will serve you more productively than a harsh challenge. Most of us simply have not stopped to think about our behavior and its impact on others. When someone does ask us in a gentle way to step back and look at our actions, we are more able to do so than if someone attacks us.

EMOTIONAL LAND MINES TO AVOID

Be prepared for defensiveness. Most of us feel defensive when we're receiving feedback or criticism, even when it's skillfully delivered. If we're speeding and the state patrol stops us, for example, most of us do not jump out of our car and declare: "Oh, thank you, officer! I'm so glad you stopped me! I could have hurt someone! Write me a ticket immediately!"

If we've noticed that our feedback frequently leads to defensiveness, another reason may be that we offer complaints without requests. As the popular psychologist Gay Hendricks points out:

> If every ounce of energy human beings use in complaining was dedicated to productive change, we could clear up many of the world's problems virtually overnight. It takes courage to turn a complaint into a request for effective action. It

requires that you think about what needs to be done rather than about what wasn't done. It requires that you get outside the negative-thinking cycle of "What's wrong with me? What's wrong with you? What's wrong with the world?" and make a courageous leap of thought to "Forget what's wrong—let's focus on what needs to be done."[1]

If we're generating a "flight or fight" mode in someone else (as discussed in Chapter 4) we may want to step back and examine whether we are expressing our emotions in the most skillful ways. If we rage at someone or alternatively, if we're holding our emotions in with a stony expression, we may trigger a fight or flight response in another. Most of us have not really thought about or practiced the appropriate expression of emotion, especially during feedback and conflict. What is the most effective way to *express* strong feelings without *dumping* them on someone?

The best way to communicate our own emotions while we're giving someone feedback is in a straightforward way. Think about it as a weather report: "It's raining and I'm angry." Our feelings change just as the weather does, and when we can report on what we experience without blaming or judging another, the other person is better able to hear what we're saying. We don't need to dramatize or hide the weather; like our feelings, it just is what it is.

While describing the effect someone's behavior has on your work can be helpful, people are more likely to be able to hear you if you use "I" statements and stay neutral in your report, stating that "I'm angry," for example, instead of "You make me angry."

When we decide it's necessary, we can, before we state the problem and communicate our request, add a clear expression of feelings. Consider the following examples:

Jane, *I'm angry*. I just realized that you didn't finish the report on time. When our reports are late, it puts the entire production schedule behind our goals. From now on, I need you to turn them in on time or let me know well in advance that you can't do it so I can find someone else.

Harry, my stomach feels queasy and I just realized that *I'm afraid*. When you yell at me when you ask for corrections, I'm afraid you're going to fire me. I need you to stop yelling and give me your corrections in a normal tone of voice.

Expressing our emotions this clearly and without drama during a confrontation takes practice. Most of us have not thought about the idea of this kind of emotional practice. How many of us ever received good modeling or suggestions from our parents or took a class on appropriate emotional expression? Yet cleanly offered emotion can make our feedback to others clearer and more congruent. If we deliver bad news with a forced smile because we're struggling to contain our anger, for example, we trigger uncertainty about our message or worse in the other person. We all have built-in radar that can be highly attuned to the emotions of others. Conversely, if we're out of control with our anger, or if we yell and use profanity when we offer feedback, the other person may freeze, flee, or fight back. When we don't offer our own feelings in an appropriate way, something frequently feels scary, false, or confusing to the other party and makes our feedback less effective than it could be.

Sometimes the problem is that we become defensive ourselves when we're offering feedback to someone. When this happens, we may want to examine whether we're speaking from what Hendricks calls discovery or from our own defensiveness.

For instance, when we're talking to someone we might notice that they start frowning and look away. Because we're sure we're correct in our assessment of them, we might be prompted to say, "I don't know why what I'm saying makes you angry. You're the one who messed up this project." Putting it this way, we've just revealed our own defensiveness, which will probably prompt them to respond in kind.

Instead, if we notice someone frowning and avoiding our gaze while we are giving feedback, we can offer something like, "I just noticed an expression on your face. I'm wondering what you're feeling about what I just said." Although it might feel awkward using this discovery method at first, you can become more skilled at the practice. Eventually, if you use this method of communicating, you will reduce the amount of defensiveness you trigger in others during feedback.

Another land mine to avoid is triggering memories in someone else of past criticism. Many times someone will explode over what you might think is relatively minor feedback. Most of us received plenty of negative and unhelpful feedback from parents and teachers as children, and workplace criticism tends to remind us of these past wounds. If someone reacts out of proportion to the event, this may be a part of the reason.

I once had an employee, for example, who was much older than me. She had been doing her work for a long time and I'm sure that she felt that her competence exceeded mine. Because she was basically a good employee, I didn't need to give her much criticism but occasionally, I had to mention a small matter and she would always bristle with indignation. In addition, she would usually engage in passive/aggressive behavior by not correcting what I asked her to do. I finally had to sit down with her and talk frankly about how necessary it was for us both to be able to give each other feedback and suggestions in order for us to be able to work together. I assured her that I valued her work and loyalty. I gently asked her if she had any ideas about how I could give her feedback in a way that she could accept more easily.

She confessed that she had grown up with an extremely critical father whose approval she had never been able to gain. His constant attacks had driven her to be a perfectionist who always wanted to do everything right. Any suggestion that she was not doing her job made her quite upset.

It took several exchanges like this for us to work out a feedback system we could both use. I had to learn to approach her carefully and always remind her that her work was excellent but that we needed to work on some small issue. It took time, but eventually, we turned the situation around.

Stick to the issue and try not to react yourself. If you don't, the problem may never be managed creatively. Take a time-out if you find yourself losing control. Be sure, however, not to give up. You may need to schedule additional sessions before the conflict moves to a higher level.

Managing confrontation effectively is an essential tool in your arsenal of creative contention. Because giving and receiving feedback is such a necessary part of the workplace environment, it's not a skill we can afford to leave undeveloped. In order to complete the feedback loop you need two other skills: the subject of the next chapter, Chapter 14, and the subject of Chapter 15.

CHAPTER 14

WHO'S ON FIRST? HOW TO HEAR AND BE HEARD

I'm not arguing. I'm just talking to myself.

—Nicolas Eisaguirre Evans, age 4

Costello: ... Who's on first?
Abbott: Yes.
Costello: I mean the fellow's name.
Abbott: Who.
Costello: The guy on first.
Abbott: Who.
Costello: The first baseman.
Abbott: Who.
Costello: The guy playing ...
Abbott: Who is on first!

Despite their efforts, the hilarious dialogue between Abbott and Costello never leads to agreement on the lineup. This classic verbal jousting provides a lighthearted look at the frustration and agitation created when one is not heard correctly. Clearly, one of the skills of creatively using and valuing conflict is the ability to listen carefully.

We may think we listen well, yet listening is an underrated skill. There are all kinds of background noises vying for our attention that have to be fended off when we're trying to listen. Your stomach growls, the phone rings, you've heard this before, you think you know what's coming next, you've got to be somewhere else in five minutes, the other person says something that makes you want to pounce so you don't hear the rest of the sentence—the list is endless. If we listen this poorly in ordinary conversation, what do you think happens in a conflict? Near-deafness sets in!

PREPARING TO LISTEN

When we're arguing during a conflict, most of us are not listening; we are, as my son says, "just talking to ourselves." Clearly, one of the most important creative conflict management skills is listening. In order to listen well, we need to prepare.

Most of us understand the importance of preparing ourselves to speak, but few of us think about preparing to listen. We take for granted that we all know how to listen. We may also assume listening is a passive activity, yet it is actually difficult to do and we are rarely prepared to listen well.

Deep listening also allows more space for the possibility of creativity and innovation. In order to listen well, we have to quiet our minds, to silence what my friend, Caryle, calls "the rock band in our heads." Most of us have a habit of taking our constant mind chatter seriously. We never stop to think about whether that makes any sense for us. Emerson once joked that 95 percent of what goes on inside our minds is none of our business.

This doesn't mean that we have to retreat to a cave or spend our lives meditating; it means that we have to consciously create a space where listening can occur, especially during conflict.

Part of the problem is our lack of understanding about how our minds work and how the mind and our senses interact, especially what we hold in our mind as "truths." Our hearing is ever present. There is no switch to turn it off. We can close our eyes, but not our ears. We live in a culture where we're constantly bombarded by sounds; our sense of balance is tied to our hearing. It's no accident that so many of us feel constantly out of balance because of the bombardment of information from inside our minds as well as external sounds.

My grandmother, Viva, became hard of hearing as she aged. At 90, her doctor gave her a hearing test and pronounced her hearing excellent. Family members continued to complain, however, that she frequently did not hear what they said or that they had to repeat themselves. The doctor tested her again and declared: "She does not have a hearing problem, she has a listening problem."

And no wonder. Approaching 90, my grandmother had raised seven children on a limited income, buried three of them (including one suicide) as well as her spouse, and served as sole caretaker for my 60-something invalid aunt. She remained the interested matriarch of a large family that included dozens of grandchildren and several great-grandchildren. Viva kept up on current events, still tended her own roses, did her own cooking and house cleaning, and supervised various grandchildren who mowed her lawn ("mow it horizontal one week, alternating diagonals the next").

Viva had heard enough. She had earned the right to be selective in what she took in and what she didn't. Most of us, however, have not earned that right. Most of us have never bothered to *really* hear anyone. We live in a culture that has forgotten how to cultivate the art of listening. Unlike my grandmother who was born before television and spent most of her life telling and listening to stories around the kitchen table, we are dominated by sight. Thousands of images flash across our minds in an hour of television or the Internet. Bombarded by rapid visuals, we've come to expect our information instantly. But listening operates on a different tempo.

We see through light. Light moves at 186,000 miles per second as opposed to sound, which travels at 1,100 feet per second. To listen, then, we must slow down far below the speed of light, far below the flickering changing images of videos and computers.

Our impatience hinders our listening and our creative conflict management. We want the world and we want it now! Yet, if we have the patience to listen, we'll learn more.

Unlike our other senses, hearing measures sounds. We can discern different colors, but we can give a precise number to different sounds. Our eyes do not let us perceive with this kind of perception. Even an unmusical person can recognize an octave. Berendt points out that there are few "acoustical illusions"—something sounding like something that, in fact, is not—while there are many optical illusions. The ears do not lie. The sense of hearing gives us a remarkable connection with the invisible, underlying order of things. Through our ears we gain access to vibrations, which lie below everything around us. The sense of tone and music in another's voice gives us an enormous amount of information about that person, his intentions, and stance toward life.

In fact, if we want to resolve a conflict and improve our relationship with someone, we might focus on the definition of *resonance*. In sound, energy resonance is transferred between objects that vibrate at the same frequency. Slowing down enough to listen well helps us develop resonance with the person with whom we have a conflict.

For example, I can be flip and glib. If you just read my words in an e-mail communication and don't hear my tone and emotion, you may think I'm seriously attacking you.

This is why it's so important to talk face to face when we're having a conflict or anticipate that we might have a conflict with someone. If we communicate via e-mail or letter, we can't really listen and we miss the subtle nuances that we might otherwise hear that reveal someone's true intentions. We also miss, of course, the visual clues that might help us understand someone, their facial expression and intention. Clearly, the ideal during conflict is to meet face to face.

Psychiatrist Edward Hallowell, in his wonderful book, *Connect*,[1] talks about the high-powered executives he treats in the Boston area. These men have everything they ever thought they wanted: great jobs, beautiful houses, lovely children, and trophy wives. Yet, they're so depressed, they're being treated with medication. This was a significant change in Hallowell's practice over the last ten years. He started to research the reasons for their depression. What he discovered was that they all talked about how their work had changed.

A typical patient would wax nostalgically about how he used to spend his time coaching people, mentoring young associates, and leading group discussions. Now, instead, he spends his days "staring at a screen," answering e-mail.

Hallowell started researching this problem and found that all of the time we spend interfacing with technology is actually changing the biochemistry of our brains and leading to clinical depression. He found this to be true in studies of adults as well as studies of children and animals. Babies, for example, who are fed and kept warm, but not held or loved, will gradually weaken and expire. Literally, we connect with others or we die.

And as we are dying in our modern workplaces where we often lack connections, we become depressed and irritable. These moods fuel unproductive conflict and make valuable conflict more difficult to manage creatively.

Clearly, we're not going to regress to a world without voice- or e-mail, but the more human connections you can create at work, the better you and your associates will feel, and the more skillfully you'll be able to listen and manage conflict. And, when you're actually in the middle of trying to manage a significant dispute, make sure you do whatever it takes to sit down and communicate face to face.

We can learn to listen. We need to start with recognition of how we're listening now. Generally, we don't bother to think about how we listen. In addition to listening well to others, we need to listen to our own feelings and ourselves in order to communicate effectively during conflict.

Sometimes listening well during a conflict is enough. Sometimes all we need to do to miraculously solve an issue is make someone feel truly heard.

GHOSTS IN THE ROOM

If we thoughtfully focus on how we listen, especially to our own thoughts and feelings, we will begin to identify what I call "ghosts in the room," when we're in conflict with someone.

To understand what I mean, think about a person you care about. When you do, you'll notice a flood of emotions and memories. To listen well is to understand that much of our present experience doesn't come from our current experience; it comes from our memory. And frequently, it's not even a memory of the person we're talking to right now, but a memory of someone long ago. We're reacting from stored memories, not fresh responses. These are the filters through which we all listen. We hear everyone through our own filter of memory, desire, perceptions, and predispositions. As the Counting Crows sing in "Mrs. Potter," "If dreams are like movies then memories are films about ghosts." Especially when we're upset during conflict, we'll find that we're rarely upset for the reason we think.

These filters that we all have are limited, even unintelligent, in the sense that they cannot respond in a *new* way to what is happening. We are busy reacting to something in the distant past. This limits our ability to be creative and innovative.

We need to learn to listen as a *witnesses*. This means to learn to listen to what is objectively there as opposed to our messy stew of memory and desire. This is not easy to do. We are often unaware of the extent to which we assume what we see is what is there. Yet, if we think of ourselves as listening as a witness, we listen better.

When I use the term "witness," I mean it in two senses: both as a witness in court—an objective, sworn witness for the truth, not for the plaintiff or the defendant—and to learn to listen as the Quakers use the term "witness." In a Quaker fellowship, they practice a way to be present for the other person and wait to speak until they hear what they call the *still, small voice inside*.

LISTEN FOR AND CHECK OUT MISUNDERSTANDINGS

Many times, conflicts escalate because of misunderstandings, especially about the meaning of language. For example, I was having dinner with several business colleagues and one woman's spouse. Two people in the couple were both retired Army majors who had been in charge of large facilities. They were talking about their experiences during Vietnam and someone asked me if my then husband had served during that war. I said my husband was a CO. They asked me of what unit. In their language, that phrase meant *commanding officer*. In fact, my ex-husband, who was raised as a Quaker, was a *conscientious objector* during the war. We all had a good laugh about the different meaning we automatically ascribe to the term "CO."

We need to take care to check our misunderstandings—indeed, to assume misunderstandings—before we assume that someone is directly attacking us or trying to escalate the conflict.

In order to do this, we have to listen as a witness. We need to distinguish between the inferences we make about experience and the experience itself. One way to do this is called the ladder of inference, developed by Chris Argyris, a professor at Harvard. He suggests that we process and create inferences about our experience at lightening speed, without noticing we are doing so. We don't notice the difference between a direct experience and our assessment of it.

We draw conclusions like this all of the time. Our conclusions take the form of reasoning that "this is the way it is." Yet, our first impressions are rarely accurate, as we can see from the CO example.

Because we're all bombarded with so much stimulation, distraction, and data, we learn early in life to focus selectively on some things and ignore others. We leap to conclusions. While such leaps are efficient and sometimes essential, our speed sometimes causes us to confuse inference with fact. Chris Argyris calls this the "Ladder of Inference."[2]

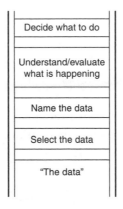

Inference ladder. (Adapted with permission from Argyris, Chris. Reasoning, Learning, and Action: Individual and Organizational. *San Francisco: Jossey-Bass, 1982)*

Because we move so quickly from data to conclusions and opinions, we don't realize we have interpreted reality, screening out certain data along the way. During conflict, we can teach ourselves and the combatants to climb the ladder of inference openly and thoughtfully. If everyone understands such ladders exist and we climb them within seconds, usually suppressing all but the final step to a decision, then we can agree to be more explicit about how we reach conclusions. We can discuss whether others have different data or interpret data differently. We need to take ourselves through these steps:

1. Objectively describe the behavior, what was said, or done or observed.

2. Describe what each person heard, saw, or observed in each person's own words.

3. Determine what generalizations were made from the selected data.

4. Describe how each person named the data, or labeled, or categorized it.

5. Determine what evaluation or conclusion was drawn.

6. Describe how each person decided to act based on the evaluation or conclusion.

For example, consider a typical workplace conflict over schedule changes. One person, for example, hears there is a going to be a schedule change and she will now have to work weekends. She uses this data to pick a fight with her supervisor, sure that he picked on her because of a previous conflict. The argument escalates before he has a chance to explain he didn't order the change or develop the schedule. She moved at lightening speed from the data—the change itself—to a conclusion that their previous conflict was to blame and decides to engage in an angry confrontation. The supervisor, feeling defensive, fights back without taking the time to examine the cause of the conflict.

If the parties are "backed up" by going down the ladder of inference through the previous steps, it becomes clear why each reached the decision to act as he or she did. More important, when the rationale underlying the decision is laid bare, people can readily see where their inferences differ and can debate on those interpretations and logic rather than just on the final decision.

CONCLUSIONS, FACTS, AND MORE GHOSTS

We form conclusions and then do not check them out, treating our initial conclusions as fact. We fail to investigate the roots of our own thinking. And even more damaging in the heat of conflict, we invest ourselves in an opinion and seek evidence that we are right and avoid evidence that we are wrong. This sends us into the *negative spiral of conflict* (see Chapter 12). We progress from our conclusions about subjects to assumptions that we invent about them and finally to belief. These beliefs tend to become dogma and resistant to change. We then see the world through the filter of our beliefs and, in fact, seek evidence that supports our opinions. This habit limits our creativity and productivity.

We can learn to listen in a way that challenges our automatic formation of beliefs, which differentiates between the stories we make up about a set of facts from the facts themselves.

Listening well helps us creatively manage conflict. Yet, slowing down our thinking and listening in this way is not easy because the landscape is not neutral. Our memories and the resultant *ghosts in the room* can be quite painful. If I say something to you that you don't like, for example, *you're stupid*, you may flash on a memory of an old teacher or parent who said the same thing. It will be difficult for you not to react emotionally, to respond from the present moment rather than from the pain of your memories. This is what we mean when we say that someone "pushes our buttons."

These ghosts from our past memory tend to cloud our listening. We listen mostly for evidence that our view of the world is right and others are wrong.

There is another way. We can listen instead at a deeper level for the source of the difficulty—whether it is in others or ourselves.

We can be *passionate* in our listening. We can learn to listen with as much energy and enthusiasm as we talk. Instead of listening for evidence that confirms our point of view, we can listen for the creative energy in the conflict—both in ourselves and in others. We listen for what challenges our view to begin to see how others see the world.

This way of listening is not easy, yet it can create extraordinary creativity in managing conflict.

Then we can take the final and hardest step: We can begin to listen for disconnects, especially disconnects between what we say and what we do. None of us is 100 percent consistent. Most of us intend to do what we say we want to do, but few of us manage to do so. Frequently, if we listen hard enough to the rock bands in our own minds, we'll be surprised to realize that we're guilty of something similar to what we're accusing the other person of doing.

To grow in our own ability to listen, we need to be still, to listen to our own minds. We need to know when our own ghosts are in the room. If we do this long enough by ourselves, we'll find we're capable of really hearing others. We will have created a clear stream in which to be present for them.

To summarize, in order to listen well, follow these guidelines:

1. **Remember filters.** We all hear what is said through our own filters. Filters can include our assumptions, biases, our own history, experience, and so on.

2. **Listen as a witness.** Ask, "how would I listen to this person if I knew I were going to be called as an objective witness in court?" "How can I listen well enough to hear the still, small voice inside of me?"

3. **Clarify.** Before you speak, make sure you understand what the other person is saying. Ask open-ended (nonleading) questions until you do.

4. **Restate.** Ask, "I think you said '....' Is that accurate?" Continue restating until your partner agrees that you heard him or her accurately.

5. **Pause before you speak.** Ask yourself which conflict style you're using and why. Is it the style that will serve you best over the long term of this relationship? Is the response you're considering likely to lead to more creativity and productivity? What response would be most likely to lead to those results?

6. **At the end of a communication, summarize the conversation and clarify the original reason for the communication.** Did the speaker want your advice, feedback, a sympathetic ear, action, or a solution to a problem? Be sure you know *why* you were asked to listen and what you're expected to do—if anything—about the communication. Many of us jump in too quickly to give advice or fix a problem before even bothering to ask if the speaker wants advice.

7. **Assume 100 percent of the responsibility for the communication.** Assume leadership in your communication. Assume it is your responsibility to listen until you understand and to speak in a way others can understand.

8. **Check out misunderstandings.** Assume miscommunication before you assume someone is trying to undermine your efforts. Back yourself and the other parties up by going over the ladder of inference.

If we follow these suggestions, we will be able to listen at a deeper level, to develop passion in our listening and to harness the conflict more productively.

CONFLICT AND CULTURE CLASH

Sometimes a conflict is actually a clash of cultures. We need to realize different cultures have very different approaches to conflict and communication. As we previously learned, diverse work groups produce more creative results, but they also require more sophisticated communication skills. If you're trying to creatively manage conflicts, you need to recognize when this happens.

For example, the dominant culture in this country values a conflict resolution model that is rather confrontational. We see ourselves in the John Wayne mode: we talk straight and we shoot straight. Yet this model is different from that used in many cultures where direct confrontation is considered rude. Instead, those cultures value the use of *mediators*. Conflict management is accomplished through a third party—a trusted family friend, priest, or advisor.

One way to find out if a conflict is culture-related is to ask the following:

- Have several attempts at creatively managing this conflict failed?
- Is the present conflict one of a series?
- Does the conflict seem emotional beyond what you would predict based upon the immediate problem?
- Are the people involved in the conflict from different cultures? Are there obvious differences in race, gender, education, age, or work groups?

In addition to the creative conflict management tools we've already discussed, the following can help resolve a cultural clash.

Gain agreement that:

There is a conflict.

We share a common goal to creatively manage it.

What we've tried so far hasn't worked.

Identify hot buttons:

Say something like: "There seems to be something that 'x' says or that I say that always sets you off. What is it?"

Clarify back to the person: "It seems that what sets you off is ...."

Look for a cultural source:

Ask something like: "With your background, is that an important concern?" or "With your background, how would you expect someone to act in this situation?"

Caution! Do not say: "With your background as an African American, woman, generation X-er, etc., is this an important concern?" There are many different aspects of our background that create our culture. Allow the co-worker (if he or she chooses) to bring up exactly what factors in his or her background drive the reaction.

Summarize the conflict as a cultural difference:

> In your own words, emphasize to the other people involved: "Where you come from, you expect ...."

Negotiate a creative dialogue:

> Say something like: "We all agreed we want to creatively manage this conflict. We've begun to understand what the conflict is about. Because we have to work together, what do you suggest we do now to creatively use this conflict to help you work together more productively?"

Keep asking until both of you can focus on specific behaviors—words and actions—that you need from the other person to work together.

Get a commitment from each side to live up to or reject the other's request. Agree to monitor the situation to make sure it is managed.

If you are the conflicted parties' boss and you're trying to mediate a solution, emphasize that you need everyone to work together effectively as a team in support of the organization's goals. If they cannot learn to work together as a team, you will have to explore other options, including discipline. Work to make creative conflict management skills a part of *their* job requirements.

Cultural conflicts can be intense yet bring creative results. For example, I worked with a group of manufacturing workers who were an even split of Hispanics and Anglos. A cultural clash had broken out over how to meet production quotas. The Hispanics favored working in groups; the Anglos focused on individual responsibility and recognition. The Hispanics were comfortable sharing both the load and the reward of their labors; the Anglos wanted more individual feedback.

Because the factory favored teams working toward a group consensus on the theory that what they decided among themselves would be likely to work, the meetings raged on for weeks, each side continuing to favor their own solution. After I started facilitating their meetings, we focused more on *why* they wanted to keep their specific systems instead of their positions or which way was the "right" way to work. The Hispanics were simply more accustomed to working as a group. It made them happier, and they were convinced it made them more efficient. The Anglos preferred working alone, and they were sure they were more productive when they used that model.

A curious thing happened as the discussions continued. Both sides began to wonder how they might work if they used the others' methods. Finally, we adopted a model that included a complex mix of the two worlds: points for both individual recognition as well as group achievement. Ultimately, by working through the conflict and valuing the process, the team boasted the highest productivity of any group in the factory.

COMMUNICATION AND POWER

Most leaders agree that good communication is essential to creative conflict and a productive workplace. As the workplace becomes more diverse, good communication is even more important. What many leaders miss, however, is an understanding that our perception of the amount of power we have in any interaction influences our communication style.

Linguists tell us that if we perceive we have less power than the person or group that we're communicating with, we will engage in what linguist Deborah Tannen calls "rapport talk" in her book, *You Just Don't Understand*.[3] This is talk designed to improve and build relationships. It is conciliatory, polite, and friendly. When using rapport talk, we say things such as, "You might be unaware that …" before delivering a negative message. We may also say things such as, "I'm not sure if this is right, but maybe we should …." We ask permission before we do things: "Would you mind if I …?" We tend to ask for the other person's advice and approval.

If we believe that we have more or equal power with the person we're talking to, we tend to use what Tannen calls "report talk." This is communication that focuses on delivering information and accomplishing tasks. This talk tends to sound like orders. When we use this talk we tend to start our sentences with "I (or we) need to do 'x.'" "I want or need 'x.'"

Some linguists, such as Tannen, believe that women tend to use more *rapport talk* and men tend to use more *report talk*. Others point to the difference in power as the key. Because women have tended to have less power in most workplaces, they tend to use more rapport talk. Studies have found that other groups that historically have had less power, such as African Americans, also use more rapport talk. Significantly, a person may use one kind of talk in the workplace and another kind of talk at home where they may believe they have more power.

The importance for diversity and conflict in the workplace is that the group that tends to use report talk may view other groups as weak or ineffectual or wasting time because they use so much rapport talk. Conversely, the group that tends to use communication to develop rapport, may view the group that uses report talk as brusque, cold, angry, rude, and so on. Many conflicts result from this difference of perception.

Ask yourself the following questions:

- Which of the two styles do you see yourself using at work?
- With whom do you use a different style?
- What is the primary style you observe people in power using at work?
- What would the benefits be to you of using a different style?
- What benefits to the organization would there be if you used different styles as appropriate for different situations?
- Is your style the one most likely to use conflict to drive creativity, productivity, and innovation?

There is no right or wrong style in all situations. The key to creative conflict management is to stop and think before you speak in order to determine which communication style is most appropriate in any given situation.

CHAPTER 15

WELCOMING A DIFFERENT OPINION: HOW TO BE CONFRONTABLE

People who don't mind telling the truth have mixed feelings about hearing the truth.

—Jerry Hirshberg, president, Nissan Design International, Inc.

A vice president in a regional health-care system is charged with merging the home care and hospice functions of two separate hospital systems. The staff of one system is furious their leader hadn't been put in charge. They complain. They sling mud. They are uncooperative. They even send anonymous, slanderous letters to the CEO. The vice president perseveres. She meets individually with every manager and supervisor to hear their concerns and deal directly with their anger. She spends an entire year building a dynamic team that would have the courage and strength to sit around a conference table and work out their disagreements to creatively solve problems. Eighteen months later, they lead the entire hospital system in bottom-line performance, customer satisfaction, and Gallup leadership results. This eagle vice president recognizes the signs that can signal big problems lurking ahead, and she sets a tenor that welcomes divergent opinions and disagreement.

When a leader creates an atmosphere that makes it safe to disagree, the leader is actually creating a much more productive and creative work place. It minimizes downtime and loss of focus and distractions that interfere with daily operations. There are numerous strategies you can use to value conflict and to make the environment safer for creative conflict management: an open door policy, using rapport talk, and maintaining confidentiality as well as others. It goes without saying that the people who have the most difficulty with making these adjustments are those who are aggressive and intimidating—the pit bulls of the organization. In this chapter, old dogs will learn some new tricks.

ARE YOU CONFRONTABLE?

Are you safe to confront? When I'm asked to coach executives who've been accused of stubbornness, abuse, harassment, discrimination, poor conflict management skills, or general "poor people management" skills, they frequently lament: "But I didn't know he or she objected to my behavior. Why didn't they tell me?"

To this popular excuse I always respond: "What have you done to make it safe for them to come to you and challenge your ideas or complain about your behavior?"

This question is usually followed by silence. The executive views confrontaphobia as the other person's problem. But if you feast on conflict like a pit bull and if you're viewed as a person who has power in the organization (these two frequently go hand-in-hand), then you're probably difficult for others to confront. You'll need to take specific steps to make it safer for people to confront you.

One of the best ways to overcome your previous reputation is to be honest about your style. At the next staff meeting, mention that your own awareness has been raised about this issue and you've realized you may not have been the easiest person to approach with a new idea or conflict. Announce that you've changed your attitude and ask for suggestions about what would make it easier for people to come to you. You might try something like this:

> I'm becoming increasingly aware of how much I need the feedback of each and every one of you to make this organization a success. I want us to be more innovative and productive. But because I've had a reputation in the past as a pit bull who approaches every conflict or new idea as a personal attack or as an opportunity to debate, I'm realizing that some of you may not have found me approachable. What could I do to make it easier for each of you to come to me with conflicts, feedback, or suggestions?

Be prepared for resounding silence.

Your reputation as a pit bull will not be easy to overcome. As I mentioned in Chapter 4 as one high-powered attorney I coached complained about the associates in his firm: "They won't talk to me; they think I'm the prince of f------ darkness."

If you continue to ask for suggestions about your approachability, however, hints will eventually arrive at your doorstep.

You may ask, "Why do I care?" Many people with an abrasive style have been successful and even gained power in the workplace. As Vick, one VP of finance complained when I gave him feedback about his brutal style that had generated a score of employee complaints, "In other organizations, my style would be viewed as an advantage. In fact, I used to receive compliments here for being a tough boss and a hard charger. People today are just too sensitive."

The reality is, the workplace has changed. An abrasive style may have been successful yesterday; it will not be successful in the future.

The intrusion of the law into people management in the workplace is one obvious reason for the change. The likelihood of an employee charging you with harassment, discrimination, or a violation of the Americans' with Disabilities Act (which now may cover psychological as well as physical disabilities) skyrockets if you have a pit bull reputation.

You may protest that you're not discriminating against any particular person because you treat everyone this way. In my experience, that argument won't fly with courts or juries. They assume that if you're abusive to everyone, you're even more abusive to people who have less power in the organization, usually women and people of color. Even if you do succeed, you will be stuck with the embarrassing defense of presenting a parade of witnesses to attest to how abusive you were to them also.

These groups will make up more of the workplace as our labor force becomes more diverse. According to the Hudson Institute in their Workforce 2020 Report,[1] by the year 2000, only 15 percent of new workers were white males and the twenty-first century will bring a huge increase in older workers, adding new diversity management issues. As a manager or co-worker, you will increasingly need to know how to work successfully with a diverse workforce.

The second reason is that with the change in the economy, the unpredictable labor market, and the interdependent way most organizations are managed, no one can succeed alone. You'll need the suggestions, dedication, and brainpower of all your people in order to prosper in the future. To elicit the best ideas from your troops, you need to encourage honest feedback.

The problem, of course, is that many people's best ideas are not offered directly to leaders but are whispered in the break room or sent in private e-mails after the meeting. People worry how their boss will react if they tell the truth or criticize the CEO. And yet often, these "secret" opinions are what companies most need.

Many organizations now evaluate both leaders and co-workers based upon how well they address issues such as diversity, consensus, and team building. You can't survive in most organizations without these kinds of skills.

If you're the boss, after announcing at your next meeting your change in your own modus operandi, I'd also suggest you start having weekly 15-minute one-on-one meetings with your direct reports or co-workers on your team. In those meetings, there should be one item on your agenda—keep asking the questions: What do you need from me or others to be successful here? What behaviors do I or others engage in that limit your success?

Again, when you first ask these questions, be prepared for silence. If you continue to ask these questions week after week, month after month, however, eventually your colleagues will tell you what they need from you. They'll be more willing to bring you new ideas. More important, you will start to see patterns in how others in the organization perceive you and what you must do to change.

You need to keep asking these kinds of questions—not because you're automatically going to change your behavior to suit others—but because you need to be able to skillfully manage their expectations about your behavior. Once you know how they want you to treat them, you can begin to have an honest dialogue about what you can both do differently in the future to make your relationship succeed.

If you're a leader in your organization, consider the model Robert Rodin, president and CEO of Marshall Industries uses. At least once a month, he invites criticism by holding a forum at one of his sites. No managers are allowed. He calls these sessions "Marshall Live" and informs the workers that it's their company, and he wants to know what's wrong with it. He vows to deal with the feedback in two weeks or less. Although he doesn't follow everyone's ideas, he makes sure that people feel heard. He's always amazed at what he hears.

If someone does summon the nerve to complain directly to you about your behavior: Stop. Try not to immediately react like a snarling pit bull. It's natural for most of us to start defending our actions with an offensive move. Instead, if we can rein in our dog-eat-dog ways and learn to *respond* rather than *react*, we may actually learn something.

When someone comes to you with a conflict, a new idea, or a criticism about your behavior, follow these steps:

1. Stop what you're doing and listen. Give the person your complete attention. If you cannot do that, schedule an appointment as soon as possible.

2. Do not get defensive. First restate what the person said to make sure you understood. Say, for example, "Let me make sure I understand what you said. I heard you say you don't want me to yell at you when I give you feedback. Is that correct?" or "It sounds as if you have a new idea about how to speed up our production schedule." Sometimes all someone really needs is to believe that you truly listened and paid attention to what they said.

3. Apologize if appropriate. If you're convinced you did nothing wrong, at least say you're sorry your behavior offended them. A good boss or co-worker should be sorry someone else is upset even if they're convinced the other person overreacted. If you really did do something very wrong, grovel.

4. Ask what specific *behavior* the person needs from you in order to work effectively with you in the future or what their specific idea or request is. Be certain you focus on behavior, not attitudes or their feelings. You can change your own behavior, but you may never be able to change how they feel. Also try to

get them to focus on what their specific idea or request is rather than complaints. If someone says you're a jerk, for example, you may respond with a questions such as "Can you tell me what you mean by that word?" or "Can you give me a specific example of my jerkiness?" or "Do you have some specific ideas about how I can be less jerky?" While it's not easy to generate creative responses when you're feeling attacked, these kinds of questions will frequently both defuse their anger as well as give you something specific to consider. When people criticize, they sometimes just hurl verbal blows without much thought. Forcing them to think about what they really mean will help you respond more thoughtfully. Your disarming response helps move you jointly into a problem-solving mode instead of a bad fight.

5. Thank them for bringing the matter to your attention and for their courage and honesty. Let them know you respect and appreciate them for talking with you directly. Unless it's impossible or outrageous, tell them you'll consider their new idea or suggestion. Try to find something in their criticism that you can agree with. If you do, you'll help defuse their annoyance. A disarming response can be a powerful one. If you start arguing instead, you'll quickly escalate the conflict and undermine the chances of a good fight. If Joe accuses you of a financial reporting error, for example, which you're sure that you did not make, you may be tempted to fight back with emotion and facts. Instead, stretch yourself to find some common ground. You may respond, for example, as follows: "Well I know I sometimes do make mistakes so anything is possible. Let's sit together while we pull up the information on the computer and see if we can straighten this out." By not immediately telling Joe that he's an idiot, you've allowed him to save face and moved you into jointly finding a solution.

6. Follow up. Make sure you schedule another meeting with them to see if your change in behavior or your response to their idea has met their needs.

7. Keep talking and keep meeting until your working relationship improves. If the two of you cannot make it work together, seek an experienced mediator to help you manage your differences.

Sometimes you're faced with a confrontation or criticism in a public setting, such as when you're giving a presentation to a group or a more formal speech. Many times these comments are intensely critical or confrontational and made by someone who has more interest in giving a speech than in truly contributing to a dialogue. In that situation, how do you skillfully defuse the confrontation?

As a speaker and workshop leader, I've frequently had to deal with pesky participants. First, I immediately move toward the speaker. This seems to give them some sort of recognition or attention that they need while putting the audience's focus on my movement, instead of the heckler. Then I thank them for their suggestion or comment with as much genuine enthusiasm as I can muster. Next, I acknowledge that we have a need for further investigation and research on that topic and invite the speaker to share his or her views with me after the program.

Throughout the entire interchange I try to remain as polite as possible. As one participant—also a professional workshop leader—remarked to me after my program, "I never thought of *politeness* as a tactic for dealing with hecklers. It seems to calm them right down. I'm going to try it next time I face one."

This technique frequently turns my fiercest foes into friends. I've had many come up to me after a speech, thank me for my comments, and offer to help with my work.

Instead of using such a skillful approach to either private or public criticism, however, most of us get sad or mad.

In order to avoid these reactions, it helps to understand why we feel the way we do. Cognitive therapists—a school of psychologists who help us focus on realizing that our thoughts drive our emotions—warn that if we're prone to depression, we may feel sad when criticized. We probably feel that way because we automatically decide the critic is right. Without investigation, we decide the critic is correct and then magnify the importance of the criticism by either over-generalizing—wrongly concluding that our whole life is nothing but a string of errors, or labeling ourselves a total idiot. Usually, this is because we have perfectionist tendencies and assume that we are supposed to be flawless and if we're not, we must be worthless.

These mental errors drive depression and low self-esteem. When criticized, we avoid the conflict and our responses will be ineffectual and characterized by avoidance and withdrawal. Roadrunners, for example, frequently respond to criticism in this way. They flee the scene so that they don't have to deal with the confrontation.

In contrast, the pit bulls among us may get mad in response to criticism. Pit bulls are frequently perfectionists who stubbornly refuse to admit that we're less than our own ideal. Somehow, we have it wired that admitting errors makes us worthless. So we start snarling and snapping at the critic, which gives us an energy rush of adrenaline and a temporary high. We hurl unsavory opinions of the critic back at him. For the moment, we feel pumped up with righteous indignation, and we may even convince the critic to slink away and lick his wounds. Unfortunately, in exchange for our momentary bliss, we've permanently crippled the relationship.

If instead, we can summon the courage to respond skillfully to criticism and feedback because we either have the self-esteem or act like we do, we can bolster the relationship while enhancing our own skills and productivity. During feedback, we take the position that we'll investigate and determine if it contains a grain of truth. We can even be grateful for the chance to learn something from the exercise. We ask specific questions until we understand their real concerns. If we're wrong, we apologize and admit it. If it's a true conflict of interests, we use the skills we've learned in this book to negotiate. If they're wrong, we find something to agree with as we diplomatically explore their errors.

Does this all sound like too much effort? Unfortunately, there's no quick and easy way to change a pit bull's reputation. You do it by changing your own behavior—inch-by-inch, day-by-day. You also do it by assuming a leadership role in managing conflict within your organization and by encouraging feedback as group learning, rather than individual criticism. This is the only way to encourage open communication and make sure that people tell you the truth.

HOW TO MANAGE YOUR OWN ANGER

The biggest challenge for most pit bulls in becoming confrontable may be managing their own anger. Although we all have issues around appropriately expressing anger, pit bulls tend to have the biggest problems. The other styles tend to suppress anger, while pit bulls tend to express anger in inappropriate ways, discouraging others from confronting them. Understanding your anger is the first step.

The current psychological research about anger management tells us our anger is all about fear, especially the fear of exposing something about ourselves and the fear of losing control.

When you feel anger, before exploding, ask yourself of what or whom you are afraid. What might you lose in the encounter? How might you be hurt? Knowing the real, underlying reason may help you control your anger.

Next, don't ignore your anger, but don't express rage inappropriately. There was a time when people thought it healthy to immediately express their anger. More recent research, however, suggests that constant ventilating actually makes us more angry rather than less. The most accepted theory is to assume a middle ground between exploding and suppressing anger.

The best course is not to ignore your anger, but to think before you express it to make sure that it's directed at the proper person in an appropriate manner. Ask yourself, am I really angry over current issues with this person, or am I expressing old issues that are tied to someone else in my past?

Your mother's advice to count to 10 remains sound. If you're still not calm enough to express intelligently and rationally what you feel, count to 100!

Once you do decide to express your anger directly to the person in front of you, you need to talk with them in private and make sure you stick with the issues at hand instead of old business.

Use "I" statements. Instead of exploding to your assistant that "You make me angry me when you keep talking on the phone to your boyfriend instead of dealing with my work," try "When I approach your desk I need you to stop talking on the phone and deal with my work."

Stay calm, but be cautious about smiling when you're expressing anger. The other person may perceive that he is being mocked by your smile and if so, it will increase his anger. Try to offer understanding of the other person's plight and give him an opportunity to save face. Most of all, understand that expressing anger appropriately will be a key to making you confrontable and modeling ways of valuing conflict.

A DEEPER LOOK AT ANGER

If you find yourself continually angry and out of control during conflict, you want to delve more deeply into the causes and cures for anger management, I recommend studying *The Dance of Anger* by Harriet Lerner, Ph.D.[2] Although originally written for women, the book is helpful for anyone who wants to understand anger on a more constructive level. As Learner puts it:

> Anger is a signal, and one worth listening to. Our anger may be a message that we are being hurt, that our rights are being violated, that our needs or wants are not being adequately met, or simply that something is not right.[3]

Lerner and other relationship experts focus on using anger productively and creatively as a tool for change in our relationships. First, this requires us to be assertive, rather than passive or aggressive. We need to identify what the real issue is. We often charge in armed for battle without a true awareness of what the war is about.

We may, for example, be angry at our boss because he reminds us of our critical father and any suggestions from him makes us bristle. Before confronting him, we may need to be clear about what we really want to accomplish and understand that we are responsible for our own reactions. What is our specific request, and what do we really want to change? What is our own bottom line? Frequently, without knowing the answers to these questions, we hurl ourselves into the fray without examining the underlying issues.

When we do confront someone, we need to use some of the communication skills identified in this chapter and throughout this book. Just blowing up and blaming may offer temporary relief, but when that passes, we may find that nothing has changed. We need to learn to stand back from the battle and the emotion, observe our own behavior, and change what we can change—ourselves.

None of these changes is easy but if we become consciously aware of what we need to do to change our part in the dance of anger, we'll have a start toward breaking old patterns of interaction. As Lerner emphasizes: "Anger is a tool for change when it challenges us to become more of an expert on the self and less of an expert on others."[4]

JUST SAY NO TO ANGER!

Cognitive therapists offer a different strategy for managing anger. Instead of looking at expressing anger or internalizing our examination of the causes of it, they advocate that we simply *stop creating so much anger!* But, you may protest, external people, things and events *make me angry* and I have no control over them.

A cognitive approach challenges this point of view.

If you believe that someone's incompetence or rudeness at work makes you angry, you're not alone. Most of us actually do believe that external events or people cause our upset. A late report from our researcher or too many mistakes in a document produced by our administrative assistant sets us off. We explode that "They're incompetent and I'm angry."

Yet if we look closer, we can see that it's not these events that make us angry, but our own reactions to these events. Cognitive therapists believe that anger—like other emotions—is created by our thoughts. We can always change these thoughts and so change the resulting emotions.

Yet some of us insist that the world really is unfair and that negative events do occur and so we have a *right* to our anger. While this may be true, we always have to ask whether it's worth it. What are we really trying to accomplish, and will it help us in the long run?

In many cases our anger is created by mental errors such as *labeling*. When we describe someone as a jerk, for example, we're seeing him in a totally negative way. We can resent the person's behavior without directing our anger to who the person is. When we label people, we set up false targets for our anger, failing to remember that we're all a mix of positive, negative, and neutral attributes. When we label someone, we decide we're morally superior, which leads to blaming and retaliation. We thirst for blood and set up a negative spiral of conflict.

Instead, we can look at the fact that this battle is really all about our own self-esteem. The other person threatens us with their attack or inattention. We need to remember that we're the only person in the world in charge of our own self-esteem and that our self-worth can only go down if we let it.

One of the other mental errors cognitive psychologists suggest causes anger is *mind reading*, assuming that we know why someone did something. If someone doesn't turn in a project on time, for example, we may assume that they didn't respect our priorities and get angry, when in fact, it may be because the co-worker was up all night with a sick child.

The third most common form of mental distortion that the cognitive school believes leads to anger is what they call *magnification*, exaggerating the importance of the negative event. When we do this, we blow up the size of our emotional reaction. We may tell ourselves, for example, that "I can't take" a staff member's mistake but is that really true? We are taking it and telling ourselves that *we can't* just escalates our emotions. Our anger won't cause them to be perfect in the way we expect.

Much of our anger comes from the idea that someone or something should be fair or just. This belief, as I've previously discussed, limits our ability to manage conflict creatively.

I'm not saying that we should never allow ourselves to feel angry, but we should ask whether our anger is productive. I have two rules that I use in my personal philosophy about anger. First, I ask myself if someone has knowingly and maliciously acted in a hurtful manner? Frequently, the answer is no. As one of my mentors once said to me, "Lynne, don't worry about what people are thinking about you, because people are *not* thinking about you. They're thinking about themselves."

We may be irritated that others are so selfish that they don't consider our needs and feelings, but their neglect is rarely intentional. Most of your co-workers these days are just too overwhelmed with their own work and personal life to take your needs into account.

Second, I try to ask whether my anger is useful. Will skillfully expressing it help me achieve my larger work and personal goal? If not, I need to find another outlet to blow off steam, such as exercising, creating art, talking to a friend, or visiting a shrink or a priest.

Sometimes our anger is justified. If, for example, we find that there are no women in management in our company and we've investigated the causes and believe that it's purely discriminatory, we may use our anger to fuel our energy to form a group to convince management to change.

When we feel angry, it's useful to list the advantages and disadvantages of feeling angry and acting in a revenge mode. Consider both the short- and long-term consequences, engage in a kind of cost benefit analysis and then decide if resentment and retaliation are really in our best interests.

As Indira Gandhi once said:

> Anyone can become angry—that is easy. But to be angry with the right person, to the right degree, at the right time, for the right purpose, and in the right way—this is not easy.

If you can learn to manage your anger so that you're *confrontable*, and if you encourage skillful confrontation in your own organization, you can move from defending and debating to listening and learning. You can evolve from debate to dialogue. You will have taken another giant step on the road to unleashing the power of a good fight.

LEARNING TO VALUE THE CONFRONTABLE ORGANIZATION

It may be helpful to you and others in your organization as you do the hard work of learning to welcome a different opinion if you understand just how critical this essential skill is for the future of your organization. Sally Helgesen, author of *The Web of Inclusion: A New Architecture for Building Great Organizations,*[5] found in her study that the ability to create open communication where people felt comfortable giving and receiving feedback at all levels of the organization was one of the key predictors of organizational success.

One of my clients Jane, started her own successful telecommunications company based on this very premise. A long-distance service "reseller," Jane's company was one of a score of such companies that made their business on the idea of buying long-distance services from the larger telecommunications companies, bundling them in unique ways, and reselling them to individuals. Both Jane and her staff came from various members of the old Bell system.

Accustomed to large, hierarchical organizations, Jane and her staff wanted a change. "We wanted to look like the telecommunications network we were selling. We devised a complex web—like a matrix, really—of interlocking people and departments. We wanted everyone to have access to anyone they needed in the organization. We wanted everyone's thoughts and ideas so we wound up with the best solutions to our problems."

One of Jane's first problems was how to design the offices. Breaking with years of Bell tradition, she put her own office out in the open with the other staffers. She toiled at a desk, no walls or even a cube to separate her from her employees. Anyone could talk to her at any time about any concerns. Jane had no secretary and no set schedule. Although this sometimes resulted in a line surrounding her desk, she welcomed the open atmosphere the design created.

"Spontaneous meetings erupted around my desk," Jane told me. "We finally put a couch next to it so people could participate without fainting from fatigue."

The informal system had another benefit: Rumors were nipped in the bud because anyone who wanted to participate in the initial discussion could. There were no secret meetings behind closed doors. Jane's power as a leader came from the extraordinary openness she was able to demonstrate. Creative solutions flowed out of the chaos surrounding Jane's desk.

Jane also instituted an electronic bulletin board where anyone could post questions about what the company was doing and why. No queries were off-limits. Postings ranged from "Why don't we have a better brand of coffee?" to "Why is our stock down this morning?" Jane, or one of her assistants, answered these queries within 48 hours or let the questioner know when the information would be available.

Perhaps most important, Jane shaped her successful company by listening and asking the right questions. When anyone would come to her with an issue, her response was always "What do you think we should do?" Or "What are your team's ideas for solving that problem?" No one doubted that Jane was anxious to seek out their opinion or to be confronted about any issue.

In part, because of the depth of inclusion and confrontability Jane was able to create, her company survived the recent telecommunications shakedown that plunged many other companies into bankruptcy. When the market tightened, Jane simply solicited the best ideas of all of her employees. Instead of the layoffs other companies had to stomach, Jane asked her people what they should do. When someone suggested offering voluntary three-month sabbaticals to those who wanted them, Jane agreed. Around 15 percent of her employees took advantage of her offer over the next two years—enough to get the company over their financial hump.

Similarly, Southwest Airlines has always created an inclusive culture where everyone from a vice president to a baggage handler knew they could offer suggestions and feedback. Everyone refers to Herb Kelleher as "Herb," and he seems to know all the employees by their first names. Once, after I gave a speech to their executives, I attempted to walk across the crowded hall with Herb to the buffet table. He stopped so often to ask how someone's divorce was going or to inquire after a new baby that I gave up in starvation and fetched lunch by myself. The new head of Southwest, Coleen Barrett, is well known for her own encyclopedic knowledge of employee birthdays, anniversaries, and work preferences.

When new employees start at Southwest, they're given a list of 100 questions to answer about the company. Everyone's door—right up to Herb's—is open to these new questioners. From an employee's first moment at Southwest, they know that they can approach anyone with questions or concerns.

What is the benefit of such extraordinary access? When other airlines were forced to lay off employees after the September 11 attacks on the World Trade Center and the Pentagon, Southwest instead assured employees that they would stand firm and asked employees to suggest any cost-saving ideas they might have. The strategy worked, and Southwest flew through the storm.

Another one of my clients, a manufacturing company, has always avoided unions in an industry that's largely unionized. How do they manage this feat, I once asked the vice president of employee relations? "If you don't want a union," he responded, "act as if you already have one."

Indeed, the company recently fought off an attempted organizing effort by stepping up its normally frenetic schedule of town meetings, management/labor baseball games, and CEO informal lunches with employees—all emphasizing access, access, access. The would-be union lost again, gaining only 10 percent of the workers' votes. In addition, profits were up for the third year in a row, running against the industry norm.

Likewise, a large school district in our state was fraught with dissention from teacher unrest, parent unhappiness, and student agitation. When the new superintendent took over, she announced that she was delegating most of her day-to-day duties to one of her deputies. Instead, she would spend her first year "listening and learning." She got an earful.

Teachers wanted more pay and more support. Students wanted open campuses and smoking lounges. Parents wanted higher educational standards. Voters wanted better administration accountability. The superintendent realized that there was only one way to achieve everyone's objectives—a new bond issue to raise money. The only problem? The past three bond issues had failed miserably.

Continuing to listen to the suggestions from the various stakeholders, she told the voters that she had adopted one citizens' group's gutsy idea: The district would receive new money from voters only if they managed to achieve specific educational objectives. No gains, no money. The bond issue passed.

Creating a confrontable organization doesn't happen overnight, and the process can challenge some of our most cherished assumptions about the way things should be. Yet as these examples illustrate, welcoming a different opinion can lead to good fights as well as increased success. Because the change itself can create conflict, in the next chapter we'll focus on another aspect of creative contention: dealing with change.

CHAPTER 16

MAKING CHANGES MAKES WAVES: HOW TO SWIM, NOT SINK

All things must change to something new, to something strange.

—Harry Wadsworth Longfellow

A large financial institution reorganizes its human resources (HR) department with the goal of overhauling employee training and development. Senior management thinks that employee skills are lagging. They bring in several new players to bring fresh energy and more capacity to the department. The result is a huge culture clash between the new and old employees that paralyzes the department.

When an organization makes changes, conflict increases. The upheaval creates uncertainty that can degenerate into turf wars, resentments, sabotage, and multiple negative behaviors. Underlying many of these behaviors are issues of culture, grief, loss, or fear of loss. These are major organizational issues that determine whether a merger will succeed or whether the employees will work to make it fail. On a smaller scale, substantial change within a single department or in reporting relationships can create crippling conflicts if not handled with foresight, thoughtfulness, and respect. Coping with change is probably one of the single most important skills in today's business arena.

Never before has so much change taken place so quickly. In the last 40 years there has been more technological advancement than in all of recorded history, and it has altered the way people, communities, and entire countries interact, work, and live. In order to use conflict creatively for good fights instead of bad, we must understand the impact of change in our organizations and on our lives.

Many times intractable conflicts are really about our resistance to change. Skillful conflict management requires an understanding of this dynamic. When we find ourselves resistant to a new idea, it's usually because we're resistant to change. Even if we don't like the way we're currently working or behaving, it's familiar. Sometimes we create unnecessary conflicts in the workplace because we refuse to recognize or admit this. If we continue to resist the change, we're unlikely to creatively harness the power of conflict.

I've worked with many groups who had conflicts between old leaders and employees and new leaders and employees. Many times, for example, when I'm facilitating a diversity workshop, the most conflicted groups will be those who represent the old versus the new as a result of mergers or acquisitions, not those who represent different ethnic backgrounds or genders.

In one such instance, I was brought in to help a large HR department manage a simmering dispute between old and new members. The old managers saw themselves as serving the more traditional role of *employee advocates*. The old VP, Joe, came from an employee relations background and emphasized representing employee needs. The newer members of the department aligned with Ron, a new high-powered vice president of HR, and saw themselves as strategic *business partners* who needed to serve the highest-ranking manager of whatever business unit they were assigned to.

After much discussion, we came up with a creative definition of their role that embraced both ideas. The reason it took them so long and required my assistance as a facilitator was not so much the substantive conflict itself as it was the whole issue of *change*. The old managers were struggling with the grieving process as they moved into a new and uncertain future. The new VP and the new managers were also struggling with the change process. Even though the move to new jobs was something they had all sought, they had to learn that even positive changes take us through the predictable stages of loss and grief. If we don't acknowledge and move through each stage, we will flounder. Frequently, because we're not conscious of why we feel upset, we will project our anxiety outside ourselves onto our co-workers. Conflicts naturally follow.

Once the group had an opportunity to talk honestly about the changes they were all experiencing and were able to express the common feelings they shared, the underlying issues were much easier to creatively explore.

THE STAGES OF GRIEF

Most of us feel comforted by the familiar. Whenever we have to learn or do something new, we go through classic and predictable stages of leaving the old ways. These stages are those of the grief process, first identified by Elisabeth Kübler-Ross in her work with the dying. Conflicts almost always involve underlying issues of grief, loss, or the fear of loss. These stages are:

> **Stage 1: Denial**—We deny the event or action is occurring. Sometimes we engage in bargaining at this stage.

> **Stage 2: Anger**—We're angry the event or action has occurred; it's common at this stage to be unaware of the real source of our anger. We may lash out at other people or events instead.

> **Stage 3: Depression**—We realize that bargaining won't work and we feel a deep sadness, usually disguised as depression, over this realization.

> **Stage 4: Acceptance**—We accept that the change will occur, adjust our lives accordingly and start planning for the future.

Be aware that most of us do not travel through these stages on a straight line. We may proceed with one step forward, two steps backward. Yet, if we're aware of the grief process and if we chart our progress, we generally move in an upward spiral to resolution and acceptance.

When we're faced with a new idea or change, it's important to take stock of where we are in the change process and work through our feelings. The only way around these feelings is through them. If we deny they exist, we block the energy that we could use more successfully for the future. If we sink too deeply into any stage, that also leaves us paralyzed. Some people remain stuck at one stage for months, years, or even a lifetime.

An awareness of the process and an active attempt to experience and move through your emotions will propel you to the future. Talking with someone—a trusted friend, minister, or counselor—who is educated about the grieving process, can be helpful. Be careful to select someone who understands grieving and who will not just urge you to move on and ignore your feelings.

Expressing your emotions creatively through writing, dance, art, or singing can also be helpful. The trick is to do *something*—not just sit back passively and assume that your emotions will take care of themselves. Taking care of our emotions responsibly, through one of these methods, is just as essential as taking care of our bodies through diet, exercise, and visits to a health-care practitioner.

MANAGING CHANGE OR MANAGING YOUR FUTURE?

Once you have started a regular process to deal with your emotions around change and how you personally handle transitions, try to expand your thinking about "change management" to "managing your future." Many organizations, speakers, and books these days emphasize change management, but I caution you about these programs. If we're only managing change, we're probably in a reactive or catch-up mode. I try to help people anticipate and plan for the future instead. Now the future is all about change, but language is so important that I avoid the words "managing change." Managing the future goes hand-in-hand with learning how to assume leadership in conflict and use it creatively.

Organizational change management programs make people focus on something that's being done to them rather than their own active participation. "Change management" programs also sometimes create the illusion this change will be the last and allows the ostriches among us to hunker down and wait it out—an "I'm going to hide until things calm down" attitude. Most organizations today are trying to encourage employees to feel "empowered" (another fuzzy word). The whole idea of change management runs counter to that goal.

You will need to acquire creative conflict management skills in order to stay happily working. Successful people stay ahead of change and anticipate the future. As Andy Grove, founder of Intel, emphasizes in his book, *Only the Paranoid Survive*, we need to learn the power of positive paranoia. In a future without jobs, we need to learn how to forecast the future, and then imagine and place ourselves in new work rather than just learning how to manage the present chaos. Future forecasting and planning is a way you can create power in the present moment.

A provocative ad I saw asked: "The World Wide Web is the Future. Do you want to be the spider or the fly?" To which I would add the twist, "Do you want to spin your own future work or just be caught in the web of change?"

To do this you will need an additional element—a "querencia." *Querencia* is a term from bullfighting, which is not a bad metaphor for how you may feel as you evolve into future workers.

In bullfighting, matadors swear every bull has a place in the ring where he feels safe, untouchable and where—no matter how much skill the bullfighter has—the bull remains unreachable as long as he is in this space—his querencia. If the bull can reach this spot, he stops running and gathers his strength. From the matador's point of view, the bull is a powerful opponent in this space. A matador must know where the sanctuary lies for each bull and make sure the animal cannot reach his own refuge.

In a future with so much constant change and the resulting conflict, you will need to create your own individual querencia. I would recommend an actual physical space—not just a psychological metaphor. Some suggestions: a house you love that's paid for or with low mortgage payments, a support social, spiritual, or neighborhood community or a trade or professional association. What cannot be your querencia in the future is a traditional job because most organizations will continue to evolve, reorganize, and change. Unfortunately, in recent history, too many of us relied upon our jobs to serve as our security and refuge.

When I coach executives and other professionals who are dealing with change and the resulting conflict, that's the first thing I ask: Where is your querencia? Once you have a sanctuary in the ring, the stress of feeling as if you're a constant target subsides. Yet, for most of us in our mobile, transient society, we haven't stopped whirling through change long enough to create a safe place. If you fit that profile, before you attempt to do anything else related to "change management" or an intense conflict: Stop. Do whatever it takes to find, create, and nurture your own querencia. Without it, you will not be able to harness the creative power of conflict.

In times of organization change and transition, conflicts increase. In order to increase your skills in managing conflict, you need to understand the relationship between change and transition.

TRANSITION MANAGEMENT

Author William Bridges, Ph.D., has been fundamental in introducing the concept of *transition management* as opposed to *change management*. Change management focuses on designing the desired change and using persuasion to move a group toward change.[1]

Transition management acknowledges that even if the change is beneficial and desirable, most people have trouble moving through the stages of change and their resistance creates conflicts. While the traditional grieving process described earlier tends to show up for individuals, groups also need to look at transition management. Frequently, it's not the outcome that people are resisting—it's the sometimes painful, disruptive, and scary movement through the transition process. Failure to acknowledge that fact and design systems to assist with the movement toward change frequently results in a failed change effort. Bridges identifies three stages of transition management:

1. **Endings.** The old way is ending and must be acknowledged. Groups sometimes design ceremonies, parties, or other ways of marking this stage. Some groups even have fun with this stage by presenting elaborate mock "funerals" for the ending.

2. **The Neutral Zone.** What I like to call the "no man's land," or "chaos zone." The old way is ending, but the new is not yet visible. In this stage, a great many people problems, productivity problems, and conflicts arise.
3. **The New Beginning.** When the new is finally in place and visible, and people are actually implementing the new system or idea. Beginnings also require acknowledgment through a ceremony, party, or other visible sign.

For example, one of my clients began a large-scale reorganization effort designed to change their command-and-control environment to a more inclusive one. The CEO expected employees to love the changes, because they would have more input into decision-making. Much to his surprise, however, workers balked. They questioned the changes, carped that the proposal was too complex, and generally stalled on implementing new processes and procedures.

At first the executive team assumed that the employees were resisting the change itself so they started a series of focus groups to better inform people of why they were installing the new methods and procedures. What the groups revealed, however, was that workers didn't object to the goal. What they were resisting was the transition process through the change itself. Their number-one question was "What resources are going to be available to help me do my job during this transition?" Without knowing *how* they personally could get through the change, the workers wanted no part in understanding the *whys* behind the change.

In your own workplace, you can start to consider how many of your own conflicts or the conflicts you observe around you at work are actually issues around change and transition. Once you recognize your own or another's reaction to change, the conflict will become easier to manage. If you can educate your co-workers about the normal and predictable stages of change, grieving, and transition, you can help use the conflict to fuel the creative edge you'll need in the future. One of the ways you can be useful in leading your organization through acquiring the mediation and facilitation skills outlined in the next chapter.

PART 4

The Power of Systems: How to Create an Organization That Encourages Good Fights

CHAPTER 17

THE DOGFIGHT REFEREES: HOW TO MEDIATE, FACILITATE, AND SURVIVE

Blessed are the peacemakers.

—Mathew 5:3

Dick Richard's assistant, Pam, and his HR director, Helen, are at each other's throats over employee schedules, leave, and overtime. He wants to keep both employees, but doesn't know how to stop the fighting so he's thrown up his hands and hired an outside mediator. She starts the mediation process by sorting the issues into three categories: historical problems, current issues, and "beyond" issues—those things that are beyond Pam and Helen's ability to resolve. To their amazement, most of their issues end up in the "beyond" category. The mediator was then able to present their joint list to Dick for him to make a decision. She was also able to give him some useful feedback about his own role in the conflict. A classic conflict avoider and roadrunner, Dick had unknowingly fueled the dispute by refusing to decide critical issues that affected the working relationship of the two women.

Tired of refereeing dogfights in the office without knowing the rules? Most managers and leaders spend at least one fourth of their time resolving disputes, yet little, if any time honing their mediator or facilitation skills. In fact, in 2001, 81 percent of workers think they have "lousy bosses," up from 63 percent just two years ago, according to a survey of 700 workers by author Gordon Miller. Clearly, most bosses need mediation and facilitation skills. Studying a few basics about the process can help leaders navigate the war zones and come out alive. Frequently, harnessing the creative power of conflict requires good mediation and facilitation skills.

MEDIATION BASICS

Mediation is a complex subject—one many experts have spent years studying and practicing to refine their skills. My own workplace training for mediators takes two to five days. Yet many of us end up mediating in the workplace whether we're prepared or not. A leader—and many employees—face daily conflicting interests that require mediation.

The basics of direct conflict resolution will serve you well in mediating workplace disputes. As a mediator, you are going to facilitate a negotiation. Perhaps the most important skill is understanding the difference between positions and interests and following the 10 steps outlined in Chapter 11. You also need to map the conflict and decide what kind of conflict you're resolving as described in Chapter 12. Positional bargaining starts with the answer. Your job is to move the parties away from positional bargaining to discover the answer that best meets the needs and interests of everyone involved.

THE MEDIATOR'S ROLE

Your job as a mediator is to use questions that will help the parties elicit their underlying needs and interests rather than staying stuck upon whatever solution they favor.

First, make sure you are the appropriate person to mediate the dispute. If both sides cannot see you as neutral, you may not be. In addition, keep in mind the following basics whenever you find yourself mediating workplace disputes:

- Remember *who* owns the problem. As a mediator, your job is not to solve the problem; you must help the parties discover the creative solution to the problem: *The solution is in their hands.* If you find yourself frustrated as a mediator, this is frequently where you've made a mistake.

- Studies have shown that small things, such as where people sit during mediation, can make a big difference. If the parties to the conflict sit across from each other, for example, the problem will escalate. If they sit beside each other, they can look at each other or not, as they choose, and may develop that necessary feeling that they are on the same team to tackle the problem, not the person.

- Understand that your first goal as a mediator should be to help the parties agree on a definition of the problem. Don't rush on this step. Many misunderstandings result from a failure to agree about what the parties are fighting about.

Adjusting your own attitude and understanding your role is the first step in the process. After that, you can begin to prepare the parties.

PREPARING THE PARTIES

Before the mediation, you need to individually prepare the parties. Talk to each party separately (preferably in person) in order to find out what their issues are and decide whether the problem is medial. Start planting the suggestion that conflicts are normal and can be valuable, and that creative solutions can help foster productivity and innovation. Suggest that conflict is an opportunity to change what's not working and acknowledge them for being willing to face the issues. In an interview, veteran mediator Judy Mares-Dixon of the Boulder-based Center for Dispute Resolution told me she recommends asking the following questions:

- What are the issues you want resolved?
- What is your sense of the issues the other party wants resolved?
- What ideas do you have for resolving the problem? (Start planting the suggestion that there are *multiple* solutions to the problem).
- What do you need to resolve this? What does the other party need to resolve this?
- How will you convince the other party of the reasonableness of your proposal?

Give both parties an overview of mediation. If they've had a bad experience with previous mediators, ask what happened. (This will tell you what was important to them.)

THE MEDIATION SESSION

When you actually start the session, be sure you've scheduled enough time and privacy. Tell the parties you may need time-outs, caucuses (individual sessions when you confer separately with each side), or breaks. Let them know you want to make as much progress as possible in this session, but that you understand either side may need to break.

Then, explain the purpose of the mediation. Make sure you do so in a way that doesn't allow one person or another to fight what you're saying. In addition, as a part of your introductory session, inform the parties that you will not decide who is right and who is wrong (unless you are their boss and have announced that you will decide the issue by a certain time if they are unable to resolve the dispute). Your role as a mediator is to help the parties resolve the issue. Explain that you understand that managing conflicts can be difficult and that the parties are going to have to work hard to creatively manage the issues, otherwise they would have been able to resolve the problem by themselves.

Explain any ground rules for the sessions. In most workplaces, people want ground rules such as no insulting, put downs, or interruptions. Explain that normal workplace policies regarding harassment, ethics, codes of conduct, threats, and violence will apply. Ask them if they need any special rules in order to concentrate and be able to stay in the room and do the work.

Some ground rules can actually *inhibit* resolution. For example, some people just can't talk about issues they feel passionate about without speaking loudly. Warn the parties about this. Explain, if applicable, any rules about confidentiality that the organization or any court has required. Be careful not to promise confidentiality. If the mediation ends up subject to internal review, administrative hearings, or court proceedings, you (or the parties) may need to disclose your discussion.

Many experienced mediators will not mediate without a signed, written agreement outlining the ground rules, confidentiality agreements, and consequences if the mediation fails. While this may be ideal, written agreements may not be practical for mediating day-to-day workplace disputes and may sometimes intimidate unsophisticated disputants and make them reluctant or unwilling to mediate.

Also, be aware that ground rules themselves can spark a conflict. I once had a woman walk out of a mediation and refuse to return because her manager started talking (in what she felt, justifiably, was a condescending way) about the rules he wanted *her* to follow! One of the ways to establish ground rules is to ask the participants to think about what didn't work when they tried to discuss the issues before.

After your introduction, ask each side to give you an overview of the problems and issues. Your job at this point is to try to reveal the needs and interests of the parties, to understand what is important to them before you ask for solutions. Ask each of them to contribute to a list of the issues and confirm that the list is correct, then pick one issue (it's good to start with one you think may be easiest to creatively manage) and brainstorm as many innovative ways as possible to solve the issue. Keep encouraging the parties to move into the *future* in this step rather than repeating what has occurred between them in the past. As a mediator, consistently try to use the suggestions about reframing and listening outlined in this book.

One of the most important skills as a mediator will be to develop the skill of deep and passionate listening. When you're in this role, you'll need to listen as a witness and constantly learn to reframe misunderstandings and misconceptions.

Also, remind them of any purpose you know they share. Ask them what they value that will be served by resolving the dispute through mediation; for example, a better working relationship, a more successful project, less personal stress, or alignment with the organization's values.

Try to keep to a pace that's fast enough so both sides believe they are making progress, yet slow enough to allow each party to carefully consider what they need and what agreements will meet their interests.

If the parties seem stuck or unable to come up with any solutions, encourage them to talk about how and why they feel stuck, and acknowledge their hard work. Perhaps taking a break will help, although make sure they do not use this as an excuse to avoid mediation. If they're still mired, ask any or all of the following questions:

- If we don't come up with a creative solution in this session, what do you think will happen? How will you meet your needs and interests? How will the other side meet his or her needs and interests?
- If both of you could be content with a solution, what would it be?
- What could the two of you propose that would really work for both of you?

After you listen to their responses, if the parties are still stuck, try the following:

- Talk about similar situations you have mediated and the solutions the parties found.
- Ask one party to give advice to the other about what would really work for them.
- Ask each party to give you advice about what would work for each of them.
- Ask each party to restate the other party's issues, needs, and interests as well as what they think would work best for the other party.

As you go through the mediation process, try to find successes wherever possible: Focus on breaking down the issues and finding solutions for some part of the problem. If you use this technique it will help keep the parties working and maintain their optimism that a solution is possible.

If you're a manager mediating between two employees, a creative way to break a deadlock is to give up on resolving their differences and have them focus on you. Ask them to discuss among themselves all the concerns they have about you as a manager and all the reasons why they think *you* should change. Request that they work together to draft a document outlining their suggested improvements. Forcing them to work together on a project involving someone else's faults will sometimes help the warring parties see that they can work together and produce other interesting and surprising results.

I suggested this to my client John, head of a successful construction company. Two of his managers of different divisions constantly clashed over resources, schedules, and procedures. Ready to throw up his hands in despair, he called me for advice. "Ask them to make a list of all the things that are wrong with *you*," I suggested. "Sure, sure," he muttered, assuming I was joking. I convinced him I was serious and, not having a better idea, he tried my technique.

Much to his chagrin and eventual amusement, they attacked the task with great enthusiasm. When he met with them to discuss the results, they presented their list with more good will than they'd had for each other in ages. As they explained their concerns such as "John needs to be more organized," one of them would sheepishly admit that he also needed to work on that skill. Vowing to change if they would also, John and his two managers made a pact that eventually broke the deadlock.

Of course, this technique will only work if the manger really means to take the results seriously, but it's an unusual and unexpected tool that can sometimes break the most intractable disputes.

Sometimes the manager as mediator *is* the problem. Using managers as mediators can blur boundaries. As conflict researchers D. M. Kolb and L. L. Putnam found in their interesting study of managers as mediators:

> [M]anagers are not natural mediators .... There are occasions when managers *will* mediate disputes, particularly when it is important to maintain a working relationship between the parties. But to the degree that managers are held accountable

for particular decisions, are concerned about precedent, and overly personalize the basis of the disagreement, they are far more likely to adopt adjudicative or inquisitorial approaches to conflict management .... [A] superior's management of conflict with subordinates looks more like the exercise of authority than third party facilitation.[1]

This research suggests that managers must work extra hard to utilize all the skills and suggestions in this chapter to truly mediate a dispute—which involves understanding that the parties must ultimately come to their own solution—as opposed to adjudicating a dispute by actually forcing a decision upon the parties.

CAUCUS

A caucus is when you, as a mediator, talk individually with each of the parties outside the mediating room. If you decide to caucus with each side, first ask if there's something in the caucus they need you to keep confidential. Ask them what they need to have this work for them. In the meeting, you can ask them to role play with you, to play with options and to try out solutions. Make certain you spend an equal amount of time with each side to make sure you do not undermine your neutrality.

Sometimes a caucus will help you understand hidden issues that block the parties from reaching a solution. For example, I was mediating between a group of doctors and their office manger. Talking with the two managing partners and the officer manager in a group resulted in a stalemate. When I asked for a caucus and spoke to the parties separately, it turned out that one of the doctors thought that the office manager had made a pass at him. Because the doctors had previously been sued for sexual harassment, he was terrified that they would face a similar charge. After asking his permission, I brought the issue up with the office manager. She was shocked to learn that he had misinterpreted her words. In fact, she had no such intention and revealed that she was in a committed lesbian relationship. When we resumed as a group, I was able to point out all of the confusion and we quickly made progress on the other issues.

FINALIZING A PROPOSAL

Once you have reached a proposal that seems to meet everyone's needs, consider committing it to writing to make sure both sides understand the solution. Also, remember to test the proposal. Testing involves asking each side questions such as: Tell me how you believe this proposal will meet your needs.

Throughout the session and at the end, acknowledge and praise the parties for their effort. Consider some sort of small celebration, such as going out for coffee or ice cream, a picnic in a nearby park, a field trip to the movies, or an unexpected afternoon off. These kinds of rewards can reinforce the idea that creative conflict management is a valued part of your goals as an organization and that you, as a mediator or leader, appreciate their ability to value and embrace the conflict.

Depending on the agreement when you started the mediation, you may or may not reveal the results to the boss of the respective parties or anyone else who requested the mediation. Be sure that you clarify the expectations of the parties around confidentiality before you begin.

FACILITATION BASICS

Facilitation is the task of leading a group through a decision-making process, whereas mediation usually involves working with two or more parties on a specific conflict. While leaders can also serve as facilitators, it's frequently useful to recruit someone objective and removed from the issue.

What makes a good facilitator? The best practitioners demonstrate the ability to structure a discussion, synthesize comments, capture ideas in text and informal graphics, encourage diverse comments, and remain neutral. Objectivity, patience, listening skills, and the ability to probe and question assumptions should be added to the list. Many leaders favor quick decisions and may not be the best facilitators.

People who have backgrounds in more than one discipline make good natural facilitators among diverse groups, those with both a marketing and finance background, for example, who can speak both languages.

Some of the mediation techniques we've considered in this chapter—such as sorting the issues—are also helpful in facilitation. Other techniques are sprinkled throughout this book, especially the next two chapters. Although more detailed facilitation techniques are beyond the scope of this book, several excellent sources are listed in the bibliography.

WHY UNPRODUCTIVE CONFLICT CONTINUES

As most leaders know, many pairs or groups, left to themselves, maintain destructive conflict. If you need to repeatedly mediate or facilitate bad fights with the same group, you may be frustrated by their behavior. Given how costly, painful, and uncreative such conflict is, why do they do this? As psychologist Kenneth Kaye concludes:

> The best answer psychologists have been able to discover is that members of a group are working together when they engage in repetitive, predictable dispute cycles. They are *collaborating to avoid something worse.*[2]

One of my clients, for example, is a construction company that has experienced phenomenal growth over the past five years, starting with a gross in the low six figures and expecting in the current year a gross of $6 million. Don, their young leader, had worked hard to build an effective team, reward good work, and involve everyone in major decision-making. With the slowdown in the economy, however, the business started to experience cash flow problems. New accounts still flocked to Don's company because of their excellent reputation, but clients paid slower and fought more over seemingly insignificant mistakes.

While Don struggled to borrow money to manage the cash flow, he found himself increasingly drawn into mediating clashes among his team and responding to their complaints. His staff began to fight constantly, usually over some petty matter such as who failed to record something, lost an estimate, forgot to pass along a message, or allowed a member of the crew to leave early. Don would mediate the current quarrel and a temporary cease fire would ensue. Yet within a few days, another battle erupted over new and trivial issues.

In desperation, Don brought me in to diagnose the problem. He couldn't understand why his formerly compatible staff seemed to love destructive fights. When I met individually with the parties, the answer quickly came to me.

Why does a temporary peace frequently lead to conflict? Psychologists find that it happens for two reasons:

1. Peace isn't really peace. The true issue hasn't been embraced, or perhaps even acknowledged and everyone knows it—at least at some level. The combatants keep fighting about trivial matters in the hopes of getting to the real issues, but when it gets too threatening they "agree" to back away.

2. Alternatively, the peace itself makes them nervous. With the resolution of some issues, the peace itself sparks new questions the collaborators aren't ready to face, such as, if we're working this well together, does that mean one of us isn't needed? Which one?

With Don's company, everyone was fighting to avoid the real issue: they were terrified because of the company's cash flow problems and the resulting change in Don's behavior. Their formerly available and nurturing leader had grown distracted and distant. Did that mean that the business was going under? Would they lose their jobs? Was there an even greater problem he was hiding from them?

When you find a group or pair mired in a cycle of sustained conflict, you may break the cycle by asking some radical questions such as: "What are you fighting together to avoid?" Or ask them, "What would you do with all this creative energy if you weren't stuck in a destructive dispute?" Or "What do you think might happen if you did something different in that situation?"

Planting the suggestion that a group is actually *working together* to achieve a common goal frequently shocks the participants out of their trance of denial. When you ask these questions, the real energy behind the conflict usually emerges. It could be anything from "she'd walk all over me" to "we'd have to face the possibility of failure" or "we wouldn't have any more excuses for our poor performance."

Most constant combatants are aware of these underlying forces but are not aware that they've been fighting to keep the entire group from having to deal with the issue. In many cases, they're actually protecting the noncombatants.

With Don's construction business, for example, the distracting disputes saved him from facing his own deepest fears about losing the business he'd worked so hard to build, and also helped him save face by relieving him from talking to his team about the extent of the business's financial problems. What he didn't realize was his staff suffered from a fear of the unknown that was more debilitating than facing the true numbers. Oddly, the solution to the continuing conflict wasn't to help the disputants work better together, but involved instead a series of frank discussions with the entire team to let them know the current financial status and the various options. Once Don was willing to let go of his "big daddy with everything under control" facade and involve his staff in the difficult problems he needed to face, they surprised him with their own creative solutions to the current crisis.

Long-standing unproductive conflicts sometimes have the unspoken agreement: "Let's you and me fight." The mutually destructive pattern of fighting will continue until someone gives the parties a more direct way to embrace the real issues they've been successfully avoiding through the continual disputes.

How do you interrupt the process so that the warriors can have a good fight instead of a bad one? First, help them identify their own individual fears that trigger the conflict. These are the underlying needs and interests that have been too threatening for them to reveal.

They may also have shared fears that you can help them recognize by forcing the group to answer the questions designed to elicit the real reasons for the conflict. In order to help the parties recognize the warning signs, you can help the individuals assemble a list of gestures and feelings that frequently lead to trouble. I call this list "hot buttons," and a simple technique is to share these lists and respond with an "ouch" if someone hits them.

Second, help the group learn to interrupt the process. Make sure someone keeps track of the traditional cycle of battles and learns to point out the repetition to the group whenever they're stalled. To do this, people have to learn to recognize their own and the shared fears that will lead to another round of unproductive battles unless they consciously choose to respond differently. Again, this involves helping them learn to respond from something other than their reptilian brain.

Finally, as a leader or facilitator, you will need to monitor the group's interactions in order to reinforce the productive and creative skills the group has learned.

Unproductive fights can be transformed into good fights, but it will take some digging and practice to bring the real issues that lurk beneath the surface of the continual bad fights to light.

SURVIVING AS A REFEREE—KEEPING THE FAITH

Mediation or facilitation takes skill and patience, yet can lead to valuable and creative results. Perhaps the most important skill you need to develop is your own patience with the process and your own listening ability. As a mediator or facilitator, you need to serve as a sort of "cheerleader," constantly assuring the parties that if they stay on task, a solution that meets everyone's needs will emerge. Work to develop your skills to referee good fights, and your reputation as a leader will flourish.

Need inspiration? Consider the experience of mediation veteran Susan Podziba, a faculty associate with the Program on Negotiation at Harvard Law School, who has facilitated dialog between Israelis and Palestinians, between environmentalists and fishermen, and between pro-choice and pro-life activists.

She proceeds from the assumption that the combatants hold the key to resolving their own conflicts. "Life isn't fair," she says. "The reality is that people everywhere have hard choices to make. My job is to challenge people to see the complexity of a situation and to encourage them to take an active part in making those hard choices."[3]

Consider also, as a model, the experience of Vancouver Island. The community clashed in a destructive conflict between loggers who wanted to continue their traditional clear-cutting and environmentalists who insisted that they stop to protect the fragile island ecology. Other community members believed that the logging industry was essential to the economy of the island. After nearly 10 years of dialog with the assistance of various mediators, the groups finally agreed on a creative resolution to the conflict. Logging continued, but with a new company that practices sustainable logging. These innovative loggers don't strip the forest for huge roads because they lift all the logs out by helicopter! They selectively cut so that large sections of the forest surround any cleared sections.

Although community members agree that the long battle was divisive and expensive, they are pleased with the ultimate creative solution, one that honors their special environment while protecting the local economy. None of this would have been possible if the participants hadn't been willing to embrace the conflict and keep working toward an innovative solution.

Looking to other successful mediation projects can help us develop our own skills as facilitators and lead our organizations to more good fights and more innovative solutions to our deepest problems.

In Chapter 18, we'll consider a frequently ignored, yet underlying source of many conflicts you may be called to mediate—no one knows *how* a particular decision should be made.

CHAPTER 18

AVOID THE RECOUNT: HOW TO ARTICULATE A CLEAR DECISION-MAKING PROCESS

The idea of a charismatic leader, someone who gets his one idea realized by sheer force of his personality, is a myth!

—Professor Paul C. Nutt

On November 7, 2000, chaos tumbled out of Florida voting booths and into communities across the country as a storm of controversy erupted over the Presidential election. Did George W. Bush or Al Gore win Florida's electoral vote? Should a "dimpled" chad count? What about a "hanging" chad? And what in the world is a "pregnant" chad? On November 6, 2000, the decision process seemed clear: registered voters cast their ballots, they're counted, and the winner takes all Electoral College votes. We've all learned it isn't nearly that simple. At the heart of the matter was the question: What exactly is the decision process?

Internal combustion can explode within your organization when decisions are made in the absence of an articulated process and a strategic communication plan. Does the popular vote within the team rule the day or does a corporate Electoral College really cast the ballots? More importantly, does everyone know the decision-making method beforehand? There are countless ways to reach a decision—circumstances call upon all of us to use a variety of strategies daily. You might take a poll about where to grab a bite of lunch with several colleagues, seek consensus about hiring a new person to join your management team, and decide alone whether to approve overtime. Each decision-making model has a role, and a good leader is flexible, using this array of techniques as appropriate. Determining the right model is a key factor in creating good fights.

If we fail to outline the decision model, the group's ability to value conflict and use it creatively will be lessened. Instead, participants are likely to constantly resist decisions that were already made, as well as quibble over the wrong issues.

Trying to help groups come to an innovative decision about issues is complex. One mistake most groups make is that they fail to talk about *how* the decision will be made. There are pros and cons to any decision process you may decide to use. The following example explains different group options.

DECISIONS! DECISIONS!

Eight people want to go out to dinner together and are trying to decide on a restaurant. The following options describe the decision process:

- **Unanimity:** Everyone's first choice happens to be a Mexican restaurant.
- **Convincing Argument:** One person likes a French restaurant. After presenting advantages, everyone is convinced this option is better than their original preferences.
- **Follow a Popular Leader:** One person wants to go to a German restaurant; everyone else wants to do whatever that person wants more than they want their own food preference, or they believe that person knows better what is best for the group than they do.
- **Implicit Majority or Voting:** If five people want to go to the Thai restaurant, two want to go to the seafood restaurant, and one wants to go to McDonald's, they could decide to go to the Thai restaurant since that is what most people want. The others agree that they do not want to get in the way of what most people want. Without a formal vote, the group goes with the majority.
- **Compromise:** Some want to go to a Thai restaurant, some want to go to the seafood restaurant, and some want to go to McDonald's; so they decide to go to a seafood restaurant this

time, the Thai restaurant next time, and McDonald's after that. Or they go to a different Thai restaurant that serves Thai dishes, seafood, and hamburgers, but none of the food is very good.

- **Intensity of Preferences:** Maybe the five who want Thai food are mostly interested in eating ethnic food, the two who want seafood don't like spicy food, and the person who wants to go to McDonald's can afford to spend only $3. Here the people who don't like spicy food have a stronger reason not to go to a Thai restaurant than the people who like ethnic food have a reason to go so it takes precedence; but, the person who wants to go to McDonald's absolutely cannot go to the other, more expensive restaurants, whereas everyone else can go to McDonald's, so they decide to go to McDonald's.

- **Meeting Everyone's Needs (True Consensus):** They decide to go to a Japanese restaurant (ethnic, but not spicy) and everyone chips in to cover the cost over $3 for the person whose cash flow is only a trickle.

*Adapted with permission from Randy Schutt's handout, "Notes on Consensus Decision-Making."

One useful process to conduct with groups is to take them through the preceding list and have them describe the pros and cons of each process. If you do this first with a group that's trying to decide how to make a decision, it will be much easier to decide which process is appropriate. No one process is right for every decision, as we shall see in the following sections.

UNANIMITY

Unanimity and consensus are often used interchangeably, but there are some important distinctions. Unanimity as a process usually occurs when everyone's first choice felicitously corresponds. Consensus is usually reached after a process of identifying everyone's needs and interests and looking for a creative solution that meets all of them. Consensus, then, is more often the *process* for reaching agreement whereas unanimity is the *result*.

The word *unanimous* comes from two Latin words: *unis,* meaning "one," and *animus,* meaning "spirit." In theory, a group that reaches unanimous agreement would proceed from one spirit. When a group commits to unanimity, they are agreeing everyone will converge and allow each person to have veto power. This means one person can delay the decision and prolong the decision-making process for hours, days, or even weeks. Conversely, some people may be reluctant to exercise this veto power and create delay. A group that decides to use unanimity is, in effect, committing to staying in dialogue until they reach an agreement that meets everyone's needs and interests.

The Latin root of *consensus* is *consentire,* which is a combination of two Latin words: *con,* meaning "with" or "together with" and *sentire,* meaning "to think and feel." *Consentire* means "to think and feel together."

Consensus is the participatory process through which a group thinks and feels together in order to reach a decision of unanimity. Unanimity is the point of closure for the group. Many groups say they use consensus even when they really use unanimity minus one, voting after a certain time has passed or 80 percent as an acceptable "consensus" point. In those groups, no one person has real veto power and yet a great effort is made to make sure all voices are heard. A true consensus would be 100 percent unanimity. Many business groups use a fallback consensus model where they agree to talk for a certain period of time and then if a consensus is not reached, the leader decides.

There is nothing wrong with deciding to use less than 100 percent consensus. What's important is to think carefully about the needs of the group, the particular decision involved, and then to make sure everyone in the group understands why that particular method was chosen.

Using consensus to reach unanimous agreement and obtain the best decision for all concerned may seem like a wonderful idea, but the reality of many groups struggling to do this may be quite different. One reason is a failure to assess when consensus should be appropriately used. A related reason may be a failure of understanding and training for the group in consensus decision-making. Some groups lack skilled leaders or facilitators who can guide them through the process. Another problem may arise when everyone says they "agree" to a certain proposal or solution yet they may mean different things—from enthusiastic support to "I just don't want to talk about this anymore."

The veto power of unanimity can also create problems for an inexperienced group or facilitator. If there's no skill at encouraging everyone to speak up, someone may drag out the discussion for days without surfacing the underlying issue. Others may refuse to agree when what they really mean is they still have questions or concerns that need to be answered. In other groups, some people may be reluctant to invoke the veto power because they don't want to feel responsible for prolonging the discussion. They may say, "I agree" when what they really mean is they don't want to take responsibility for holding the group back. Some solutions to these issues are presented in the next chapter.

The advantages to a unanimous decision reached through consensus is that everyone feels heard and the organization knows it has found a solution that is likely to be *sustainable*—one that will not have to be reversed and that meets everyone's needs and interests.

CONVINCING ARGUMENT

This solution favors the orators in the group and those who think and talk well on their feet. These people may or may not have the best solution for the individuals and the group. What they do have is a clear understanding of their own interests and a high level of ability to communicate their interests to the group.

The advantage of this method is that it tends to be quicker than consensus. Many people may feel reluctant to take on someone skilled in this kind of argument so they will quickly agree. Sometimes a group will get lucky and the most persuasive members will also be those who will happen upon the best solution for all concerned. Sometimes the issue is not important enough or so few people are affected that it's simply not worth a long discussion.

The problem is, if the issue is important to the group, this method of decision-making can create long-simmering resentments among those members who simply go along. They may dig in their heels or take a stand over seemingly petty issues. The leader or facilitator may find himself or herself quite confused as to why something seemingly trivial has erupted into a major dispute.

This method may also create problems for the group at the implementation stage. Some members may go along with the decision, but later indulge in delays, sabotage, forgetting, or other passive/aggressive techniques in order to interfere with implementation.

FOLLOWING A POPULAR LEADER

A strong and charismatic leader can often simplify decision-making by convincing a group to follow his or her lead. This works as long as the leader has a deep understanding of the different needs and interests of individuals and groups within the organization and an alignment with the best future for the organization.

Problems occur when a leader becomes removed from the individual needs of the group, especially when an organization grows. Then, no matter how enlightened the leader, he or she may make decisions that do not work well for all stakeholders. At this point, the group may experience the same kind of problems as those that result from one person using convincing argument.

COMPROMISE

Compromise is a process where everyone agrees to give up part of what they want in order to reach something that everyone can follow. What's interesting about this method is that many people view it as quite enlightened. Yet the reality is that it means everyone is settling for less than what they really want. This may mean no one is really happy since no one gets what he or she wants most.

The advantage is that there is less a sense of winners and losers since everyone gives something in order to come up with a solution.

IMPLICIT MAJORITY OR VOTING

This method means that majority rules. The advantage is that it's frequently quicker than the other methods and the result is that people become less frustrated with the decision-making process.

The disadvantages are that some people, departments, and groups are left out of the process and their needs and interests are not met. In addition, the group may not make the best decisions since the process doesn't seek to utilize all of the ideas, suggestions, and minds of the group. The whole idea of consensus decision-making is that the process requires everyone to think deeply about the problem, resulting in better quality and more innovative decisions. As the Quakers say, everyone has a piece of the truth. Putting the pieces together helps the group come up with a more creative, and ultimately more satisfying and sustainable decision, than the organization would have otherwise.

INTENSITY OF PREFERENCES

This decision-making method may be best when only a few people really care about a decision and the issue is relatively minor. There are some things in which many people simply have no stake. If this is the case for a particular issue, allowing the needs of these few to dominate may be a good solution. A leader or facilitator needs to be very skilled, however, to make sure the needs and interests of those who do not participate in the process are really minor and they don't care. In addition, for important issues, this method doesn't give the group everyone's best thinking to come up with the highest, most creative and best decision.

USING THE BEST PROCESS

Before making a decision, a leader or group needs to step back from the process and ask which method is the most appropriate for any particular decision. Make a list of the pros and cons of any particular method. You can then make an informed and thoughtful decision about which process best meets the needs of the group.

Paul C. Nutt, a professor of management at Ohio State University's Fisher College of Business, has been studying for 19 years the question of why smart companies make dumb decisions. Nutt's research focuses on how executives make decisions and whether those decisions succeed or fail. After examining strategic decisions at 356 companies, he found that half such decisions were abandoned, partially implemented, or never adopted. Nutt offers three ideas for making sure decisions will translate into action.[1]

First, his research yielded an overwhelming statistic so compelling that one wonders why any executive acts unilaterally except in the most extreme situations. When executives impose their ideas on the organizations, they frequently do so because they believe they're acting like "take-charge" leaders. Only 42 percent of the decisions that used this approach were actually adopted, Nutt found. When executives conferred with colleagues and rethought long-term priorities, they had a 96 percent success rate for decisions.

Next, keep exploring new options. Everyone likes a decisive leader, yet the business world is now so complex, being decisive can lead to leading blindly. When executives failed to investigate alternatives once they'd made a decision, 60 percent of those decisions were dropped or never adopted at all. Leaders need to constantly broaden their scope, Nutt advises. In the absence of asking the proverbial "What if?" a leader can unwittingly send his team and organizational performance plunging over a cliff to catastrophic results.

Third, we all have a piece of the truth. Only one fifth of the leaders Nutt interviewed consulted staffers when making decisions. Most ramrod their decisions through by persuasion (41 percent) or by edict (40 percent). Each approach usually failed. Persuasion failed in 53 percent of the cases; edict in 65 percent. Nutt stresses that the problem isn't just that decisions lack merit, it's that staffers resent the railroading. To counteract their feelings of impotence, underlings proceed to undermine their leaders by dragging their feet on implementation or using other passive-aggressive behaviors.

If you go through the process of evaluating which decision-making option to use and then train your group how to consider different options, the quality of your decisions will improve. If you're the leader, it will be important for you to model the openness that you're asking the others to follow.

RESISTING A PREMATURE URGE TO MERGE

To be creative and make the best decision, a group must first generate lots of options. Many factors, however, sometimes prevent this. A leader or facilitator may need to help the group resist the urge to prematurely merge. If the group's leader is overly directive, the group resists hearing outside opinions, the group experiences time pressures, or the group has a norm that defeats divergent thinking, the group may reach a decision too quickly.

Deadlines, if they're real, can concentrate the mind and help a group stay on task, but an artificial deadline can kill creativity and lead to bad decisions.

The tragic end for the U.S. space shuttle *Challenger*, in which six astronauts and the "teacher in space," were killed, may be partly due to time pressures in the decision-making process. Delayed once, the time window for another launch was closing. The leaders of the decision team were concerned about public and congressional perceptions of the entire space shuttle program and its continued funding. Today, the decision-makers wish they had taken more time to make the decision to launch and had listened to a few vocal dissenters.[2]

An overly directive leadership style can also discourage the pursuit of creative options, especially if a leader signals how he or she wants the group to converge at the outset. Group members may not want to risk their status with the leader by disagreeing. Most organizational histories contain at least one story about someone who challenged a leader and suffered the consequences.

When William Niskanen was chief economist at Ford Motor Co. in 1980, his free-trader views clashed with his superiors' new protectionism in the face of increasing Japanese competition. Niskanen was canned. CFO Will Caldwell explained to him, "In this company, Bill ..., the people who do well wait until they hear their superiors express their views. Then they add something in support of those views."[3] While times may have changed toward encouraging more diverse thinking, many groups still carry this unspoken message.

The leadership problem is compounded by the tendency of many leaders to favor quick thinking and quick decision-making. Creative group decisions, as we've discussed, take time. Effective decision-making requires a balance between exploration and speed.

MAKING A PACT WITH THE DEVIL

The perils of groupthink can be avoided by appointing a devil's advocate. President Kennedy, for example, took this tact by appointing his brother, Attorney General Bobby Kennedy, to serve in that role during critical policy decisions after the Bay of Pigs fiasco.

In the Roman Catholic tradition, a devil's advocate is an official of the Congregation of Rites whose duty is to point out defects in the evidence upon which the case for beatification or canonization rests. While it's a good practice to favor encouraging *everyone* to act as a critical thinker, challenging premature convergence, sometimes assigning a formal devil's advocate role is useful.

To be most effective, the devil's advocate must have the absolute support of the group leader rather than being a token. He or she should also be clear what the actual contrary decision is and should be able to act as if they totally believe in it. Finally, the role should rotate among group members to prevent the advocate from being a mere token and also to prevent the group from confusing the advocate with the devil himself!

In one study of team decision-making, for example, several groups of managers were formed to solve a complex problem.[4] Told that their performance would be judged by a panel of experts in terms of the quantity and quality of the solutions generated, the groups were identical in size and composition, with the exception that half of them included a "confederate." The researcher instructed this person to play the role of devil's advocate. This manager was to challenge the group's conclusions, forcing the others to critically examine their assumptions and the logic of their arguments. At the end of the problem-solving period, the experts compared the recommendations made by both groups.

Significantly, the groups with the devil's advocates had performed much better on the tasks. They generated more alternatives and their proposals were judged as superior.

After a short break, the groups reassembled and were told they would perform a similar task during the next session. Before they started discussing the next problem, however, the researchers gave them permission to eliminate one member. In every group containing the confederate, he or she was asked to leave. The fact that every high-performance group expelled their unique competitive advantage because that member made others feel uncomfortable speaks volumes about how most managers react to conflict, as one participant stated: "I know it has positive outcomes for the performance of the organization as a whole, but I don't like how it makes me feel personally."[5]

While this study was an experiment, the decision to expel the "devil" of an organization for being a "trouble maker" happens in real life. In 1984 Ross Perot sold Electronic Data Systems (EDS) to General Motors (GM) for $2.5 billion and immediately became GM's largest stockholder and a member of the board of directors. GM desperately needed EDS's expertise to update and coordinate its massive information system. Roger Smith, GM's chairman, thought that Perot's fiery "the crazy aunt in the attic" spirit would reinvigorate GM's stogy bureaucracy. Perot leapt into the fray and immediately started criticizing GM policy and practice. He squawked that it took longer for GM to produce a car than it took the country to win the Second World War. He lashed out at GM's bureaucracy, claiming it fostered conformity at the expense of results. By December of 1986, Roger Smith was fed up with Perot's "reinvigoration." GM paid dearly to exorcise its devil, giving Perot nearly twice the market value of his stock ($740) million to silence him and extract him from the board.[6]

Other CEOs have been more receptive to the concept of playing or receiving a devil's advocate. Such leaders establish norms that make spirited debate the rule rather than the exception. They also realize that making decisions is a process, not an event.

Chuck Knight, for example, for 27 years the CEO of Emerson Electric, accomplished this by relentlessly cross-examining managers during planning reviews, no matter what he actually believed about the proposal under review. He asked aggressive questions and expected intelligent responses. Knight dubbed the process the "logic of illogic" because of his willingness to test even thoughtful arguments by raising unexpected, and occasionally trivial, concerns. Yet his reign produced a steady stream of smart investment decisions and quarterly increases in income.[7]

Bob Galvin, CEO of Motorola in the 1980s, took a different tact. He constantly asked surprising hypothetical questions that stimulated innovative thinking. Subsequently, as chairman of the board of overseers for the Malcolm Baldridge National Quality Program, Galvin startled his fellow board members when, in response to a question about broadening the criteria for the award, he suggested narrowing them instead. After a lively discussion, the board did in fact broaden the criteria, but his unexpected suggestion sparked a creative and productive conflict.[8]

FOSTERING GOOD FIGHTS THAT LEAD TO GOOD DECISIONS

Good fights are fueled by clear discussions of the decision-making process. Many bad decisions arise from using the wrong process. Leaders must also model the openness necessary to convince participants that they haven't already made up their minds. Leaders or facilitators must also resist the early urge to merge, perhaps even enlisting the devil or his advocates when appropriate.

CHAPTER 19

GETTING TO YES WITHOUT GOING TO WAR: HOW TO BUILD CONSENSUS

> *In our present society the governing idea is that we can trust no one, and therefore, we must protect ourselves if we are to have any security in our decisions. The most we will be willing to do is compromise, and this leads to a very interesting way of viewing the outcome of working together. It means we are willing to settle for less than the very best— and that we will often have a sense of dissatisfaction with our decisions unless we can somehow outmaneuver others involved in the process.*

—Caroline Estés

In 1954 the U.S. Supreme Court rendered a landmark decision in the case of Brown v. Topeka Board of Education. *In a historic nine to zero vote, the Supreme Court shattered the notion of "separate but equal" and began untangling the web of racial segregation. In the hope of finding common ground, Chief Justice Earl Warren spent the five months between arguments and the issuance of the opinion cultivating consensus, repeatedly gathering the Justices to discuss the many issues involved in the case. To come to agreement, he went to lunch 20 times with one particular Justice. Chief Justice Warren believed adamantly that the country would be best served if the Court could render a clear and unanimous opinion—and his remarkable leadership in garnering that decision changed the course of history.*

Achieving true consensus is an arduous task that is often misunderstood by leaders. Gaining consensus is a process by which members of a group gather and agree to keep talking until they reach a solution that addresses the needs of all the stakeholders. It can be a time-consuming process that requires skilled facilitation, but can add significant gains in creativity and innovation.

Many organizations today want to use consensus in order to fully utilize the ideas and talents of all of their people. As explored in

Chapter 18, there are advantages and disadvantages to this approach. Consider the seven tools in the sections that follow if your group thinks it wants to use consensus.

STEP ONE: CONSIDER WHETHER CONSENSUS IS APPROPRIATE

First be sure you've considered how this decision should be made. Is consensus really required?

Many leaders tell me they "manage by consensus." Just their terminology always makes me question whether this is truly their approach. Consensus is not something that can be "managed." Usually, when leaders says this, what they mean is that they already have in mind an approach, but want to give their group the idea they are interested in their input. They will convene some kind of an open forum in order to go through the appearance of listening to other ideas. This approach can backfire since, although people may be enthusiastic the first time this occurs, they will soon realize something else is going on.

One of my clients, for example, asked me to help them revamp their group brainstorming process. Although this large financial institution had effectively utilized this method to design creative financial packages in the past, as the company grew, the process stalled. Debates dragged on endlessly, participation waned, and people groaned when invited to participate in a meeting using their brainstorming methodology. When they brought me in, they thought the problem was that newer people didn't understand the system or the ground rules. After I interviewed the executive team and watched one of their meetings, however, the true problem emerged.

The CEO, Rich, oozed charisma and power. He'd started the company with little more than a few thousand dollars and a dream, and built it into a billion dollar deal shop. All eyes swiveled toward him whenever anyone made a comment or offered a suggestion. Although he declared he valued the process of group decision-making and the creativity inherent in working through the process, Rich's face gave him away. Raised eyebrows or rolled eyes instantly signaled his lack of enthusiasm for what someone said. Most participants felt sure that Rich had made up his mind before the meeting, but wanted to create the illusion of participatory decision making by leading them through the process. He fooled no one. Consequently, his employees saw no point in going through the motions.

Sometimes a leader is a bit more sincere in the process. He or she has a basic approach outlined, but will listen if someone comes up with an idea or objection that has not been considered. In either event, this is not a true consensus.

A true consensus means going in with an open mind in order to consider all the needs and interests of the entire group. The group agrees to keep talking until a solution that truly addresses all of the needs and interests of all stakeholders has been reached. This is a time-consuming process.

It also requires each member of the group take the responsibility of speaking up in order to make sure the group hears their concerns as well as truly listening to the issues of others. Consensus requires each member to give up their beloved positions and focus on under-lying needs. Most groups need a fair amount of training, discussion, and practice in order to make this work successfully.

STEP TWO: FOCUS ON NEEDS AND INTERESTS, NOT POSITIONS

Be sure that you start by identifying needs and interests of each group member and avoid positions, as we've discussed in previous chapters.

This step requires each member of the group to take seriously the difference between positions and needs and interests outlined in Chapter 11. They need to avoid positions, which are predetermined solutions to the problem, and focus instead on meeting the needs and interests of each person, department, or group. The process takes a lot of active listening and creativity.

STEP THREE: USE A FACILITATOR

Consider using a facilitator for contentious meetings so that everyone can be heard and so that all interested parties can participate. This is this best way to help the group recognize that everyone has a piece of the truth.

Ideally, a facilitator is a disinterested party who has no stake in the outcome. Such a person can come from outside the organization or from another department or group. Their job is to focus on the group process—to make sure the group is focusing on solving the problem and not getting distracted on personality issues. A professional facilitator can also stay alert for process problems and solutions, which also frees the leader from the role of running the meeting so that he or she can join in the discussion and participate.

One tool that facilitators find useful is to have each member use laminated, color-coded strips of paper they hold up when they want to speak or express agreement or disagreement with another speaker. Especially with large groups, this helps the facilitator keep track of what's happening and quickly "read" the group. Similar strips can also be used to keep track of group process. One side of the strip can be used to express an opinion and the other side to raise process issues. Especially for members of the group who may have much to offer, but who do not feel comfortable speaking up in meetings, this process can help them contribute to the group in a non-threatening way.

Some strips I have used successfully with groups (the left side below is for decisions/the right for expressing process concerns):

> **Green**—I agree with the proposal/with what's being expressed.
>
> **Blue**—I'm neutral about the proposal/I have a question or comment.
>
> **Orange**—I have an individual (as opposed to a group) concern about the proposal/I have an individual question or comment.
>
> **Red**—Veto; I believe the proposal harms the organization/ Stop the process; there is something about the way we're discussing this issue that harms the organization.

Using these strips allows the facilitator to easily read where the group is on an issue. A facilitator can also use the strips to take straw polls on a particular issue and to keep track of who wants to speak.

Facilitating a successful meeting involves skill and art. An outside, experienced facilitator can bring many different process ideas to a group. This frees the group from process concerns to focus solely on creativity solving the problem.

For example, one exercise I use as a facilitator is to post various suggestions around the room after a brainstorming session. I then allow the participants to circulate around the room with colored markers, marking the ones they agree with and writing down questions or concerns. In addition to allowing the group to move around the room, which tends to increase creative thinking, this process helps those who have trouble speaking up.

Always remember when conducting meetings that the fear of public speaking is the number one fear of many people—second only to drowning! This fear manifests for many creative people in large and small group meetings. What this means is that you miss the creative energy of people who have that particular style of interaction.

"Everyone has a piece of the truth" is an old Quaker saying. The Quakers, who have perfected the art of consensus decisions, know that it takes many different perspectives in order to come up with the best solutions to any particular problem. They acknowledge and know the power of group wisdom to solve any problem and realize that no one person can do it alone. When the group is stuck or polarized in any creative problem-solving session, this is a good way to encourage the group to think differently.

Calcified positions are frequently the result of someone assuming their way is the only way. Sometimes just stopping the process and reminding the group of this issue is helpful.

STEP FOUR: CONDUCT A WRITTEN SURVEY

When you know an issue is likely to be contentious, consider first conducting a written survey.

Ask for the parties' thoughts on the subject and about their individual, department, or group needs and interests. Avoid asking for positions, decisions, or solutions at this stage. Avoid backing people into positions; allow for "wiggle room" and creative group solutions. Written surveys allow people to think carefully and individually rather than to take positions in a group meeting.

Again, this suggestion helps bring forth the creativity, thoughts, and ideas of each group member. Many people communicate better through the written word than in meetings. It's also true that many people do not think well on their feet.

Written surveys also encourage people to think before they speak. After living with my then husband for 20 years, who tends to be a brilliant, absent-minded professor kind of introvert, I've come to learn the value of thinking before talking. This was a revelation to me. I used to be the kind of person that if you asked me a question, I would answer it. I may or may not know the answer, but I always had an opinion and wouldn't hesitate to express my views. As an extrovert, I tend to feel left out of meetings if I'm not talking.

Because of the work I do, and because of my research and understanding on the way personality style impacts conflict, I've learned to think before I talk (at least most of the time). Written surveys, through paper or e-mail, force those of us who tend to speak first to slow down and think about the issue. It also allows the leader or facilitator to retrieve the valuable thoughts of those who are more comfortable expressing themselves in a written format.

Sometimes it is helpful to tabulate all or part of the survey and distribute it before the meeting. Sometimes you may not want to take that step. Tabulated written surveys offer the advantage of allowing everyone to see what others are thinking. The disadvantage is that tabulation may serve to deter people from expressing thoughts that are outside the mainstream when you actually have a meeting. There's no right or wrong answer to this issue other than to think carefully before you do—or do not—tabulate the results and distribute them.

In some cases, written surveys can also help you formulate, eliminate, or expand the issues that need to be discussed. Often, especially if an issue is controversial or emotional, you may need to limit the discussion to just a piece of the issue.

In mediation, we call this eating the elephant bite by bite. Sometimes a group needs to experience success in coming to agreement upon a part of the issue before moving on to something larger. Sometimes the leader or a facilitator, after studying the written surveys, will realize that a meeting is unnecessary. Sometimes a new issue or a different way of framing the question will emerge.

In any event, formulating the problem successfully can make all the difference in the outcome of the discussion.

STEP FIVE: FORM SUBGROUPS

If it appears that only some people in a meeting are polarized and positioned, ask them to form an ad hoc team or subgroup.

This suggestion can be extremely successful for bringing together a polarized group. At the end of a meeting to discuss a particular problem, you may realize that the group is hopelessly deadlocked. You may be able to identify certain people who seem to be the most intractable. Appointing these people to work together as an ad hoc team or subgroup can help.

Encourage the most polarized and opinionated members to go through a consensus building process on their own and to make recommendations to the entire group. This gives the subgroup ownership of both the problem and the solution. It also forces them to work together. Make sure they understand the rules from this book or other resources you want them to follow. Also encourage them to first agree upon how they will agree. If the polarized parties can converge upon a solution, the rest of the group will be likely to follow their recommendations.

Be prepared for some surprises. I have watched some groups go through this process and have seen interesting results. Sometimes the members of the polarized group have long-simmering conflicts. When forced to work together to present a solution to the group, they sometimes form new alliances. The remainder of the group—

accustomed to those members carrying all the various objections of the group—starts squabbling among themselves or sometimes even objects to the ad hoc group's proposed solution, surprising the leader who thought the formerly silent group members had little interest in the issue.

I have seen leaders inexperienced with true consensus give up at this point, convinced that "this consensus stuff doesn't work." The reality is that the process is working beautifully. The leader has now forced everyone to play his or her true hand. Rather than allowing some members of the group to remain silent and forcing the more noisy members to raise all the issues, more people are taking responsibility for speaking up and voicing their own previously hidden needs and interests. Now the leader and the group can go on to craft a solution that truly meets everyone's needs, even though that process may take longer than expected.

STEP SIX: ALLOW SUFFICIENT TIME

Building a true consensus takes extra time on the front end, but avoids time-wasting and foot-dragging as well as many other negative consequences on the back end. As a leader or group trying to decide if true consensus is necessary or desirable, you need to constantly ask whether you can make the necessary time available. Failure to do so can contribute to the entire process going awry.

If people have legitimate interests that are being ignored, the only way to make sure they are met is to force people to go through a true consensus process. Otherwise you are left guessing about their concerns. If they have substantive interests that are discounted in the final solution, these issues will rebound to haunt you. People will delay acting upon necessary implementation steps for the solution, they will raise procedural objections and even sabotage the enactment of the proposal. Forcing everyone to consider the best solution for the organization and all concerned on the front end may ultimately save you time.

It can be hard to remember this when you're in the midst of the endless discussions frequently required to reach a true consensus. As a member of a co-housing community (a community built for neighborhood interaction) that makes all decisions by consensus, I've had many painful experiences around this issue. Patience is not my strong suit. I sometimes want to scream in frustration at my fellow community members. Since I frequently do not care about the underlying substance of the decision, I want to jump in and push for a decision, any decision, just to get it over with so we can stop talking about the issue. Yet, I have seen many creative and sustainable solutions come from this process.

For example, many of the parents in the community thought we should cover all the window wells in order to prevent injury to small children. Nonparents objected, citing the need for light and air in the basement rooms. The discussion dragged on for months. Subgroups formed, fumed, and met. Finally, when we were all ready to throw up our hands and admit defeat, Bob, a skilled carpenter, designed a window covering out of strong plastic mesh. The covering protected wayward toddlers yet allowed in light and air. Problem solved.

Many of my business clients experience frustration with the slow process of consensus, which is why I also counsel them to consider whether a true consensus is really required or wise. Once they decide it is, I advise them to take a deep breath and wait out the process.

One book that has helped me increase my own patience with the process is *A Different Drum: Community Building and Peace*, by Scott Peck, in which he profiles many different types of business and community organizations that use consensus. He profiles one spiritual residential community of monks he followed through more than 20 years of successful group living. On one important issue, it took the community an entire year to reach consensus. He (and the community) viewed this as a successful solution.

In our modern world, we want decisions now. The Internet age has contributed to our impatience. In addition, many people feel businesses, in order to compete, need to be able to change directions quickly.

I don't disagree with this assessment of the modern, global climate. Yet I still think there's much room for thought on many decisions. Many quickly made decisions have to later be reversed, resulting in huge losses of time and money. Taking the time to reach a true consensus on the front end can save you later on.

Think back to the time and skill Earl Warren used to reach a true consensus on the Supreme Court. Such diplomacy pays off in the end.

STEP SEVEN: EDUCATE YOUR PEOPLE

Before you begin, it's useful to educate your group about the pros, cons, and processes involved in consensus decision-making.

Many problems with so-called consensus decision-making could be avoided if people were educated in the true meaning of consensus, how and when to use a facilitator, group process, and the realistic time required for the process. When people do not understand basic concepts of consensus building such as everyone has a piece of the truth and the difference between needs and interests, they will simply continue to use their old tools in a new process. You can avoid this problem by educating them about consensus and sharing with them the theories and tools of this book.

WHAT DO WE MEAN BY AGREEMENT?

Many times, a manager or leader will stress that he or she wants a "consensus," "everyone's agreement," or "everyone's buy-in" on an idea. Yet, many times those same leaders have left a meeting to discover that everyone's agreement was not what they thought.

Saying, "I agree" with the proposal may mean many things, including any of the following:

"This is great! I can't wait to get started."

"I'd agree to anything right now. I'm sick of discussing this issue."

"I'll go along to get along."

"It's better than the alternatives I've seen, but it doesn't really address my issues."

Similarly, saying, "I disagree" may also mean different things to different people. It may mean:

"Wait! I haven't had time to digest the idea and decide what I think."

"I'm angry with you. I'd disagree with any proposal you have at this point."

"This offends my core values."

"I like another proposal better."

"I would agree if we could change one minor part."

Groups create confusion when they don't take the time to sort out all of these variables that describe, "I agree" and "I disagree." This may result in stalemates or in groups agreeing to proposals that are never implemented or are actively sabotaged.

To avoid this problem, after you think you have agreement about a proposal, consider using a "variables of agreement scale." This scale allows participants to rate their agreement with the proposal from enthusiastic endorsement through the middle ground of abstention to blocking the proposal.

Not all agreements require the enthusiastic support of the entire group. Such support is essential when the stakes are high, when the decision is not easily reversible, or when the issue has been difficult to solve. Groups may also want enthusiastic support of issues where there is a need for a stakeholder buy-in on the issue or if there's a need to empower group members because the members will be expected to use their own judgment and creativity to implement the decision. Such decisions require that each member understand the reasoning behind that decision.

Enthusiastic support is often necessary, for example, for major strategic initiatives, new business ventures, or major changes in the goals or direction of an organization.

A less important decision around day-to-day tactics or when fewer members of the group are involved in implementation would require less support. A way to determine how much "agreement" you really have about an issue is to have people assess their standing on the scale in the following section.

VARIABLES OF AGREEMENT

When you finally believe you have a true consensus, you need to test it against the variables of agreement scale.

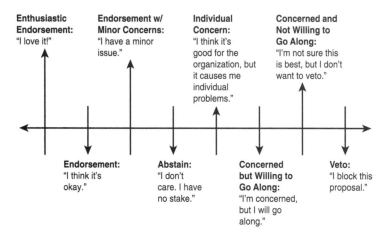

Variables of agreement. (Adapted with permission from Kaner, Sam. Facilitator's Guide to Participatory Decision-Making. *Gabriola Island, BC: New Society Publishing, 1996)*

A facilitator, either through polling the individuals, having them mark on a scale, or asking for a show of different-colored cards responding to the scale, can quickly see if the argument is solid and how sustainable the agreement is. By recording the results and presenting them to the group, this scale allows the group to see whether the agreement has the degree of support the group needs.

For example, I worked with a team of executives for a large corporation who were polarized over the direction of the company. While new business was strong, their initial undercapitalization had taken its toll over the years and they were short of cash. Some of the leaders wanted to continue to aggressively seek new markets, others wanted to pull back and wait. After going through a consensus process where the CEO pushed prematurely for a decision, we asked everyone to fill out the "Variables of Agreement" Scale. It soon became apparent to the CEO that he had lukewarm support at best. He decided to go back to discussing options until he had a stronger agreement, realizing that such an important decision required a stronger consensus of the group. Although the discussions raged over several weeks, and were at times quite frustrating, they finally hammered out an acceptable plan.

CHAPTER 20

SURFING THE WAVES OF CONFLICT: HOW TO MANAGE WHEN THE CONFLICT TIDE REFUSES TO RECEDE

I don't give them hell. I just tell them the truth and they think it's hell.

—Harry S. Truman

Steve Miller gazes out the window of his office with folded arms. A reformed pit bull, he's not a man comfortable with defeat. He's done everything the conflict resolution specialist they hired suggested: mediated with his team, listened endlessly to their concerns about the restructuring, even informed his team that they were facing discipline if they couldn't manage their differences. Nothing worked. All the talking and worrying feels like a waste of Steve's valuable time and effort.

"Surfing the waves of conflict" is a term I've borrowed from veteran community facilitator Rob Sandelin. As readers of this book may have guessed by now, I'm an optimist when it comes to managing conflict. I truly believe that we can meet the seemingly conflicting needs of most people most of the time if we're simply willing to put enough time and effort into the process.

Sadly, however, even I have to admit that some conflicts stay stuck despite our most valiant attempts. This may be because the other parties simply won't participate at the level we need in order to work our way through the issue or because our true needs and interests are ultimately incompatible. In that situation, what do you do?

Sandelin suggests an interesting alternative, "conflict surfing." He offers the idea that while some conflicts truly are not resolvable, you can "surf them with agility and understand the wave as you ride it."

Sandelin's suggestion points to intriguing solutions. While resolution may not provide the neat solution we'd hoped, we can both surf and understand the wave of the disagreement. Surfing skillfully can in itself lead to solutions, although not those we'd originally planned.

WHAT IS A SOLUTION?

Sometimes, the reason we can't resolve a conflict creatively is that we're sure we know what the solution *should* be. One way of surfing is to drop back from the waves into calmer seas while we consider whether our view of what "resolution" looks like is too narrow.

In my personal life, I've had this experience many times. As my then husband and I struggled to save our marriage, for example, we both thought that resolving the issues would lead to keeping our family together—a solution we both thought that we wanted. Yet the longer we wrestled with our unique and challenging situation, the more we came to the sad conclusion that we had no common ground for keeping the marriage together. We both adored our two children, however, and were passionately committed to their welfare.

We hashed out a plan that put their needs first. We would keep our house in the community where our kids felt safe and happy. John and I would move in and out, sharing time and duties equally with the children.

The children stayed put in the neighborhood and school. Little about their life changed, except that they no longer enjoyed the company of both of us at the same time. For now, we've spared them the disruption of traipsing between two households. We also maintain a strict policy of not discussing our differences in front of the children or using them as cannon fodder in the war over our private feelings. We share dinner together as a "bi-nuclear family" about once a week and hold a family meeting afterwards where everyone has a chance to raise issues and share concerns.

While the situation involves complex logistics and continual negotiation, our children are responding well to what could have been a tragic outcome. Obviously, this solution would not work for every family. The arrangement succeeds for us mainly because I travel frequently for business and John stays in the house when I'm out of town. Also, we're both flexible about trying to accommodate everyone's needs and interests and we've maintained a level of caring and good will for each other even though we're divorced. We've also managed to continue to put our children first. As my daughter, Elizabeth, responded one day when I asked how she felt about the divorce, that "it doesn't hurt *my* feelings."

While I'm sure that someday she will be more in touch with the impact our divorce will ultimately have on her life, for now, we have managed to "surf the divorce wave" in a way that—while not resolving the marriage—did reorganize our family in a way that works for everyone (even though the original conflict was not resolvable in the traditional way).

LAST-DITCH QUESTIONS

Sometimes we can move a conflict that feels hopeless by asking what I call "last-ditch questions." These questions may help raise doubt in the minds of the parties about whether clinging to their own views is really in their best interest. Asking what mediators call "reality testing" questions can sometimes help bring parties back to the table, or at least help them surf the waves if they walk away. Doubt can be useful because by walking away, the parties are assuming that they have better options waiting. If we can raise the specter of doubt, we may help them see when that isn't true.

If you're mediating between warring factions, ask the questions alone with each party. If you're negotiating with someone else, try to raise these issues in a way that sounds truly open-ended and curious. The most common reality testing questions are:

- What do you think *I* will do if we don't reach agreement?
- What do you think *you* will do if we don't reach agreement?
- What advice would *you give me* if we don't reach agreement?

Here are some additional queries mediation expert Christopher W. Moore recommends in his book, *The Mediation Process*[1]:

- Do you think you can win in court (or other public setting such as before a commission or in the legislature)?
- How certain are you? 90 percent? 75 percent? 50 percent?
- What risks are you willing to take?
- What if you lose?
- What will your life be like then?
- What impact do you think your victory in court (or other arena) will have on your ongoing relationship with the other party?
- Will you ever be able to work together again?
- Who else might be affected?
- What would they think of your position?
- Would you be proud to publicly announce this stance?
- Would others whom you respect feel it is reasonable?
- If you were in the other party's place and this proposal were made to you, would you accept it?
- Could you accept it over the long run?

These questions help educate the other side about the reality of walking away. Lee Iacocca skillfully used these kinds of queries when Chrysler Corporation was facing bankruptcy in 1979. As he tried to negotiate with Congress for a loan guarantee of the bailout, most legislatures refused to even discuss the issue because they didn't believe that the government should rescue private businesses.

As the Congressional hearings progressed, Iacocca educated the legislators by examining what would happen if they refused his proposal. He asked, for example: "Would this country really be better off if Chrysler folded and the nation's unemployment rate went up another half of one percent overnight? Would free enterprise really be served if Chrysler failed and tens of thousands of jobs were lost abroad?"

Focusing on what it would cost the government in unemployment insurance and welfare payments if they laid everyone off, he said: "You guys have a choice. Do you want to pay the $2.7 billion now, or do you want to guarantee half that amount with a good chance of getting it all back?"

Gradually, Congress realized how many people in their own districts depended upon Chrysler work. Iacocca walked away with his requested $1.5 billion loan guarantee.[2]

If we ask these kinds of questions with care and curiosity, we may be able to move someone to keep talking. At the least, I find, it will help us go forward with a better understanding of the other party or parties' issues and helps us surf the wave of an irresolvable situation.

As a part of the process, we also need to ask ourselves the same questions. This requires that we know our own "exit point," the point at which it makes more sense for us to walk away than to continue to expend energy in trying to creatively manage the conflict with the other parties. We can do a cost benefit analysis of staying or "voting with our feet." Yet we need to constantly test our exit strategy with these kinds of queries to make sure that leaving is the best option. Sometimes just reminding ourselves that we're not trapped can help us continue the work of creative conflict management.

MOBILIZE THE THIRD FORCE

If you're sinking under the waves of conflict, consider mobilizing what negotiation expert William Ury calls "The Third Force." The third force may be team members who have an interest in the conflict, although not one as intense as the parties who have been striving to manage the situation. This is one time where triangulation may be appropriate. Try to find out if others can influence the parties to keep working toward a solution. Try to enlist them in opening up the minds of people who seem closed to creativity.

The third force can also be some external authority such as the party's boss, a judge, or arbitrator. Someone with power in the situation may be able to engage the parties in a way that you have not been able to do. Many times, for example, a judge will recognize that the parties have not reached a settlement and so will bring the parties together and either indicate a solution that favors one party, bringing the other back to the table, or hint at a solution that neither party finds favorable.

If you're mediating between workplace combatants, their boss may be able to remind them that creatively resolving conflict is in their job description.

On the world stage, there's been no better example of this strategy than the Dalai Lama. Forced to flee Tibet with his countrymen after the brutal Chinese take-over, and realizing that negotiation with the Chinese government would be futile, he has managed over the years to mobilize the press and many political supporters for the idea of restoring Tibet. While the Chinese have not yet relented, they have softened their stance on many issues. Clearly the Dalai Lama is able to do what many of us are not: Take the long view. While he's frequently stated that he understands that a solution may not be imminent, perhaps not even in his lifetime, he's never given up hope that one may someday arrive.

The third force, then, can be the media or a political constituency that shares your interests. I once consulted with a group of women in a major corporation, for example, who were unhappy with the progress of women in the company. After many negotiations about the issues with upper management failed, they formed an ongoing "Women of 'ABC' Corp," group in order to continue to address their issues. They contacted the local paper and had a reporter attend their meetings. Stories started to filter out into other media. Eventually, the CEO asked to meet with representatives of the group and founded a successful women's initiative to speak to their concerns.

In using the third force, however, be sure that you've explored all your other options. Triangulating or going public with your concerns can sometimes back the other parties into a corner and thwart your ultimate goal of creatively managing the conflict. Yet used as a strategy when you've exhausted all other options, it can sometimes produce effective results. At a minimum, it will remind you that you always have the power to control your own options—including your own exit plot.

CONSIDER UNILATERAL ACTION

If all of our attempts to convince, cajole, or persuade others to participate in a way that creatively manages the conflict fail, we can take the responsibility for dealing with our piece of the puzzle, even if no one else will play the game by our rules.

You always retain the power to take unilateral action. Most of the strategies we've discussed so far in this book require a certain amount of willingness and cooperation on the part of our co-workers in order to change the organization. Sometimes, however, people may promise to change while dragging their heels on actually doing so. Even so, you have more power than you might expect as a single individual. You can still incubate positive change. By modeling for others the changes you would like to see in them, you can be effective in increasing your influence on the organization.

I worked with Bill, a young vice president of a pharmaceutical corporation. The company had recently merged with a much larger organization, creating layers of bureaucracy that both Bill and his group resisted. At some point, Bill realized his team's own actions were undermining its effectiveness, and he decided to persuade his fellows to abandon their protest. His words fell on deaf ears. They didn't budge. He tried again. They dug their heels in farther. He circled back for another round. They shunned him. Finally, he briefly flirted with the idea of firing the entire lot. The momentary respite of that fantasy gave him the will to try something else, something more subtle. He stopped talking and just acted. Calmly, without a word, he just changed his own behavior and abandoned the notion of changing the group's approach.

Bill followed the rules the new ownership demanded. When appropriate, he continued to advise his team of his own decisions to "go with the flow." He dealt with his employees, as well as his supervisors, in a fair and even-handed manner, avoiding the politics and passive/aggressive sabotage that some of his teammates delivered. He stopped lecturing his group on how they needed to follow his example and surrender to the enemy. He remained a calm and cheerful example of leadership.

Gradually, his employees adjusted and followed his lead. Although they continued to insist that they liked the old regime better, they slowly adapted to the new ways. Their resistance melted in droplets, but as they say, "the rock will wear away."

Today, Bill is an executive vice president and his team leads the world in sales for their global conglomerate. While people sometimes still talk about the "good old days," they don't actively resist the efforts and directives of headquarters. In five years it's likely that they'll end up referring to these times as the good old days, too!

While one individual may not be able to change a whole system, you can always control your own behavior within the system and whether you continue to work for the organization. When you give up fighting with the other combatants without expecting that they change, you inspire by example, instead of convincing by argument.

As you take on the role of leading in this way, it helps to tell your co-workers what to expect and then to be sure that you act in step with those expectations. Make sure you use "I" statements and talk only about your own behavior, instead of the behavior of others. Also outline the ways in which you will change, instead of asking for others to change or focusing on their past behavior.

For your own sanity, give up hoping that others will appreciate your efforts. They may someday, but in the meantime, if you're using unilateral action, you need to attend to our own business. If you do notice tiny changes in the direction you want others to move, appreciate their efforts, no matter how small. Last but certainly not least, spend some time thinking about why the system seems so resistant to change and what kinds of healthier systems you could encourage.

One of my clients, Diana, an HR manager who has a long-running feud with John, a marketing director, used this technique. John had continually ignored and even sabotaged various HR policies that he considered a waste of his time and energy. Diana, however, had to deal with an indignant parade of employees who disliked John's management style. She tried to persuade John that he was violating good management practices, as well as company policy. No matter what approach she tried, he rebuffed her efforts.

After talking with me, she devised a new plan. Trapped in a no-win game, Diana caught John working late one night and informed him that she was no longer going to harangue him about the problems he was causing employees. She realized that he didn't want or seem to need her advice and so she would stop the campaign. Diana told him that she would inform employees that John would be handling his own HR problems henceforth. She explained her new policy without anger and advised John that she was open to suggestions about how they could make their relationship work better.

For once, John was shocked into silence. While not willing to initially acknowledge her efforts, over time, as employee complaints started landing on his desk, he started to seek Diana out for advice and counsel. Today, while Diana still ruefully describes John as one of her "problem children," the unilateral truce seems to be working.

While such disarmament may appear to demonstrate weakness during the throes of battle, it can actually lead to a more lasting peace than continuing a futile fight.

There are many examples in history of unilateral action that has resulted in creative conflict management. In 1948, for example, after the end of World War II, Soviet leader Joseph Stalin blockaded West Berlin, insisting that Allied troops leave the city. The Western Allies considered blasting through the blockade with an armed convoy but feared starting World War III. Instead, they choose the unilateral action of mounting a huge airlift of food and supplies to the isolated Berliners. Frustrated, Stalin called off the blockade and agreed to negotiate.

Sometimes we can use skillful words to turn a stalled situation around. During the American Civil War, for example, President Lincoln spoke sympathetically about the Southern rebels in a public address. Fully aware that he would need to try to unite the country after the war, he started the process of healing with his own unilateral action. When a staunch Unionist lambasted him for speaking kindly of his enemies when he should be destroying them, Lincoln answered with his classic reply: "Why, madam, do I not destroy my enemies when I make them my friends?"

Unilateral disarmament can be preferable to a forced settlement. Many historians believe, for example, that forcing unacceptable terms on the Germans after World War I helped fuel World War II. One of the conditions the Axis insisted upon in the Treaty of Versailles was staggering reparations to pay for the costs of the war. The payments devastated the value of the German Mark. Cartoonists during that time, for example, depicted German housewives using wheelbarrows of essentially worthless marks to buy a loaf of bread.

Most of the world had such revulsion to the idea of another war that they pinned all their hopes for a future peace on the League of Nations, the predecessor of today's United Nations. Yet the forced—and many believe untenable—settlement of World War I allowed Hitler to gain power and helped spark World War II.

Sometimes the best unilateral action is to walk away. That's what schoolteacher Christine Pelton decided. After discovering that nearly a fifth of her biology students had plagiarized their semester projects from the Internet, the Piper, Kansas, teacher sought and received the backing of the district to fail the 28 sophomores. Yet after parents complained, the school board reversed the decision. Her integrity at stake, Pelton resigned when she couldn't convince the board to change their stance. "The students no longer listened to what I had to say," she said. "They knew if they didn't like anything in my classroom from here on out, they can just go to the school board and complain."[3]

Pelton didn't feel that she could maintain her own honest standards if she stayed. In this case, the costs to her own personal integrity would have been too great. When conflict violates our own sense of self and what's most important to our identity, sometimes the best solution is to walk away.

When all your other frantic efforts at conflict management have simply whipped up the waves, consider grabbing your board and going surfing. Surfing can involve paddling away from the conflict forever, if necessary, as in quitting a job or firing an uncooperative employee. Surfing can also involve asking the last ditch questions or considering unilateral actions. Sometimes surfing means hanging in the midst of conflict for longer than you anticipate, but still riding the waves as skillfully as the Dalai Lama, instead of expecting the waters to recede.

While you're contemplating your options, keep in mind the power of culture to incubate eagles, the subject we return to in the last chapter.

CHAPTER 21

SAVING AN ENDANGERED SPECIES: HOW TO INCUBATE EAGLES

> *It's okay to spend a lot of time arguing about which route to take to San Francisco when everyone wants to end up there, but a lot of time gets wasted in such arguments if one person wants to go to San Francisco and another secretly wants to go to San Diego.*

—Steve Jobs, Apple Computers

Joe Dishman spent six years working endless hours as an associate in a major law firm. His track record and work ethic were impeccable; his personality was not. He was a notorious pit bull. Nonetheless, the other partners felt Joe's results spoke for themselves and they rewarded him by making him a partner. Joe's new position only made his bulldog personality worse. Associates quit because of his aggressive barking and partners avoided him. Finally, Joe became so miserable he sought help. Slowly, he began a metamorphosis by trying new communication tools in small interactions. Joe made the comeback of his career, becoming an eagle in his firm. Rifts with partners were healed. He became a mentor to young associates. He could disagree without it becoming a personal grudge. His influence, power, and happiness grew exponentially.

The workplace has undergone dramatic shifts in the last several decades, which require employees to embrace an inclusive culture. Successful, cutting-edge organizations are thinking out of the box, turning obstacles into opportunities and capitalizing on the strengths of a diverse workforce—they are creating eagles. If your organization wants to join the ranks of the "best practice" companies, it is incumbent that staff members are skilled at creatively managing conflict and that they engender a culture of inclusiveness that is solution oriented. Creating a strong culture fosters a team environment that can give the organization tremendous synergy. However, without such a culture, the company can fall prey to unproductive conflicts that will reduce effectiveness, profits, and performance.

LEADERS AND THE POWER OF CULTURE

A client—the CEO of a high-tech company—recently called me. For several years my company had provided consulting and training services to his company. He finally decided to fire Frank, his CFO—a technically brilliant man who was lacking in "people skills." Employees constantly carped about the CFO's abusive, abrupt, and intimidating manner.

When the CEO delivered the news that he could no longer defend the manager against the rising tide of employee complaints (and even one pending lawsuit), Frank's surprised response is typical of many I hear in today's workplace: "In some companies, my style would be considered an advantage! People around here are just too sensitive!"

Another client decided to upgrade the computer department in his company from data management to a true information technology department. On the advice of a headhunter, he hired someone from a large computer firm, an old-fashioned hierarchical company. The ensuing cultural wars shocked my CEO client. Long-time employees reacted with anger and tears to the dictatorial regime of the new manager. The CEO found he had no time to run his thriving and complex company. Instead, his days were spent trying to mediate disputes among the new manager, his team, and other departments.

A third client reorganized its large HR department and brought in several new players to invigorate the team. The result? Another culture clash! The old team insisted workers need HR representatives who are *employee advocates*. The new managers wanted to move up the ladder of corporate success. They were convinced the way to do that was to raise the visibility of HR and make HR representatives *business partners* with the leaders of their business units. When I came in to facilitate a session to creatively manage this dispute, some of the people were not even speaking to one another.

What is the common denominator in all of these situations? The leaders in these organizations had not spent enough time and energy thinking about *culture*—that invisible glue that holds organizations together and determines organizational effectiveness. Especially lacking was a failure to think about how they want the culture to address and creatively manage the inevitable and valuable conflicts each organization faces on a daily basis. A lack of agreement about a common culture frequently shows up as constant and unproductive conflicts.

I'm amazed that even somewhat successful organizations have spent so little time thinking about what kind of culture they want to create and what kind of employees will assist them in building that culture as well as how to shape, deliver, and reinforce that message. A clear culture can become an organization's brand: a powerful tool in attracting and retaining top talent. The executive team may have spent a few hours working on a superficial and platitudinous mission statement they then proceed to plaster on the walls of employee lunch rooms and insert into the employee manual, but the kind of culture I'm talking about will only result from two things:

1. Top leaders walking the talk
2. Constantly engaging employees in ongoing discussions about culture

When organizations take the time to do this kind of work, the culture they want to create becomes what Margaret Wheatley, in her book, *Leadership and the New Science*, calls a "field of vision"—a powerful structuring field where certain types of individual behavior and events are guaranteed. Such a structuring field is especially important in communicating how you want people to manage conflict. All of the organizational research has shown that culture is one of the most important factors in creating a healthy, long-lasting company.

In order to shape the future, leaders need to encourage other leaders and serve as models to create energy fields that shape organizational culture, especially how they model and value conflict management. Wheatley sees leaders as "broadcasters, talk radio beacons of information, pulsing out messages everywhere … stating, clarifying, discussing, modeling, filling all of the space with the messages we care about."[1]

Leading in the future will require even the best executives to acquire new skills. The old order in the workplace is clearly crumbling, but the new has not yet emerged. In between, a great many misunderstandings occur. If not skillfully managed, these misunderstandings escalate into unproductive conflicts.

For example, I was asked to conduct a diversity project for a major law firm. They had gone through a number of steps of the project over a series of months, but kept putting off the one key phase: having a series of focus groups with partners and associates to help us determine the issues we'd need to address in diversity trainings. When I finally met with the Executive Committee to find out why they kept dragging their feet on scheduling those meetings, the chairman blurted out:

> But we don't want some of our partners meeting with associates. They're idiots. They'll say all the wrong things! They'll make the associates want to leave! They just don't understand these issues. In fact, I don't even like them. I haven't talked to some of them in years.

Now this is an interesting way to run a law firm, but it doesn't lead to productivity, teamwork, and profitability. It's impossible to keep toxic partners, managers, or supposed leaders away forever from lower level employees. If the firm doesn't have leaders who will "walk the talk," reinforcing the culture they want to create, there's no way it will ultimately accomplish its goals.

The reality is that today's new workforce trends call for new leadership attitudes. Organizations now face historic shortages of skilled employees to fill many positions, making it essential to retain productive employees and attract the best new employees. Worker loyalty is at an all-time low, with people changing jobs so frequently that leaders have no time to build cohesive teams. Those workers who are available are much more diverse and have a different work ethic, creating the need to lead differently. Increased employee litigation and unproductive conflict distracts leaders from their mission. Setting aside the time to create, discuss, and shape organizational culture is one part of the solution to these problems. Leaders must force ongoing conversations at every level about the power of culture in an organization, especially about how to creatively manage the inevitable and increasing conflicts.

As discussed in Part 1, one of the best ways to address the issue of purpose and culture is to strive to make community building a part of your own purpose. Many successful business leaders now see community building as a pragmatic business decision.

Larry Weber, for example, is founder of Weber Shandwick International, part of the Interpublic Group of Companies, a $7 billion advertising and marketing conglomerate. He believes new leaders succeed because they've abandoned the military management style and instead are what Weber calls the "provocateurs." Provocateurs, he emphasized in a recent interview,[2] see themselves as community builders, with the customer at the center. These days most customers are nomads who are looking for places to camp out. The more engaging, useful, or attractive provocateurs can make their communities, the better their chances are of attracting and keeping customers.

Weber cites Rick Wagoner, CEO of General Motors, as a new-style provocateur inside an old-style company:

> Every day, he has to deal with a dozen or more constituencies that he can't control, from customers to employees, strategic allies, business partners, legislators, and labor unions. Wagoner sees it as his job to get those constituencies to work together for the benefit of the GM community. If he can strengthen the GM community, then GM will succeed.[3]

Weber believes that provocateurs understand that a CEO must see his or her primary job as "to engage in deep, constant dialogue with all the company's constituencies." Weber exhorts leaders to "build a community, not a company," noting that "the strength of a business is measured by the strength of its relationships."[4]

ORGANIZATIONS AND PURPOSE

Most organizations now have some kind of mission statement. If thoughtfully crafted, these statements can help organizations achieve their goals and create a powerful culture. Consider including conflict management as a part of your organization's mission.

For example, I helped one of my clients, a large transportation district, craft the following addition about conflict to their general mission statement. You can see it also intersects well with the organization's union contract.

Goals Statement for Conflict Resolution

The Transportation District, as an organization, recognizes that conflict is a normal and predictable part of working together. Therefore, we adopt the following goals relating to conflict resolution:

1. We are committed to increasing our skills in resolving conflict.

2. At all levels of the organization, we strive to resolve conflicts in a productive and creative way, without threats, harassment, or violence.

3. Nothing in this goal statement is meant to conflict with the Collective Bargaining Agreement or other policies.

Section 1: Management-Union Relations

The Employer agrees to meet in good faith with the duly elected representatives of the Union and attempt to resolve all questions arising between them. The Union fully agrees that within its ability each of its members shall render faithful service in their respective positions as outlined in the clauses of this Agreement and will cooperate with the management of the Employer in the efficient operation of the system in accordance with the rules, regulations, and operating conditions as announced by the Employer, and will cooperate and assist in fostering cordial relations between the Employer and the public.

We combined elements with their usual mission statement with the mission statement on conflict. We then included a statement about their goals for labor/management relations since they were a unionized organization. You can see the parallels between the two statements. Reprinting these two together helped the organization come together around the issue of conflict with the union.

What is the mission of your organization? What are its goals? How would it help your organization reach its goals if you included your mission for conflict resolution?

One of the most powerful statements, in my experience, is to emphasize that you recognize, as a group, that conflict is a part of life, can be valuable and that it's your goal to skillfully manage conflict. This can serve as a revelation to those in your organization who are constantly frustrated by the very existence of conflict. They need to know their leaders understand conflict is normal and healthy. Yet, leaders also need to make it clear that *skillful* and creative conflict management is something they consider a part of everyone's job description. Just making these statements and serving as role models for their enactment can help to resolve many problems around conflict.

FOSTERING A CREATIVE CULTURE

What other organizational characteristics most encourage a creative and conflict-positive culture? A group of creativity researchers[5] used the Department of Labor's classification of the characteristics of U.S. organizations to determine what organizational values led to innovation, and identified four factors:

1. People orientation, such as collaboration, supportiveness, and team orientation
2. Risk taking, such as a willingness to experiment and aggressiveness
3. Attention to detail, such as precision and results orientation
4. Stability, such as security of employment

These results suggest an organizational culture that supports risk taking, collaboration, quality, and security is likely to be innovative and "high performance." They also found using teams and information-sharing led to higher levels of group interaction and fostered creative decision-making. Organizations with these characteristics in their culture will be most able to generate good fights and the resulting innovation.

Perhaps one of the most critical components of fostering a creative culture is encouraging risk-taking. How do you encourage reasonable risk? Dick Liebhaber, executive vice president of MCI, has observed: "We do not shoot people who make mistakes. We shoot people who do not take risks."[6]

Organizational norms, top management walking the talk, and managers encouraging risk, help encourage creative risk-taking. Without encouraging risks, it's difficult for anything creative to emerge. Researcher Amy Edmonson,[7] for example, studied the effects of "psychological safety" in a large number of teams in an office furniture manufacturing company. Psychological safety "is characterized by a shared belief that well-intentioned action will not lead to punishment or rejection." She measured safety with a survey instrument that included statements such as "it is safe to take a risk on this team." Edmonson found the level of psychological safety felt by team members affected learning behavior and led to higher team performance. She also found that team leadership needed to create the climate for risk-taking that led to enhanced performance.

Leaders must also be careful how they respond to failure in order to encourage risks. A superintendent at Chaparral Steel, for example, championed a $1.5 million arch saw for trimming finished steel beams. When he brought the saw back to the site, it totally failed. After a year of unsuccessful tinkering, the saw was replaced. The superintendent was promoted to vice president of operations, surprising outsiders who "can't believe you can make a mistake like that and not get crucified."[8]

Leaders can learn to deliver honest feedback in a way that encourages creativity and risk-taking. Alan Horn, for example, chairman and CEO of Castle Rock Entertainment, is careful when first presented with creative ideas such as screenplays or ideas for marketing. He tries to cultivate a "heartfelt, internalized respect for what these people do." When they present a new idea:

> I want to remember that they are *completely* vulnerable at that moment. My job is not to kill them but to find the bright, creative, special parts of their proposal and focus on those

first, to ease their anxiety, make them feel less vulnerable. Then I have to find a graceful way into the parts of what they've brought that need improving.[9]

Feedback delivered in this way helps create a culture that welcomes risk-taking and innovation. Such a culture helps incubate eagles.

CONNECTIVITY

Nurturing connectivity is also critical to fostering a culture of creative conflict. For example, one of my clients, the CEO of a high-tech company, makes it a point to wander through his various groups of developers to look for ways in which different programming research can be shared in new and innovative ways.

Other clients foster connectivity through the web by creating sites related to specific projects and making sure that workers around the world can access the site to share and learn.

ADDITIONAL ORGANIZATIONAL TACTICS

The research on creative conflict confirms a strong culture organized around a clear purpose helps lead to conflict-skilled organizations. Nurturing risk-taking and connectivity also helps. In addition, researchers Kathleen Eisenhardt, Jean Kahwajy, and L. J. Bourgeois III, reporting on their findings in the *Harvard Business Review*,[10] identified five other cultural tactics that helped companies skillfully manage conflict to drive creativity and productivity. The successful teams were able to separate the person from the problem, disagree over strategy significance, and still get along with one another. The tactics were ...

- They worked with more information and debated on the facts.
- They developed multiple solutions to raise the level of debate.
- They injected humor into decision-making.
- They maintained a balance of power.
- They used a fall-back instead of a true consensus.

Let's look at how successful teams used all of these factors.

FOCUS ON THE FACTS

The researchers found more information is better because it encourages people to focus on issues, not personalities. Companies who managed conflict skillfully claimed to "measure everything," including facts about the external environment. As one CEO explained his process, "we over-MBA it." Otherwise, teams waste time in pointless debate over opinions and biases. Without timely and accurate information, people rather than issues become the focus, creating interpersonal conflict. Managers with high degrees of interpersonal conflict rely more on "hunches and guesses" than on current information.

The researchers found "a direct link between reliance on facts and low levels of interpersonal conflict." With facts, people moved swiftly to the central issues. In the absence of facts, people instead suspect others' motives. "Building decisions on facts creates a culture that emphasizes issues instead of personalities."

MULTIPLE ALTERNATIVES

Sometimes leaders assume they reduce conflict by focusing on only one or two alternatives in order to minimize the possible disagreements. Yet the researchers found that teams with low interpersonal conflict do just the opposite. They purposefully float multiple alternatives, sometimes even suggesting options with which they disagree, just to promote debate.

Considering multiple alternatives lowers bad fights and increases good ones, because it diffuses conflict, choices become less black and white and people can shift positions more easily. More creative options emerge, sometimes taking part of several different solutions. The process itself becomes more creative and enjoyable—people focus more on the problem instead of on personalities.

THE POWER OF HUMOR

The researchers found teams that handle conflict well make explicit and often contrived attempts to relieve tension and promote collaboration.

They find competition exciting. In the teams with unhealthy inter-personal conflict, humor was absent.

The successful teams used humor as a healthy defense mechanism to protect people from the stress that arises in the course of making strategic decisions. The humor also put people in a more positive mood. Many researchers have found that people in a positive mood tend to be not only more optimistic, but also more forgiving of others and more creative.

BALANCED POWER STRUCTURES

Organizations with autocratic leaders as well as extremely weak leaders both generated high levels of unhealthy interpersonal conflict. The lowest level of destructive conflict comes from teams with balanced power structures in which the CEO is the most powerful, but the other members of management wield substantial power in their own areas of responsibility.

QUALIFIED CONSENSUS

The most successful teams didn't seek true consensus all the time. Instead, they used a kind of *fall back* or *qualified* consensus. The group talked and tried to reach consensus. If they couldn't within a relevant period of time, the most senior leader made the decision. Remarkably, the teams that insisted on resolving substantive conflict by forcing consensus displayed the unhealthiest interpersonal conflict. Insisting on consensus in all issues leads to "endless haggling."

As one VP of engineering put it: "Consensus means that every-one has veto power. Our products were too late and they were too expensive." What the researchers found was that people wanted to be heard; they wanted their opinions and ideas treated with respect, but that people were willing to accept outcomes they disagreed with if they believed that the process used to come to a decision was fair, and that the leader didn't just seek their opinion as a ruse.

In sum, these five tactics, in addition to emphasizing common goals, lead not to less conflict, but to more healthy and productive conflict. What these researchers affirmed is that if there is little conflict over issues, there's also likely to be poor decision-making. Conflict over issues, not personalities, is valuable. The successful teams avoided groupthink, which has been a primary cause of failure in both public and private sectors. The researchers found "the alternative to conflict is usually not agreement, but apathy and disengagement."

ORGANIZATIONAL CONFLICT MANAGEMENT

Once you establish a mission statement around conflict for your organization such as storytelling and facilitating, you'll want to consider structures that support creative conflict management and help incubate eagles. A successful model for the conflict-skilled organization involves the following:

- A creative conflict management mission statement
- Leaders who model skillful conflict resolution through walking the talk
- Skilled mediators to resolve conflicts that people cannot resolve directly
- Skilled coaches to advise people in the midst of conflict
- Conflict management skills training specifically tailored for leaders, mediators, coaches, and all employees
- Accountability

The first element of this program—a mission statement—was discussed in the first part of this chapter. The other elements also require careful consideration.

BASIC CONFLICT MANAGEMENT SKILLS TRAINING

An organization that wants to successfully and creatively manage conflict should consider basic conflict management training for all employees. These trainings should be four to six hours in length and cover the organization's overall mission, policies, and procedures around conflict as well as the basic conflict management skills employees need. The sessions should be designed to be practical, hands-on, and experiential. Participants should experience a successful conflict resolution exercise as well as gain an understanding of the theories and steps involved. The session should emphasize the power of attitude about conflict to encourage employees to value and embrace conflict in order to drive innovation.

The most successful organizations will make such trainings mandatory for all employees.

ADVANCED TRAINING FOR COACHES, FACILITATORS, AND MEDIATORS

After completing the basic training, those with the interest and ability to serve as coaches, facilitators, and mediators should go on to advanced training. This training would help people learn two skills:

1. Providing confidential coaching to those in the midst of conflict
2. Serving as coaches, facilitators, and mediators for those who cannot creatively manage conflict themselves

Organizations should consider training one coach/mediator for every 50 to 100 employees. This training would also be highly interactive, focusing on mediation and coaching skills beyond the basics. The training should take two and a half to five days.

EXECUTIVE BRIEFING

Ideally, executives should take both levels of training since surveys show they spend at least one fourth of their time resolving and mediating conflicts. At the least, executives should be briefed as to the basics of the program in a one to two hour session and receive a taste of the regular training.

If you skip this step, you won't have executives who understand the process and "walk the talk." They tend not to encourage their subordinates to go to the other session and do not use the same language to manage conflicts. Although it can be difficult to convince the executives to take the time to sit through even a short briefing, it will be well worth the effort in the long run.

ACCOUNTABILITY

The last piece of the puzzle to creating a conflict-positive organization is to focus on accountability. None of the other moves will create the level of cooperation, community, and teamwork you need in your organization without this important element.

For example, one of my clients is a large manufacturing company. I was hired by the president, Helen, to conduct my conflict management workshop at their annual executive retreat. She'd told me one of their problems was that some people on the executive team used a pit bull style of conflict resolution while others triangulated conflict. The workshop was a success based on the feedback and participation; in fact, the executives wanted to expand the session to a full day class and bring it to all of their other managers. Over the next month, I conducted day-long workshops for their entire management team across the country. Again, the feedback was positive.

In my last meeting with Helen, she thanked me for making the workshops a success but lamented that—even though we'd provided the skills—one VP was still a problem. His behavior included incredible displays of rudeness, attacks, and constant criticism of the other executives and managers, yelling profanity and a general inability to be a team player, even though he was good at his own substantive area of expertise.

"I just don't understand why he won't change," she sighed. I asked the obvious question: "Have you talked to him about his behavior?" Helen responded that she had, several times, but nothing shifted.

I then went on to emphasize to her the difference between a talk about his behavior and making him accountable for his behavior. She'd never enforced any *consequences* for his inappropriate behavior. I suggested that she needed to make improving his behavior a part of his performance plan, complete with consequences up to and including termination if he failed to meet those requirements. She revealed she was concerned about losing someone who was substantively good at what he did, yet Helen understood failure to do so would continue to undermine the entire executive team. Miraculously, when she followed my advice and included accountability for his behavior, he started to improve his skills.

You have the right and, indeed, the responsibility as a leader or manager to insist that all of your workers make creative conflict management a part of their job description. Just giving them the skills may not be enough if you fail to follow through with significant consequences for their failure to act.

HOW THE SYSTEM WORKS IN PRACTICE

With this system in place in a conflict-positive organization, most conflicts would be managed directly between the involved parties. If they are unable to do so, the participants could request individual coaching sessions from designated coaches. If that fails, they could then request mediation. Leaders could also refer associates to mediators to resolve disputes.

This approach allows an organization to take a systemic approach to creative conflict management and will result in significant savings in lost productivity, time, and energy. This system also prevents a rise in the negative spiral of unproductive and personal conflicts, lawsuits, and other costly conflicts. Finally, this system will help you harness the power of a good fight to improve productivity and innovation. The time an organization invests in this system and training will bring dramatic results for all involved and incubate many eagles within your organization.

LEADERSHIP AND STORYTELLING

Much has been written in recent years about leadership in general and the need for all employees to become leaders, not just employees. Yet these writers miss two significant nuances: the need to give people *meaning* in their work and the power of *story* as a tool for encouraging meaning and for serving as a model for the "why" behind conflict management. People must have common goals or resolution is not possible. Many organizational conflicts result from disbelief in or a lack of understanding about:

- Why the organization exists.
- Why the organization does what it does.
- What the organization's true goals are.

Skillfully using stories can help change this dynamic.

Glenn Gienko, executive vice president of human resources for Motorola in Schaumburg, Illinois, agrees that leadership and story-telling are keys to making constructive conflict a part of the fabric of an organizational culture. As he recalls:

> Fifteen years ago during an officers' meeting, in which every-one was celebrating the success of the company, one employee stood up in front of his peers and their spouses and proclaimed that Motorola's quality stunk. The willingness of [that lone] employee to speak against the grain ultimately turned into Motorola's highly praised Six Sigma quality effort. Today, we tell this story over and over as a way to show employees what constructive dissent can do for a company.[11]

Futurist Rolf Jensen, director of the Copenhagen Institute for Future Studies, argues:

> Storytellers will be the most valued workers in the 21st cen-tury. All professionals, including advertisers, teachers, entre-preneurs, politicians, athletes and religious leaders, will be valued for their ability to create stories that will captivate their audiences.[12]

Jensen claims that in the years ahead we will move into what he calls the Dream Society:

> In today's Information Society, we prize those who can skill-fully manipulate data; in tomorrow's Dream Society—focused on dreams, adventure, spirituality and feelings—we will most generously reward those who can tell stories. ... In the

future, the notion that work should be no more than a means of obtaining something else will disappear. People will, of course, be paid for working, but money will not be the main reason for working. People will require meaning in their work.[13]

Current surveys of Generation-Xers place meaning high on the list of what they look for in a job. Aging baby boomers—having passed through their materialistic stage—will also demand meaning in their work, not just management.

Organizations will have to develop a collective meaning to survive and to resolve the ever-escalating conflicts. Companies in the future will also have to show that they have values and contribute to society.

Leaders will be increasingly called upon to help give meaning to employees. Of course, before you can help others find meaning in their work, you have to find it in your own. Meaning fuels the sometimes-challenging work of conflict management.

Can all honest, legal work have meaning, dignity, and value? Yes, I believe it can. If you doubt me, read Victor Frankl's classic work, *Man's Search for Meaning*, about finding meaning in his work as a prisoner in a Nazi concentration camp. There may be more difficult environments, but I can't imagine where or when.

Even if your current job doesn't fit your long-term passion, find meaning in the support the work provides as you plan for more passionate future work. Find meaning in doing what you do with excellence and integrity. Mother Teresa noted, "We do not do great things. We do small things with great love." Ultimately, if you can't find meaning in your work, leave. The dilemma is this: The future will require such a level of commitment that you will not be able to sustain your work with anything less than all out dedication.

One way to give meaning to your work and to work of those you lead is through storytelling. As we moved into Jensen's Dream Society, in the later part of the twentieth century, it's no accident we elected an actor, Ronald Reagan, as president of this country and a playwright, Václav Havel, as president of the Czech Republic.

How powerful are stories? "Everybody is a story," writes Dr. Naomi Remen in her book, *Kitchen Table Wisdom: Stories That Heal:*

> When I was a child, people sat around kitchen tables and told their stories. We don't do that so much anymore. Sitting around the table telling stories is not just a way of passing time, it is the way wisdom gets passed along. The stuff that helps us to live a life worth remembering. Despite the awesome powers of technology many of us still do not live very well. We may need to listen to one another's stories again.[14]

Loneliness is the hidden wound of our time—the price many have paid for embracing such frontier values as independence, self-reliance and competence. It's also a price paid by those who frequently change jobs. In the future, leaders will be increasingly called upon to remember we are all connected and can become a community, to help organizations work more cooperatively and to move toward goals with humor, meaning, purpose, and quality companionship. A good story provides a compass for a group's mission. Skillful conflict management builds trust and creates connections and helps a group work together to accomplish its mission.

As leaders, how do we discover and develop our own stories to inspire others? Look at your *wounds*. There is power in the wounded leader. As Nietzsche wrote, "life breaks all of us eventually, but some of us grow back stronger in the broken places." Ironically, our greatest strengths come from these wounds, from what makes us vulnerable, because our vulnerability also makes us human. And in our humanity lies our ability to connect with and lead others. At the heart of most wounds is a conflict. The healing of most wounds involves connection.

The ability to appropriately reveal our wounds and vulnerability, makes the most powerful leaders. Bob Dole, despite his physical wounds, was not. It's why Clinton won a reelection (despite his many mishaps) and Hillary may not. It's why Marilyn Monroe, "the vulnerable blonde," is a timeless cultural icon and Madonna never will be. (Unless, of course, parenthood brings Madonna to her knees, as it does most of us).

How do we develop storytelling ability? After we look at our wounds, ask what we can teach from that place of wounding. What do you know because you bought that knowledge with your life?

Learn also from other great storytellers. Read and listen to a diverse collection of artists. Recently, for example, I've been inspired by such different sources as a novel by Haitian Edwidge Danticat, *Krik? Krak!*, and the Academy Award winning documentary about Maya Lin, *A Strong Clear Vision*. Danticat evokes the conflict, terror, and heartache, along with the wonder of her native Haiti, telling the story of a people who resist the brutality of their rulers through the powers of imagination and community. Through her work, those of us who find the news from Haiti too painful to hear can understand the place more deeply than we ever thought possible. Out of her wounds, and the many conflicts in her country, Danticat weaves her life and culture into a powerful force to move us to understanding and action. Similarly, you can use your own life and culture to move your organization closer to its goals.

Maya Lin, the architect who at 20 beat out hundreds of more established architects to win the contest to design the Vietnam Veterans' Memorial, recounted how wounded she felt in the conflict when people attacked and misunderstood her design. Yet she found that out of that wound came the inspiration to design more and even greater work. Her story inspires us all.

Tell stories. Use them in your work. Search for the stories of others in songs, novels, poems, and dance. Practice them first if you must—in front of your kids, a Toastmasters' group, or your book club—but weave them into the memos and reports you write and the meetings and trainings you lead.

When you do, you will have taken an awesome step into the future toward leadership in conflict management through the power of storytelling. You will help your organization move forward to become a conflict-positive organization.

SUMMARY

In summary, an organizational culture that fosters creative conflicts and incubates eagles exhibits these traits:

- The organization's mission, values, and priorities are clearly expressed and modeled through leaders who walk the talk and reinforce the culture through storytelling.

- Risk-taking is encouraged; people take intelligent risks; and mistakes are viewed as learning opportunities.

- Diversity is welcomed and valued; workers are educated in diverse thinking and conflict styles.

- Decision-making is shared; people are encouraged to participate in making decisions in their area of expertise.

- Group wisdom is respected by making use of diverse teams to solve problems; because of a belief in the creative potential of the group, conflict is valued.

- Members of the group understand that conflict is a part of life and are trained in creative conflict management with the ability to disagree about issues instead of personalities; they understand we all have a piece of the truth.

CONCLUSION

There was reason to fear that the Revolution, like Saturn, might devour in turn each one of her children.

—Pierre Vergniaud

After September 11, 2001, we all have to ask the question: What value does this book have? What will the idea of valuing conflict bring to that tragedy? How is what we've learned and have to offer on this subject healing for the country and the world?

I'm in Valley Forge, Pennsylvania, conducting a workshop for one of our clients. Ironically, the subject is Managing a Respectful Workplace. My co-presenter is talking and I've taken a break, walking up to the cafeteria to drink tea.

Winding my way through the dull gray building, I overhear Cathy, the cashier in the cafeteria, telling someone about planes crashing. I can't resist asking what she said: "Two planes crashed into the World Trade Center," she responds.

For some reason, my mind decides that the planes crashed into each other and then into the building, a bizarre occurrence, but, my brain thinks, an accident.

I walk back downstairs to the workshop and our client contacts at the back of the room have heard the news, too. They're buzzing with rumors. No one knows, but the news reports suspect terrorists. In a blur over the next hour, we hear about the crash into the Pentagon and in western Pennsylvania. We make announcements but proceed with the workshop, telling our class that we'll let them know if anything new happens. I spend my breaks upstairs in the cafeteria, glued to the television.

We're grounded in Philadelphia for three days before we can escape. We watch the news, drink Scotch, and eat steak and fries. I manage to drag myself to the airport hotel treadmill where I walk and watch more TV. By the end of the second night I watch a movie in my room, a slick and silly romantic comedy, *Someone Like You*, unable to bear the news images any more. I call my family each night, promising the kids that I'll arrive home the next day. I tell them the same thing for two more days; they're confused and worried.

On the third day we arrive at the airport at 6:00 A.M. for a 7:55 flight. One thousand people jam the ticket counter, snaking in a line that winds in and out of the terminal. The line crawls along but people are quietly cheerful, glad to be alive with the chance of escape after days of promises and delays.

Finally, around 7 A.M., it's obvious that we're going to miss our flight. Bruce, my traveling companion and a former rugby player, decides to try to bluff his way through security, even though we've been told that we have to show boarding passes which we do not have. I hold our place in line in case he doesn't make it. I can't stand still and dance nervously from foot to foot. Bruce finally calls my cell after 15 minutes to yell, "I'm through!" happy as if he'd made a goal.

I have to charge outside the airport to blast through the mob. I'm running now, afraid to miss my flight but concerned that by racing I may attract the attention of a nervous security force. I finally arrive at the security gate and an older dark-haired woman tries to send me back, telling me I don't have today's date stamped on my ticket, which we've been told we must do.

That's when I lose it. Tears form as I point with shaky fingers to the date. She looks doubtful but finally waves me through to the x-ray machines. Security stops me again; they've selected me for a bag search.

My tears flow openly now; I'm shaking. All the pent-up fear, fury, and frustration of the past few days crash down on me. A woman searches my bag, asks me to show her my nail scissors, which the scanner has picked up. I hand them over.

Would you like to fill out a form and get them back later? She wants to know? "No, no, I don't care," I say, weeping openly now. She smiles at me and pats my hand. "There, there," she says.

I sprint for the gate. Bruce sits calmly, reading the paper. I blurt out my travails. He informs me that our flight is delayed, weather in Philadelphia.

My stomach churns: adrenaline nausea kicking in. I ask Bruce to watch my bags and I go to the bar to buy a meal of eggs benedict, prepackaged, airport food. I sit at the bar and watch TV, chewing numbly. I stare at the unreal images, burning into all our brains, shown over and over like wallpaper: planes crashing into the towers.

We finally take off after several more delays: lightning on the boarding ramp, rain, weather. The flight is uneventful, most passengers sleeping off their exhaustion. I'm wide awake with nervous energy but thrilled to be heading home to my kids.

WHAT IS THE RELEVANCE OF VALUING CONFLICT AFTER THE TRAGEDY?

Over the next week I grapple with the issue and wonder. Where did we go wrong as a country and a world in all the Middle East negotiations? Where did we fail to address the voice of the Muslim world? Could we have listened better? Could we have embraced the conflict at an earlier stage? Allowed the change to occur that was trying to occur? What creative solution did we miss?

What did we ignore that drove this group to such extremes to get our attention? What could we have done differently or better? Clearly now we've been forced to a military response but could we have had a different result at an earlier stage?

And what about those—such as my friend Michael, a Jew who has lived in Israel—who says that this is the work of madmen, that we couldn't have negotiated with those who were as corrupt as the Mafia, who want nothing but power. Is he right? Was there no room here for anything but violence?

I argue with the conflicting voices in my own head, wondering and worrying. I don't believe that we caused this tragedy, but is there a way that we could have prevented it? Is there a way we could have had a dialogue instead of a debate? A debate that ultimately escalated into violence?

I do not know the answer to these questions. I am not wise enough to know yet I do believe that—as a civilized society—we must continue to keep raising these issues, we cannot just blindly charge ahead letting our words become cannon fodder.

OUR ROLE IN CONFLICT

One thing is clear. The world has never been more in need of the attitudes and skills you've learned in this book. With weapons of mass destruction in the hands of insatiable governments and terrorists, the necessity for creative and productive approaches to conflict management has never been more acute. If you've worked diligently through this book and you've begun to adopt the attitudes and use the concepts, you'll be well on your way to playing your part in the effort to move the world to peace.

I believe that all our actions have consequences, that our own efforts—however small they may seem—ripple out like waves, affecting many others we may not see or know. Know that your own words and behavior make a difference and that my thoughts and prayers are with you as you go forward.

Lynne Eisaguirre
Golden, Colorado
January 17, 2002

APPENDIX A

BIBLIOGRAPHY

Allen, N., and Hecht, T. D. "Team-Organization Alignment and Team Behavior: Implications for Human Resource Management." *Human Resource Management Research Quarterly*. 2000, Volume 4, Number 3.

Amabile, Teresa M. "How to Kill Creativity." *Harvard Business Review*. September 1998.

Andert-Schmidt, D. *Managing Our Differences: Meeting the Demands of Diversity*. Shawnee Mission, KS: National Press Publications, 1995.

Arad, Sharon, Mary Ann Hanson, and Robert Schneider. "A Framework for the Study of Relationships Between Organizational Characteristics and Organizational Innovation." *Journal of Behavior*. 1997, Volume 31, Number 1.

Argyris, Chris. *Reasoning, Learning, and Action: Individual and Organizational*. San Francisco: Jossey-Bass, 1982.

Axelrod, Alan. *Elizabeth I CEO: Strategic Lessons from the Leader Who Built an Empire*. Paramus, NJ: Prentice Hall Press, 2000.

Bennis, W. *On Becoming a Leader*. Menlow Park: Addison-Wesley, 1989.

Birkhoff, J., C. Mitchell, and L. Schirch, eds. *Annotated Bibliography of Conflict Analysis and Resolution*. Fairfax, VA: Institute for Conflict Analysis and Resolution, George Mason University, 1995.

Bolton, R., and D. Bolton. *People Styles at Work*. New York: AMACOM, 1996.

Briggs, M. *Myers-Briggs Type Indicator.* Palo Alto, CA: Consulting Psychology Press, 1991.

Briggs, M. I. *Introduction to Type.* Palo Alto, CA: Consulting Psychologists Press, 1985.

Brown, C. D., C. C. Snedeker, and B. Sykes, eds. *Conflict and Diversity.* Cresskill, NJ: Hampton Press, 1997.

Burke, T., and A. Genn-Bash. *Competition in Theory and Practice.* London: Croom Helm, 1998.

Bush, R. A. B., and J. P. Folger. *The Promise of Mediation.* San Francisco: Jossey-Bass, 1994.

Caudron, Shari. "Keeping Team Conflict Alive." *Training & Development.* September 1998, Volume 52, Number 9.

Cloke, K., and J. Goldsmith. *Resolving Conflicts at Work: A Complete Guide for Everyone on the Job.* San Francisco: Jossey-Bass, 2000.

Cloven, Geoffrey, "The Ultimate Manager." *Fortune.* November 22, 1999.

Couter, Diane L. "Genius at Work: A Conversation with Mark Morris. *Harvard Business Review.* October 2001.

Cox, T., Jr. *Cultural Diversity in Organizations.* San Francisco: Berrett-Koehler, 1993.

de Bono, E. *Conflicts: A Better Way to Resolve Them.* New York: Penguin Books, 1986.

———. *Six Thinking Hats.* London: Penguin Books, 1990.

Doyle, M., and D. Straus. *How to Make Meetings Work!* New York: Berkley, 1993.

Edmondson, Amy, Richard Bohmer, and Gary Pisano. "Speeding Up Team Learning." *Harvard Business Review.* October 2001, 125.

Eisenhardt, K. M., J. L. Kahwajy, and L. J. Bourgeois, III. "How Management Teams Can Have a Good Fight." *Harvard Business Review*. 1997, 75(4), 77–84.

Esquivel, Michael A., and Brian H. Kleiner. "The Importance of Conflict in Work Team Effectiveness." *Team Performance Management*. 1996, Volume 2, Number 3.

Fernandez, J. P. *The Diversity Advantage*. San Francisco: New Lexington Press, 1993.

Fisher, R., and S. Brown. *Getting Together: Building Relationships as We Negotiate*. Boston: Houghton Mifflin, 1988.

Fisher, R., and W. Ury, with B. Patton, ed. *Getting to Yes: Negotiating Agreement Without Giving In, Second Edition*. New York: Penguin Books, 1991.

Gilbert, Roberts. *Extraordinary Relationships*. New York: John Wiley & Sons, Inc., 1992.

Gundling, E. *The 3M Way to Innovation: Balancing People and Profit*. Tokyo: Kodansha International, 2000.

Halberstam, David. *The Reckoning*. New York: William Morrow & Co., 1986.

Hamel, Gary. *Leading the Revolution*. Boston: Harvard Business School Press, 2000.

Handy, C. *The Age of Paradox*. Boston: Harvard Business School Press, 1995.

Harvey, J. B. *The Abilene Paradox and Other Meditations on Management*. San Francisco: Jossey-Bass, 1996.

Hirshberg, J. *The Creative Priority: Putting Innovation to Work in Your Business*. New York: HarperBusiness, 1999.

Hoffer, E. quoted in Leonard Silk, "On Managing Creativity," *Business Month*. 1989, Volume 133, Number 4.

Hogan, R. C., and Champagne. *Personal Style Inventory*. King of Prussia: HRDQ, 1979.

Jackson, Susan E. *Team Composition in Organizational Settings: Issues in Managing and Increasingly Diverse Work Force in Group Process and Productivity*. Beverly Hills, CA: Safe, 1992.

Janis, I. L. *Crucial Decisions: Leadership in Policymaking and Crisis Management*. New York: Free Press, 1989.

————. *Groupthink, Second Edition*. Boston: Houghton Mifflin, 1982.

————. *Victims of Groupthink*. Boston: Houghton Mifflin, 1972.

Judge, William Q., Gerald E. Fryxell, and Robert S. Dooley. "The New Task of R and D Management." *California Management Review*. 1997, Volume 39, Number 3.

Kaye, Kenneth. *Workplace Wars and How to End Them: Turning Personal Conflicts into Productive Teamwork*. New York: AMACOM, 1994.

Kheel, T. W. *The Keys to Conflict Resolution*. New York: Four Walls Eight Windows, 1999.

Landau, Sy, Barbara Landau, and Daryl Landau. *From Conflict to Creativity*. San Francisco: Jossey-Bass, 2001.

Leonard, Dorothy, and Walter Swap. *When Sparks Fly: Igniting Creativity in Groups*. Boston: Harvard Business School Press, 1999.

Leonard-Barton, Dorothy. *Wellsprings of Knowledge*. Boston: Harvard Business School Press, 1995.

Lerner, Harriet. *The Dance of Anger*. New York: HarperPerennial, 1997.

Mayer, B. *The Dynamics of Conflict Resolution: A Practitioner's Guide.* San Francisco: Jossey-Bass, 2000.

Mongeau, P. A., and M. C. Morr. "Reconsidering Brainstorming." *Group Facilitation.* 1999, 1(1).

Moore, C. *The Mediation Process: Practical Strategies for Resolving Conflict, Second Edition.* San Francisco: Jossey-Bass, 1996.

Moorhead, Gregory, Richard Ference, and Chris Neck. "Group Decision Fiascoes Continue." *Human Relations.* 1991, Volume 44, Number 6.

Osborn, A. F. *Applied Imagination: Principles and Procedures of Creative Problem-Solving.* New York: Scribner, 1963.

Packard, David. *The HP Way: How Bill Hewlitt and I Built Our Company.* HarperBusiness, 1996.

Pascale, R. T. *Managing on the Edge: How the Smartest Companies Use Conflict to Stay Ahead.* New York: Simon & Schuster, 1990.

Pascale, R. T., M. Milleman, and L. Gioja. *Surfing the Edge of Chaos: The Laws of Nature and the New Laws of Business.* New York: Crown Business, 2000.

Peters, T. J., and R. H. Waterman. *In Search of Excellence: Lessons from American's Best-Run Companies.* New York: Warner Books, 1982.

Remen, Rachel Naomi. *My Grandfather's Blessings.* New York: Riverhead Books, 2000.

Roberts, Gilbert. *Extraordinary Relationships.* New York: John Wiley & Sons, Inc., 1992.

Rosner, Bob. *Working Wounded: Advice That Adds Insight to Injury.* New York: Warner Books, 2000.

Senge, P. "Turning the Creative Tension On" (interview with Bill Staples). *Edges.* 2000, Volume 12, Number 1.

Shaw, M. E. *Group Dynamics: The Psychology of Small Group Behavior.* New York: McGraw-Hill, 1976.

Simmons, Annette. *Territorial Games: Understanding and Ending Turf Wars at Work.* Amacon Books, 1997.

Southworth, N. "Canadian Team Builders Turn U.S. Heads." *Globe and Mail.* August 28, 2000.

Sutton, Robert. "Weird Ideas That Work: 11½ Practices for Promoting, Managing and Sustaining Innovation." *Harvard Business Review.* September 2001.

Sternberg, Robert. *Successful Intelligence.* New York: Simon & Schuster, 1996.

Tannen, D. *Talking from 9 to 5.* New York: Morrow, 1994.

———. *The Argument Culture: Stopping America's War of Words.* New York: Ballantine, 1999.

Thomas, K. W., and K. W. Kilmann. *Thomas-Kilmann Conflict Mode Instrument.* Palo Alto, CA: Consulting Psychologists Press, 1974.

Tjosvold, D. *The Conflict-Positive Organization: Stimulate Diversity and Create Unity.* Reading, MA: Addison-Wesley, 1992.

Tjosvold, D., and M. M. Tjosvold. *Psychology for Leaders: Using Motivation, Conflict and Power to Manage More Effectively.* New York: Wiley, 1995.

Ury, W. *Getting Past No.* New York: Bantam Books, 1991.

Wetlaufer, Suzy. "Common Sense and Conflict." *Harvard Business Review.* January/February 2000, Volume 78, Number 1.

APPENDIX B

FOOTNOTES

INTRODUCTION

[1] Rosner, Bob. *Working Wounded: Advice That Adds Insight to Injury.* New York: Warner Books, 2000.

[2] Hamel, Gary. *Leading the Revolution.* Boston: Harvard Business School Press, 2000.

[3] Moore, Christopher. *The Mediation Process: Practical Strategies for Resolving Conflict, Second Edition.* San Francisco: Jossey-Bass, 1996.

[4] Fisher, Roger, et al. *Getting to Yes: Negotiating Agreement Without Giving In, Second Edition.* New York: Penguin Books, 1991.

CHAPTER 1

[1] Pascale, Richard Tanner. *Managing on the Edge: How the Smartest Companies Use Conflict to Stay Ahead.* New York: Simon & Schuster, 1990.

[2] Hamel, Gary. *Leading the Revolution.* Boston: Harvard Business School Press, 2000.

[3] Sutton, Robert. "Weird Ideas That Work: 11½ Practices for Promoting, Managing and Sustaining Innovation." *Harvard Business Review.* September 2001: 96–103.

[4] Ibid.

[5] Packard, David. *The HP Way: How Bill Hewlitt and I Built Our Company.* HarperBusiness, 1996.

[6] Sutton, Robert. "Weird Ideas That Work: 11½ Practices for Promoting, Managing and Sustaining Innovation." *Harvard Business Review.* September 2001: 96–103.

[7] Ibid.

[8] Quotes and modified portions reprinted by permission of Harvard Business Review from Eisenhardt, Kathleen M., Jean L. Kahwajy, and L. J. Bourageois, III. "How Management Teams Can Have a Good Fight." *Harvard Business Review.* July/ August 97, Volume 75, Issue 4. Copyright 1997 by Harvard Business School Publishing Corporation. All rights reserved.

[9] Wetlaufer, Suzy. "Common Sense and Conflict." *Harvard Business Review.* January/February 2000, Volume 78, Issue 1.

[10] Ibid

[11] Janis, Irving. *Groupthink: Psychological Studies of Policy Decisions and Fiascoes.* Boston: Houghton Mifflin, 1982.

[12] Ibid.

[13] Ibid.

[14] Ibid.

[15] Ibid.

[16] Pascale, Richard Tanner. *Managing on the Edge: How the Smartest Companies Use Conflict to Stay Ahead.* New York: Simon & Schuster, 1990.

CHAPTER 2

[1] Hallowell, Edward M. *Connect.* New York: Pantheon, 1999.

[2] Putnam, Linda L. "Productive Conflict: Negotiation as Implicit Coordination." *The International Journal of Conflict Management.* July 1991, Volume 5, Number 3.

[3] Baron, Robert A. "Positive Effects of Conflict: A Cognitive Perspective." *Employee Responsibilities and Rights Journal.* 1991, Volume 4, Number 1.

[4] Ibid.

[5] Ibid.

[6] Ibid.

CHAPTER 3

[1] Quotes and modified portions reprinted by permission of *Harvard Business Review* from Eisenhardt, Kathleen M., Jean L. Kahwajy, and L. J. Bourageois, III. "How Management Teams Can Have a Good Fight." *Harvard Business Review.* July/August 97, Volume 75, Issue 4. Copyright 1997 by Harvard Business School Publishing Corporation. All rights reserved.

[2] Quotes and modified portions reprinted by permission of Harvard Business Press from Leonard, Dorothy, and Walter Swap. *When Sparks Fly: Igniting Creativity in Groups.* Boston: Harvard Business School Press, 1999. Copyright 1999 by Dorothy Leonard and Walter Swap. All rights reserved.

[3] Ibid.

[4] Ibid.

[5] Ibid.

[6] Judge, William Q., Gerald E. Fryxell, and Robert S. Dooley, "The New Task of R&D Management." *California Management Review.* 1997, Volume 39, Issue 3.

CHAPTER 4

[1] Leonard, Dorothy, and Susan Straus. "Putting Your Company's Whole Brain to Work." *Harvard Business Review.* July/August 1997, Volume 75, Issue 4, p. 110.

[2] Ibid.

[3] Ibid.

CHAPTER 7

[1] Charan, Ram. "Why CEOs Fail." *Fortune.* June 21, 1999, p. 69.

CHAPTER 9

[1] Cloven, Geoffrey. "The Ultimate Manager." *Fortune*. November 22, 1999.

[2] Ibid.

[3] Michaels, Ed, Helen Handfiled-Jones, and Beth Axelrod. *The War for Talent*. Boston: Harvard Business School Press, 2001.

CHAPTER 10

[1] Shaw, M. E. *Group Dynamics: The Psychology of Small Group Behavior*. New York: McGraw-Hill, 1976.

[2] Jackson, Susan E. *Team Composition in Organizational Settings: Issues in Managing an Increasingly Diverse Work Force in Group Process and Productivity*. Beverly Hills: Safe, 1992.

[3] Janis, Irving. *Victims of Groupthink*. Boston: Houghton Mifflin, 1972.

[4] Janis, Irving. *Crucial Discussions: Leadership in Policymaking and Crises Management*. New York: Fire Press, 1989.

[5] Amabile, Teresa. "How to Kill Creativity." *Harvard Business Review*. September 1998.

[6] Ibid.

[7] Diane L. Coutu, "Genius at Work: A Conversation with Mark Morris." *Harvard Business Review*. October 2001.

[8] Ibid.

[9] Ibid.

[10] Quotes and modified portions reprinted by permission of Harvard Business Press from Leonard, Dorothy, and Walter Swap. *When Sparks Fly: Igniting Creativity in Groups*. Boston: Harvard Business School Press, 1999. Copyright 1999 by Dorothy Leonard and Walter Swap. All rights reserved.

[11] Ibid.

[12] Ibid.

[13] Ibid.

[14] Sternberg, Robert. *Successful Intelligence*. New York: Simon & Schuster, 1996.

[15] Hirshberg, Jerry. *The Creative Priority: Putting Innovation to Work in Your Business*. New York: HarperBusiness, 1999.

[16] Ibid.

[17] Ibid.

[18] Tannen, Deborah. *The Argument Culture: Moving from Debate to Dialogue*. New York: Random House, 1998.

[19] Ibid.

CHAPTER 11

[1] Osborn, A. F. *Applied Imagination: Principles and Procedures of Creative Problem Solving*. New York: Scribner, 1963.

[2] Quotes and modified portions reprinted by permission of Harvard Business Press from Leonard, Dorothy, and Walter Swap. *When Sparks Fly: Igniting Creativity in Groups*. Boston: Harvard Business School Press, 1999. Copyright 1999 by Dorothy Leonard and Walter Swap. All rights reserved.

CHAPTER 13

[1] Hendricks, Gay. *A Year of Living Consciously*. San Francisco: Harper, 1990.

CHAPTER 14

[1] Hallowell, Edward M. *Connect*. New York: Pantheon. 1999.

[2] Argyris, Chris. *Reasoning, Learning, and Action: Individual and Organizational*. San Francisco: Jossey-Bass, 1982.

[3] Tannen, Deborah. *You Just Don't Understand: Women and Men in Conversation*. New York: William Morrow, 1990.

CHAPTER 15

[1] Hudson Institute. *Workforce 2020: Work and Workers for the 21st Century.* Indianapolis: Hudson Institute, 1997.

[2] Lerner, Harriet. *The Dance of Anger.* New York: HarperCollins, 1997.

[3] Ibid.

[4] Ibid.

[5] Helgesen, Sally. *The Web of Inclusion: A New Architecture for Building Great Organizations.* New York: Currency/Doubleday, 1995.

CHAPTER 16

[1] Bridge's stages are spread throughout his many useful books and articles. See, for example, William Bridges, Ph.D., *Transitions: Making Sense of Life's Changes.* Reading, MA: Addison-Wesley Publishing Company, 1980.

CHAPTER 17

[1] Kolb, Deborah M., and Linda L. Putnam, "The Multiple Faces of Conflict in Organizations," *Journal of Organizational Behavior.* Volume 13, 1992.

[2] Kaye, Kenneth. *Workplace Wars and How to End Them: Turning Personal Conflicts into Productive Teamwork.* New York: AMACOM, 1994.

[3] Rosenfeld, Jill. "She Stands on Common Ground," *Fast Company.* January/February 2000.

CHAPTER 18

[1] "Smart Companies, Dumb Decisions." *Fast Company.* Issue 11, October 1997.

[2] Moorhead, Gregory, Richard Ference, and Chris Neck, "Group Decision Fiascoes Continue." *Human Relations.* Volume 44, Number 6, 1991.

³ Halberstam, David. *The Reckoning*. New York: William Morrow & Co., 1986.

⁴ Esquivel, Michael A., and Brian H. Kleiner, "The Importance of Conflict in Work Team Effectiveness." *Team Performance Management*. Volume 2, Number 3, 1996.

⁵ Ibid.

⁶ Ibid.

⁷ Garvin, David A., and Michael A. Roberto, "What You Don't Know About Making Decisions." *Harvard Business Review*. September 2001.

⁸ Ibid.

CHAPTER 20

¹ Moore, Christopher W. *The Mediation Process, Second Edition*. San Francisco: Jossey-Bass, 1996.

² Ibid.

³ Bellamy, Clayton. "Honest Not the School Board Policy." *The Denver Post*. February 7, 2002.

CHAPTER 21

¹ Wheatley, Margaret. *Leadership and the New Science: Learning About Organizations from an Orderly Universe*. San Francisco: Berrett-Coehler Publishing, 1992.

² Judge, Paul C. "Provocation 101." *Fast Company*. January 2002, pp. 110–111.

³ Ibid.

⁴ Ibid.

⁵ Arad, Sharon, Mary Ann Hanson, and Robert Schneider. "A Framework for the Study of Relationships Between Organizational Characteristics and Organizational Innovation." *Journal of Creative Behavior*. Volume 31, Number 1 (1997): 42–58.

[6] Peters, Tom. "Prometheus Barely Unbound." *Academy of Management Executive.* 1990, Volume 4, Number 4.

[7] Edmondson, Amy. "Psychological Safety and Learning Behavior in Work Teams." *Administrative Science Quarterly.* 1999.

[8] Leonard-Barton, Dorothy, *Wellsprings of Knowledge.* Boston: Harvard Business School Press, 1995.

[10] Quotes and modified portions reprinted by permission of Harvard Business Press from Leonard, Dorothy, and Walter Swap. *When Sparks Fly: Igniting Creativity in Groups.* Boston: Harvard Business School Press, 1999. Copyright 1999 by Dorothy Leonard and Walter Swap. All rights reserved.

[7] Quotes and modified portions reprinted by permission of *Harvard Business Review* from Eisenhardt, Kathleen M., Jean L. Kahwajy, and L. J. Bourageois, III. "How Management Teams Can Have a Good Fight." *Harvard Business Review.* July/August 97, Volume 75, Issue 4. Copyright 1997 by Harvard Business School Publishing Corporation. All rights reserved.

[11] Quoted in Shari Caudron, "Keeping Team Conflict Alive." *Training & Development.* September 1998, Volume 52, Issue 9.

[12] Jensen, Rolf. *The Dream Society: How the Coming Shift from Information to Imagination Can Help Your Business.* McGraw-Hill: 1999.

[13] Ibid.

[14] Remen, Naomi, M.D. *Kitchen Table Wisdom: Stories That Heal.* New York: Riverhead Books, 1996.

INDEX

N

O

P

W

Wagoner, Rick, 257

waigaya, 12

Web of Inclusion: A New Architecture for Building Great Organizations, The, 186

Weber, Larry, 257

Welch, Jack, 88-89, 93

Wheatley, Margaret, *Leadership and the New Science*, 255

"witness" listening, 161-162

workgroups
    creativity, avoiding squelching, 99-100
    diverse workgroups, 109-112
        building, 100-105
        embracing, 105-109

wounded leaders, 270

written surveys, building consensus, 231-233